W9-BAE-115

DATE DUE

APR 0 6 2010		
APR 2 1 2014		

Bloom's Modern Critical Views

Bloom's Modern Critical Views

KURT VONNEGUT
New Edition

Edited and with an introduction by
Harold Bloom
Sterling Professor of the Humanities
Yale University

BLOOM'S
LITERARY CRITICISM
An imprint of Infobase Publishing

Bloom's Literary Criticism
An imprint of Infobase Publishing
132 West 31st Street
New York NY 10001

Library of Congress Cataloging-in-Publication Data

Kurt Vonnegut / edited and with an introduction by Harold Bloom.—New ed.
        p. cm.—(Modern critical views)
    Includes bibliographical references and index.
    ISBN 978-1-60413-167-3 (alk. paper)
    1. Vonnegut, Kurt—Criticism and interpretation. 2. Science fiction, American—History
and criticism. I. Bloom, Harold.
    PS3572.O5Z7534 2008
    813'.54—dc22

                                2008037161

Bloom's Literary Criticism books are available at special discounts when purchased in
bulk quantities for businesses, associations, institutions, or sales promotions. Please call
our Special Sales Department in New York at (212) 967-8800 or (800) 322-8755.

You can find Bloom's Literary Criticism on the World Wide Web at
http://www.chelseahouse.com.

Cover design by Ben Peterson

Printed in the United States of America
Bang BCL 10 9 8 7 6 5 4 3 2 1

This book is printed on acid-free paper.

All links and Web addresses were checked and verified to be correct at the time of
publication. Because of the dynamic nature of the Web, some addresses and links may
have changed since publication and may no longer be valid.

Contents

Editor's Note

My Introduction briefly but admiringly considers both *Slaughterhouse-Five* and *Cat's Cradle,* noting that Vonnegut was at work rewriting the wonderful Book of Jonah throughout his literary career. As an acquaintance of Vonnegut, I found him to be as kind and generous a person as I have ever known.

Kathryn Hume offers a retrospective view of Vonnegut, noting his benign stance, while Oliver W. Ferguson admires the narrative perplexities of *Galápagos.*

The dystopia of *Player Piano* is studied by Donald E. Morse, after which he contemplates the negative reception of *Breakfast of Champions.*

Mónica Calvo Pascual finds in *The Sirens of Titan* a desperate defense of free will, while Tamás Bényei salutes risk-taking in *Breakfast of Champions.*

Player Piano, Vonnegut's first novel, is read by Peter Freese as a knowing prelude, after which Fumika Nagano concentrates on the Little Boy of *Cat's Cradle.*

Josh Simpson, admiring Vonnegut's trilogy, dwells on the frontiers of schizophrenia in that trio of fantasies.

The theory of evolution is hailed as Vonnegut's quasi-theology by Gilbert McInnis, while in this volume's final critique Kevin Brown assesses Vonnegut's particular mode of humor.

HAROLD BLOOM

Introduction

KURT VONNEGUT (1922–2007)

On December 19, 1944, Kurt Vonnegut was captured by the Germans during the Battle of the Bulge; he was twenty-two years old. Sent to Dresden, he survived the firebombing of the city on February 13–14, 1945, in which 135,000 Germans were killed. That is the biographical context (in part) for the novel, *Slaughterhouse-Five; or The Children's Crusade* (1969).

Since Vonnegut had begun publishing novels in 1952, it is clear that nearly a quarter-century had to go by before the trauma of 1945 could be transmuted into the exorcism of *Slaughterhouse-Five*. I have just reread the novel after thirty years, remembering my shocked admiration for it when it first appeared, and not looking forward to encountering it again. As it should, *Slaughterhouse-Five* remains a very disturbed and disturbing book, and still moves me to troubled admiration. I prefer *Cat's Cradle*, but *Slaughterhouse-Five* may prove to be an equally permanent achievement.

The shadow of Céline's *Journey to the End of the Night* never quite leaves Vonnegut's starker works, including *Slaughterhouse-Five*. I myself read the anti-Semetic Céline with loathing; one sees what is strong in the writing, but a Jewish literary critic is hardly Céline's ideal audience. So it goes.

It is difficult to comment upon *Slaughterhouse-Five* without being contaminated by its styles and procedures, which is necessarily a tribute to the book. In "structure" (an absurd term to apply to almost any novel by Vonnegut), *Slaughterhouse-Five* is a whirling medley, and yet it all coheres. Billy Pilgrim, as a character, does not cohere, but that is appropriate, since his schizophrenia (to call it that) is central to the book.

1

The planet Tralfamadore, where Billy enjoys pneumatic bliss with Montana Wildhack, is certainly more preferable to a world of Nazi death camps and Dresden firebombings. The small miracle of *Slaughterhouse-Five* is that it could be composed at all. Vonnegut always writes from the survivor's stance, where all laughter has to be a step away from madness or fury. So indeed it goes.

Somewhere in the book, the Tralfamadorians tell Billy Pilgrim that their flying-saucer crews had verified the presence of seven sexes on Earth, all of them necessary if babies are to go on being born. I think that is one of the useful moral observations I will keep in mind whenever I recall *Slaughterhouse-Five*.

II

Bokononism, a religion that freely acknowledges its status as a fiction, is one of the two lovely ironic inventions of *Cat's Cradle*. The other is "karass," the doctrine of hidden soul families, which curiously resembles the Kabbalistic notion of *gilgul*, Isaac Luria's idea of the transmigration of souls. In Lurianic Kabbalah, soul families are united by the root of a common spark.

As an ironist, Vonnegut is too kindly to sustain comparison with Jonathan Swift, whose *A Tale of a Tub* is one of the ironic masterpieces of the ages. I prefer *Cat's Cradle* to Vonnegut's other fictions precisely because it seems so well aware of the limits of its irony. Barely below the surface of the book one can discover many of Vonnegut's nostalgias: a longing for the earthly paradise, an exaltation of an ideal familial love, and the hopeless hope for a rational utopia, a redemptive reversal of the Faust myth, and a profoundly personal identification with the ironically successful prophet, Jonah.

Bokononism is necessarily more an ironic humanism than it is a spirituality. Vonnegut, in my view, does not intend Bokononism as another pragmatic nihilism. Its secret is in *karass*, with the implication that almost anyone can belong to one's soul-family. "Ye must love one another," is Vonnegut's authentic belief, which transcends irony.

An author who has been rewriting the Book of Jonah all his life is probably aware that it is read aloud complete on the afternoon of the Jewish Day of Atonement. *Cat's Cradle* may seem too funny to be an atonement, but that is the achievement of Vonnegut's art. A Jonah who can move us to laughter is a valuable resource, perhaps our final ironist.

KATHRYN HUME

Vonnegut's Melancholy

Vonnegut has just published what he says will be his final novel. This is an appropriate time, therefore, to try to come to terms with the totality of his output. Characterizing the array of books he has produced over the last 45 years is no easy task. Although a few of his novels can loosely be called science fiction, one would not read him for the pleasures of that genre. *Slaughterhouse-Five* made him famous as an anti-war novelist, but war is not his only or even his chief concern. He is a humorist, but if you want a *cheery* laugh, you can do better elsewhere. His attitude toward most social structures is satiric. He is hostile to most kinds of institutional power, and he sympathizes with the poor—sixties characteristics still present in his most recent novel. He has certainly been successful—his own Absolut Vodka ad, high fees for public speaking—yet the popularity of his fiction comes neither from providing emotional candy of romance or adventure nor from pleasuring the professoriat.

What is the nature of Kurt Vonnegut's enterprise? For some novelists, the enterprise is patent. Trollope's is to present institutional politics, usually within the framework of a nominal love story. Faulkner portrays a cross-section of society in a small locale as the inhabitants live out the residual effects of the War between the States. Silko records native ways in the modern world, and gives body to old myths in hopes of aiding the demise of non-tribal cultures. Mailer

Philological Quarterly, Volume 77, Number 2 (Spring 1998): pp. 221–238. Copyright © 1998 University of Iowa.

and Pynchon target the interactions between people and power, while Updike examines the erosion of Protestant faith as it comes up against secularism and modern sexual mores.

When we turn to Vonnegut, we see that he comes across as a novelist of ideas (rather than of action or character),[1] and his enterprise is to tackle problems—usually social problems, but sometimes artistic and personal. In novels of ideas by such writers as Thomas Mann, Doris Lessing, Umberto Eco, Italo Calvino, John Barth, and Salman Rushdie, we find the initial problem or question teased out, analyzed, explored, and tested. In *The Sentimental Agents*, Lessing defamiliarizes political rhetoric. Rushdie's novels ring many variations on the dictator looming over the lowly individual, who tries to find some standpoint from which political action is possible. In novels after *The Sotweed Factor*, Barth tries to generate stories that might help free him from his excruciatingly self-conscious knowledge of the hero monomyth. Vonnegut overtly explores an idea in *Breakfast of Champions* when he considers the implications of treating humans as machines. Usually, though, Vonnegut does not work the idea through very elaborately. His presuppositions about people and about the nature of reality create impasses, preventing him from considering solutions that might seem logical to someone not sharing those presuppositions. This, I shall argue, is the unseen pattern that characterizes Vonnegut's fiction. Intellectual quest is derailed by presupposition; the forward motion dissipates into stasis, and what supplants it is melancholy emotion.[2]

To identify and distinguish between what Vonnegut tries to achieve and what he actually achieves, one must analyze the recurrent elements that characterize the unusual reading experience that his fiction offers. I shall outline his presuppositions, the problems he tackles, and the dynamics that transform intellectual endeavor into emotions. Then we can examine the core elements in his vision, including the relationship he establishes with the reader. Along the way, I shall try to locate his fiction in relation to that of other contemporary writers. What he produces is so much *sui generis* that critics do not connect him to other figures of this period, yet without such comparisons (whether to Vonnegut's advantage or disadvantage), one cannot truly understand what he has been doing so long and so successfully for specific audiences.

Let us start with Vonnegut's presuppositions. His fictive worlds rest upon them, and he treats these presuppositions as universals rather than as contestable assumptions about the nature of reality. They have considerable impact upon what Vonnegut can permit himself to do in his narratives. Three stand out as central to his endeavor: the random nature of the world and life in it; people's helplessness and lack of control; and each individual's isolation and inability to collaborate fruitfully in larger social organizations.

The absurdity for which Vonnegut is famous derives from the randomness he projects upon the world. Chance accidents, unforeseeable consequences of minor actions, frequent reversals and wild, unmotivated swings of fortune are always part of a Vonnegut novel. In *Deadeye Dick,* we learn that Rudy's father saved Hitler's life when Hitler was an art student. An offhand kindness that anyone would have performed can thus plunge the world into horrible slaughter. Wilbur Swain will start life classified as an idiot yet will become president of the United States. Malachi Constant inherits a huge fortune, loses it, becomes a mind-controlled zombie, lives in strange happiness on Titan, and freezes to death when he returns to earth. Walter Starbuck starts life as the cosseted protégé of a millionaire, becomes a penniless ex-con, and then vaults to chief executive of the largest private fortune in the country before heading to jail again. The actual coincidences may be unimportant, but Vonnegut trumpets their presence. In *Breakfast of Champions,* Kilgore Trout gets dog shit on his jacket, and the narrator's voice remarks that by coincidence he knows the person who owns that particular dog, and he regales us with an account of the dog's pathetically limited life. In *Galápagos,* a paranoid soldier breaks into a store, and the narrator remarks, "If he had not burglarized that shop, there would almost certainly be no human beings on the face of the earth today."[3] Opening that particular door permits six desperate female children to get beyond a barricade and beg at the hotel; they will be the mothers of the new humanity. Such remarks and situations contribute to the feeling that life's turns are not susceptible to rational control.

The world is random, and humans, not surprisingly, are helpless. Vonnegut presupposes that people cannot control their circumstances, and this powerlessness often manifests itself in blatant symbolic form. Paul Proteus of *Player Piano* is quintessentially unable to control his own response when hitched to a futuristic polygraph; the lack of control here echoes his failure to control the Luddite revolution. Neither Malachi Constant nor Winston Niles Rumfoord in *Sirens of Titan* governs his own actions; each is a helpless agent serving Tralfamadorian needs. In *Slapstick,* gravity's becoming a variable force means that everyone is subject to uncontrollable changes; people find themselves too heavy to crawl one day, practically floating the next. In *Timequake,* the expanding universe contracts slightly, and everybody relives ten years, unable to change anything, as if they were actors in a play. Whether a character's big brain tells her to commit suicide or whether a grotesque boy is forcibly separated from his sister by parents, Vonnegut's characters face ineluctable pressures exerted against their core identity.

Because they cannot control their portion of the world even in everyday ways, Vonnegut characters tend to feel inadequate. The few who do not suffer from inferiority complexes—Senator Rosewater, for instance—are as close as Vonnegut comes to giving us villains. The senator's son, Eliot Rosewater, is the patron saint of people who feel worthless. Rabo Karabekian of *Bluebeard* feels inadequate to his calling, for his soul and his unfashionable artistic abilities combine to deprive him of a viable artistic vision. The three Hoenikker children in *Cat's Cradle* drift without friends or real work, so they try to control their lives by buying love and jobs with their slivers of ice nine. Dwayne Hoover's inadequacies are symbolically realized in his echolalia, and Billy Pilgrim's, in his psychic withdrawal while hospitalized after the war. *Slapstick's* Wilbur Swain considers himself only a dull, stupid half-person when separated from his sister, and he is haunted by the might-have-been of their combined genius.

Vonnegut's most urgent presupposition concerns the loneliness of people. His major characters are surrounded by a chilly space separating them from other people. Paul Proteus finds himself at odds with his regimented society, and does not manage to communicate fully with anyone, even his friend Ed Finnerty. Malachi Constant is isolated by his fortune, and then by being brain-wiped. Billy Pilgrim does time in a Tralfamadorian zoo, which many critics interpret as his psychotic withdrawal. Although loneliness appears in the early novels, Vonnegut foregrounds it in *Slapstick* (1976). He solves the problem by supplying everyone with a computer-generated middle name and number, which allows them to form nation-wide extended families. The success of this solution is fleeting at best; later protagonists like Walter Starbuck, Rudy Waltz, Leon Trout, and Gene Hartke are isolated by jail, guilt, ghost status, and experience in Vietnam. The *Slapstick* resolution brought Vonnegut no lasting relief from the psychological pressures this presupposition exerts on his imagination.

Vonnegut's vision of loneliness is crucial to his picture of life. The protagonists, with few exceptions, have poisonously bad relations with parents, with siblings (if any) and with their own children. Their marriages may seem true partnerships, but something about the relationship proves seriously defective. In *Mother Night*, Howard Campbell's marriage makes him a Nazi. Starbuck marries a war-waif in *Jailbird*, and his American childishness and ignorance never really win respect from someone who survived the concentration camps. Usually, though, the characters cannot bond with others; they might as well be Teflon-coated. The psychological damage caused by the typical Vonnegut parents may explain this failure to bond with others; it also explains characters' inability to feel appropriate emotions and their extremely limited talent for enjoying life. A few enjoy reading Kilgore Trout stories, but aside from that, few pleasures can register on the minds of these isolated people. The bedrock of Vonnegut's vision is this: the individual is a non-aggregative unit. Vonnegut considers social structures just gatherings of separate individuals, and even institutional hierarchy is unable to create bonds that overcome the forces of separation.

These presuppositions are one characteristic element of Vonnegut's corpus. Another is his orientation as a novelist of ideas. Many of Vonnegut's novels show utopian leanings: he presents serious social problems and wants to find answers. In others, the problems are personal and artistic. In *Player Piano* (1952), he challenges humanity's headlong craze for replacing individuals with machines. *Sirens of Titan* (1959) shows him wondering if humans have free will. *Mother Night* (1961) projects in Campbell's troubles some artistic problems of Vonnegut's own: their creative output is reviled or wildly praised, often for the wrong reasons, and while both artists feel their work has value, they cannot explain what that value is. In *Cat's Cradle* (1963), he backs into the problem that will become explicit in *Slaughterhouse-Five*, namely how he should deal with his Dresden experience in writing, and he does it by changing fire to ice. *God Bless You, Mr. Rosewater* (1965) is his first engagement with the inequitable distribution of wealth. *Slaughterhouse-Five* (1969) is his attempt to find a way to say something intelligent about a massacre, which he solves by splitting narrative focus, letting Billy Pilgrim be the person whose emotional fuses are blown by the experience—so through him we experience it subjectively—while the narrator, talking of his drinking jags and his return to Germany for a visit, can present a more externalized version.[4]

The Dresden novel was a milestone. Vonnegut had spent the interest from this artistic nest egg in earlier novels and with *Slaughterhouse-Five*, he blew the capital. He needed new ideas, and found them. *Breakfast of Champions* (1973) shows him wondering if he can avoid taking the pain of living seriously by interpreting life in a mechanistic fashion. One need not feel the suffering of others if a woman who dies in childbirth is a defective baby-bearing machine, the man who abandoned her is a disappearing machine, and the little girl ruthlessly trained in swimming for the Olympics is an outboard motor. Even brain chemicals are mechanisms; a mass-murderer committed the deed because of the bio-mechanical signals sent by a small cancer in his brain, and the Vonnegut persona mentions his own experience with undesirable brain-chemical patterns now controlled by pills. *Slapstick* (1976) tries to solve the problems of loneliness. *Jailbird* (1979) takes Vonnegut back again to trying to redistribute wealth. *Deadeye Dick* (1982) parallels living with guilt on a personal and national scale: the person deadens himself and renders his life useless; the nation takes a different tack, represses the memory, and returns to the crime and commits it again and again. *Galápagos* (1985) blames our big brains for the precariousness of our future, and solves the problem by devolving humans to the level of seals. *Bluebeard* (1987) asks questions about high and popular art. *Hocus Pocus* (1990) returns to living with war guilt. Vonnegut uses *Timequake* (1997) to consider the nature of his own writing, and again raises the issues of free will, men being replaced by machines or computers, and extended families. Of these, the most important issues explored are loneliness, war memories, the threat to human happiness offered by machines, and the inequitable distribution of wealth. Other issues, often used to create the background rather than the foreground, include disease, and the emotional damage done to children by inadequate parents.

When Vonnegut's presuppositions come up against ideas like this, the most frequent result is a strange derailment of the intellectual quest. The pattern appears full-blown in *Player Piano*. When Paul Proteus is on trial, the lie detector forces him to recognize that one of his motives for rebelling is hatred of his father, who engineered the brave new world Paul has lived in. He ponders how sordid personal motives may still have valuable results, and blurts out, "The most beautiful peonies I ever saw . . . were grown in almost pure cat excrement."[5] Vonnegut makes this important point, but does not develop it; that would demand facing human ties that are binding (even if damaging) and would demand acknowledgment that humans need not be helpless. Rather than go in that direction, Vonnegut breaks off the courtroom scene with a riot in the streets, and with this chaos, the unreliability of the world reasserts itself and blocks the development of an idea. Similarly, a Kilgore Trout scenario in *Timequake* shows a pilot who refused to drop a third atomic bomb on Japan. He is being tried, when a crack opens in the Pacific that swallows the island, plane, bomb, and courtroom.

In a similar vein, consider what Vonnegut does when confronting poverty and the uneven distribution of wealth. In *God Bless You, Mr. Rosewater* and *Jailbird*, he imagines schemes for dispersing large fortunes among the poor, but his methods are limited by his assumptions about mankind's lack of aggregative and cooperative ability. Eliot Rosewater works as a lone individual and gives driblets of money to other lone individuals. He solves the problem to his own crazed satisfaction (but only for a handful of people) by making them into an artificial family who can draw on the trust he administers. *Jailbird*'s Mary Kathleen O'Looney once worked for the Communist party in America, but by the time she has a fortune to disburse, she has no ties to any suitable organization. Her chief beneficiaries are prosperous lawyers and bureaucrats.[6] The problem of how humans should organize to accomplish things bothers other writers too. Pynchon, for instance, cannot see any good coming from any organization, but his point of resistance is that cooperation will inevitably be corrupted by power. Vonnegut has so much trouble imagining simple cooperation that he pays little attention to power or corruption. Power is misused to bully or silence people in *Deadeye Dick* and *Hocus Pocus*, but in most of his worlds, power is so neutralized that characters in *Slapstick* can yearn to become Vera Chipmunk-5 Zappa's slaves. Evidently even the master-slave bond will be so weak that it will produce none of the traditional ills.

Man's relationship to the machine constitutes another idea that comes up abruptly against Vonnegut's presuppositions.[7] He construes it in three different fashions: (1) Men invent machines that render men unnecessary and therefore unemployable and worthless (*Player Piano,* and referred to in other novels, especially *Galápagos*); (2) craftsmanship disappears in the world of mass-production, and Vonnegut sorrows for men whose cleverness lies in their hands (*Player Piano,* and referred to in other novels, especially *Hocus Pocus* and *Timequake*); (3) he notes the sexual charge that some men get from activating powerful equipment (*Galápagos*)—an attraction also touched upon by Pynchon in *Gravity's Rainbow,* Hoban in *Riddley Walker,* and Callenbach in *Ecotopia.* Utopian writers must face the issue because most recent utopias limit permissible technology. Vonnegut poses the problem of the engineering impulse, but finds no solution. Vonnegut rightly concludes in *Player Piano* that the drive cannot just be repressed by revolutionary fiat: Bud Calhoun cannot refrain from tinkering, even though before the rebellion he had created a machine that had replaced him at work. To find a humane solution, Vonnegut would have to believe that humans could collaborate effectively. The utopian theorist Charles Fourier deals with such problematic human impulses by creating uses in his utopia for all natural drives: he deliberately develops social functions that will make use of inveterate gossips and of children's love of playing in dirt, for example.[8] Fourier would have created roles for people with this engineering impulse. Fourier, however, enjoyed the advantage of believing that humans can cooperate and organize effectively. Because that solution is blocked by Vonnegut's presuppositions, we are given the defeated emotions of Paul Proteus, the wry despair at human use of machines that makes Vonnegut eliminate such machines altogether in *Galápagos,* and the admiring nostalgia for craftsmanship in *Hocus Pocus,* though that skill and care had been lavished upon trying to build a perpetual motion machine—the unattainable mechanical ideal, and one that would render humans truly unnecessary.

Similar presuppositional dynamics govern Vonnegut's handling of a frequent background problem: disease. For instance, he uses diseases to generate random catastrophes: in *Galápagos,* a virus renders all mammals sterile and wipes out most higher life on earth, and the genetic flaws that create *Slapstick's* Swain twins are responsible for many of the wild swings of their fortune. Most of the diseases that catch his attention, however, affect the mind, and serve to show that humans are not truly in control of their own motives and actions. We find Tourette's syndrome causing uncontrollable obscenities in *Slapstick;* brain cancer making someone into a mass murderer in *Breakfast of Champions;* and—but for a random throw of genetic dice—Huntington's chorea threatening the sanity and longevity of the new human species in *Galápagos.* Our helplessness when confronted with our own brains shows in

Breakfast of Champions, where the mind is said to fall prey to "bad chemicals" and it has no immunity to crazy ideas. In *Galápagos,* we also find the problem cast in terms of our big brain, which could hold "so many contradictory opinions on so many different subjects all at once, and switch from one opinion or subject to another one so quickly, that a discussion between a husband and wife under stress could end up like a fight between blindfolded people wearing roller skates" (66). Big brains can persuade people that war is a good idea. Once intrigued by an idea, big brains make their owner's life hell until he or she tries the idea out. The boy who thinks of firing the bullet from the cupola at random in *Deadeye Dick* is an example of someone irretrievably ruined by a big brain whim. Big brains are also curiously governed by irrelevancies. Big brains are unable to take problems seriously if they themselves are adequately fed. Forests of the northern hemisphere will be killed by acid rain because the well-fed inhabitants cannot bestir themselves to halt the disaster. Vonnegut links his own waning creativity to the "little radio in [his] head [that] stopped receiving messages from wherever it is the bright ideas come from."[9] Disease and mental problems are thus presented to reinforce Vonnegut's sense that people cannot control their circumstances.

This dynamic—of logic frustrated by presupposition—controls one of Vonnegut's most heartfelt issues: the linked problems of bad parenting and aloneness. His solution for both is the same: extended families. If a child is at odds with its parents, he feels, it should be able to seek solace with an aunt and uncle two blocks away. The lonely person should be able to draw on such kin when in need of company or help. Every novel with the possible exception of *Jailbird* paints an exceedingly hostile picture of the protagonist's parents. The fathers are distant and usually domineering; the mothers are weak, often alcoholics, emotionally cold, and offer no protection for the protagonist against unreasonable demands from the father. One result of such parenting is the protagonists' inability to feel "appropriate" emotion. Their brain-circuits for enjoyment remain undeveloped (*Timequake,* 16) and too much anger has to be repressed, with the result that Leon Trout and Gene Hartke feel very little at killing Vietnamese, and Frank Hoenikker feels virtually nothing over his part in destroying the world through ice-nine. Without emotional response, you make no friends or attachments. Their aloneness, and Vonnegut's image of humans as non-bonding, stems at least partly from this parental emotional abuse.

With a grand flourish, Vonnegut claims to solve this set of problems in *Slapstick.* At first, we might conclude that he had escaped his usual pattern. Discovering "relatives" on the other side of an armed struggle does reduce people's willingness to engage in massacres, and people of the same name do help each other out. However, this computer-generated scheme does not really provide the emotional supports of the folk family (as he calls it in *Fates*

Worse than Death). That pattern—the extended, local family of his childhood—does not work in our profession-oriented high-tech society, because people move away from their initial family location to get education and then to get specialist jobs, a process he details in *Timequake*. While *Slapstick*'s artificial extended family creates contacts everywhere, they are contacts that work better for adults than for a child looking for a sympathetic aunt down the street; there might be no Raspberry-11s within walking distance. A relative of the sort Vonnegut believes would help mitigate bad parenting must live within a few blocks, and preferably there would be several.

In other words, Vonnegut has dreamed up a solution, but that solution is compromised and constrained by his presuppositions. What he has produced in the *Slapstick* scheme is a collection of unattached individuals—his non-aggregative basic units—who live scattered all over the country, and whom one contacts by looking them up in a directory. Once the country has broken down, one finds relatives by chance and random accident. Not surprisingly, the solution did not slake his thirst for family nurturance, despite the happy verbiage bestowed upon the scheme in the novel. Logically, what his problem calls for is an artificial village, one that permits people to leave and join another village when they move elsewhere. Something more like the solution he wants is described in Aldous Huxley's *Island*, where groups of neighboring families form mutual adoption clubs and consciously work to help children escape the pressures of the nuclear family. His present presuppositions do not permit him to think in terms of artificial village or block community, however, because such an arrangement demands cooperation and friendship and at least some happy, sensible couples. His characters are too isolated to create such a logical arrangement.

Many of the novels end without their tensions being resolved. *Sirens of Titan, Mother Night, God Bless You, Mr. Rosewater, Jailbird,* and *Hocus Pocus* produce little sense of true relief. If not internal, the tensions may be external. *Galápagos* shows what Vonnegut may consider a real solution, but when I have taught this novel, my students vehemently reject the idea that such a solution can be considered a valid answer to the problem. For them, the tensions remain unresolved. Only *Bluebeard* offers the relaxation of a happy ending, in that the artist manages to paint the one huge picture that joins his skills and his soul into a sum greater than the parts. His soul and his "meat" end up shaking hands in reconciliation.[10] Evidently this happy state of affairs failed to release any pressures in Vonnegut's imagination, because the next novel, *Hocus Pocus,* is among his most depressive and depressing. Even *Slapstick,* a relatively cheerful novel on the personal level ostentatiously finishes with the *Märchen* formula "Das Ende" rather than "They lived happily ever after." Readers engage with Vonnegut's issues, but neither intellectually nor emotionally receive satisfaction. Vonnegut is too honest to produce false happy endings, and his bleak results challenge readers to consider whether or not happier philosophies are built upon strictly imaginary foundations. However, his inability to find premises other than his presuppositions does produce undeniable limitations in the intellectual and emotional parameters of his work.

These presuppositions, ideas, and dynamics are what seem to me to underlie Vonnegut's artistic endeavor. To round out our sense of what it is Vonnegut does as novelist, we need to look now at the core elements of his narratives, the characteristics that turn up in most or all of his novels. One such core element that makes reading the novels unusual is the relationship established between reader and an authorial voice. It does not appear in his first two novels, but in the introduction to *Mother Night,* he talks about the random accident that caused him to be born American rather than German, and from then on, the persona or characters with a similar outlook keep us reminded of the author and his wryly glum assessment of humanity and history. In *Cat's Cradle,* the obvious transformation of fire into ice reminds us that Vonnegut saw destruction through fire. The narrator's tone—if not necessarily the details—sound very much like Vonnegut's persona in *Slaughterhouse-Five:* in the earlier novel, John says "When I was a younger man—two wives ago, 250,000 cigarettes ago, 3,000 quarts of booze ago. . . . I began to collect material for a book to be called *The Day the World Ended.*"[11] In the Dresden book, the Vonnegut persona talks about his drinking jags and cigarettes and his attempts to write a book about the massacre. In that novel, Vonnegut crosses over from existence in an introduction to character in the novel, and he keeps that position in *Breakfast of Champions.* We learn about his cycles of depression and anger, now tamed by pills. We are told that suicide is a temptation, thanks to his mother's example. We find out that he gives Kilgore Trout his father's legs and feet. Other such intimate authorial details abound. By *Slapstick,* he has dropped out as a character, but an authorial voice is present in the introductions of *Slapstick, Jailbird,* and *Deadeye Dick.* In *Galápagos,* we find no authorial presence, but the narrator, Leon Trout, is full of Vonnegutisms, such as his labelling imminent deaths with an asterisk, a minor variant on Vonnegut's own "So it goes." *Bluebeard* does not feature Vonnegut directly, but much that gets said about representational and abstract art, about kitsch, about pop writing and art novels is of authorial concern. *Hocus Pocus* locates inherited insanity in an Indiana family and gives the protagonist versions of Vonnegut's own parents yet again. The Vonnegut voice returns in *Timequake,* however, and dominates that novel.

Intimacy with the author makes readers feel personally intimate with the work, and Vonnegut rewards his fans by putting in references that only they will fully appreciate, thus increasing the sense of friendship. In *Timequake,* he argues that "Any work of art is half of a conversation between two human beings, and it helps a lot to know who is talking at you" (144-145). Vonnegut's worlds are cumulative and interrelated. While his fictive creation is no Yoknapatawpha County, one novel will refer to people figured in another, and Midland City is the site for several of them. Characters map onto each other, sharing the same or a very similar name and thereby representing some larger quality that concerns Vonnegut. His three Bernard O'Hares (*Mother Night, Slaughterhouse-Five,* and *Slapstick*) are Americans in uniform, however different their behavior. His von Koenigswalds are all Nazis.[12] Fred T. Barry appears in the Midland City settings, a pillar of the civic community who profiteered from war-related industries. Rabo Karabekian is a minor character in *Breakfast of Champions,* but becomes protagonist of *Bluebeard.* The Rumford family turns up more than once, as does the shyster lawyer Norman Mushari. Kilgore Trout figures as character or as author of stories read by characters in at least seven novels. Since many of Trout's plotlines are parables of the absurd and futile and grotesque, and since Vonnegut and his characters cherish these stories, they contribute a note of continuity that helps unify the corpus.

If one ignores superficial differences, one finds that nearly all the plots contain utopian or dystopian features, or a massacre, or that extension of a massacre, an apocalypse.[13] The utopian elements are Vonnegut's attempts to solve social problems and make society better and more just than it is: *God Bless You, Mr. Rosewater, Slapstick,* and *Jailbird* all fit. *Player Piano* and *Mother Night* are dystopian, the latter in the sense of looking at a seemingly perfect marriage as a kingdom of two and wondering why it can make its participant into a Nazi war criminal. The massacres are all different in scale and importance in their plots, but we find them in *Sirens of Titan, Slaughterhouse-Five, Breakfast of Champions* (very modified in Dwayne's spree), *Deadeye Dick* (the neutron bombing), *Bluebeard* (the Armenian massacre), *Hocus Pocus* (jailbreak killings), and *Timequake* (those killed when the timequake ends). Apocalypse is most obvious in *Cat's Cradle* and *Galápagos.* These concerns give a serious quality to Vonnegut's work. He worries about large issues, and his authority, to some extent, derives from having survived the Dresden firebombing. Given that his utopias do not blossom into ideal societies, these plot elements add their bit to the pessimistic nature of his vision.

A mixture of fantasy and realism is another Vonnegut trademark. Whether set in the recent past (World War II and its aftermath, the Vietnam War and its aftermath, Watergate) or the future, most of the novels have a spacey quality that defamiliarizes the historical settings and locates all the actions in Vonnegutland. World War II intertwines with Tralfamadore, and the presence of Kilgore Trout plot summaries in several books serve this distancing function. Eliot Rosewater's strange hang-ups make an Indiana setting stranger than we thought Indiana could be. Kilgore Trout's visiting Midland

City, and the neutron bombing of the same render a similarly "familiar" Ohio location strange. The room at the top of the Chrysler building and the sub-subways in New York open up doors to strangeness in *Jailbird*. The Japanese take-over of the prison in *Hocus Pocus*, though based on real possibilities, is made to seem strange, even hallucinatory. The extremes in the corpus are *Sirens of Titan* (fantastic) and *Bluebeard* (realistic), but in most we find a realistic base (needed for relevance) and a fantastic distortion that distances us from a specific period, the better to encourage new perspectives—the sort of viewpoint that lets the child remark loudly that the emperor has no clothes.

The search for community is another element present in many of Vonnegut's novels. In this concern, he resembles many current writers. In a book on contemporary American fiction that I have just finished writing, forty or so of approximately one hundred books discussed are concerned with community in fairly central ways. Much non-Anglo ethnic fiction defines itself by means of its sense of local culture against what is perceived to be the soulless lack of true human relationships among Anglo-Americans. Naylor's *Mama Day* shows a functional African-American community while *Linden Hills* shows one warped by its relationship to white values. Nobel Laureate Toni Morrison is well known for her analyses of group experience and interactions. Leslie Marmon Silko and Louise Erdrich concern themselves with Native American enclaves manifesting different levels of assimilation to the mainstream. Rudolfo Anaya shows Chicano culture as it begins to feel the pressures of the Gringo mainstream. Regional writers and those focusing on place (Updike in the Rabbit tetralogy, Kennedy in his Albany cycle) pay a good deal of attention to the idiosyncrasies of that regional community. Utopian writers like Callenbach, LeGuin, and Piercy are by definition concerned with imagining an ideal social pattern. Pynchon in *Gravity's Rainbow* and *The Crying of Lot 49* looks at the black market and the W.A.S.T.E. system of communication used by marginalized groups. DeLillo, in *Libra*, analyzes the intelligence network as a shared way of life. Bruce Sterling's *Islands in the Net* gives us electronic community. All are concerned to see what might work, what might lessen the chill distance between people that so horrifies and depresses Vonnegut. Where he differs from them is that he is able to muster less faith than they in human relationships. He tips his hat to Alcoholics Anonymous as a truly effective support-system, and he longs for the traditional folk family, but he rarely shows nurturing networks actually functioning.

Such absence of community is one of the many causes for Vonnegut's melancholy. He is pessimistic about government and social organization. When he evaluates humans individually, he is just as glum. Virtually none of Vonnegut's characters enjoys life. Plenty of people in real life do not love their jobs or their spouses, or they are frustrated at the stupidity and cruelty of humanity, but many learn to shrug such frustrations off and develop compensatory interests: children, golfing, gardening, community and church work. The middle-class world is full of such distractions, and even in impoverished circumstances children and community activities can bring pleasure. Such nourishing and self-protecting interests do not relieve the unhappiness of Vonnegut protagonists. Their inability to feel much emotion—thanks to the psychological damage caused by their parents—may explain their failures to enjoy anything else. Not much pleasure (aside from reading Kilgore Trout stories) can register on their consciousness, and this anesthetic, depressive condition resonates through the emotional tone of the stories.

The reasons for the melancholy become clearer when you ask how Vonnegut feels about people. Basically, he seems unable to believe in them or work up strong emotions over them. Heroism and tragedy are both impossible; those forms demand powerful positive emotions and commitments that are inconceivable in his world of isolation and randomness. Vonnegut is genuinely sorry for the poor or ill-treated, but he does not manage to love them, as one can see if one contrasts him with Toni Morrison, who cares passionately about people, and whose characters are capable of caring for others. For her, every life matters, no matter how imperfect, and most of her main characters are far from ideal: Sula killed a playfellow; Milkman Dead is extremely selfish; Sethe murdered her baby to prevent its being enslaved. Tragedy is both possible and nearly inevitable, so intensely do her characters reflect the radiant energy of Morrison's concern. Vonnegut's characters aspire to little; the emotional intensity does not exist in his world. Of recent writers, perhaps Richard Brautigan comes closest to Vonnegut in terms of a shared melancholy. Their similarities show up most obviously in *So the Wind Won't Blow It All Away* and *Deadeye Dick*, both books about boys who shoot someone accidentally and have their lives ruined as a result. Most of Brautigan's characters are wispy and low-key, and he too introduces spacey and fantastic elements.

***

Where Brautigan and Vonnegut part ways is in their humor, and this humor is probably the factor that has made Vonnegut so popular throughout his career. What Vonnegut produces is brooding meditations on our being stuck in a world of random forces. He follows his meditative ideas as far as they will take him, and is scrupulously honest about working within the parameters that his presuppositions allow him, even though these bar him from happy solutions or heroic despair. He is full of liberal beliefs regarding what needs to be improved, but knows that the liberal agenda has not produced the hoped-for progress, and, moreover, he doubts that any social organization can cooperate in ways that might result in desirable change. His attitude is thus glum, but the humor makes it gently and not bitterly depressed.

The books are smart and funny. They show sensitivity to human pain, and intelligent sympathy for failure. Unlike many jokes, the humor is not directed at classes of people: women, Poles, hicks, lawyers. Most of the humor is situational and relies on the unexpected connection of two disparate concepts: high-ranking Nazis playing a ping pong tournament; a plague called the Green Death proving to be microscopic Chinese; the national anthem described as "gibberish sprinkled with question marks."[14] The humor often works itself out in Kilgore Trout's plot summaries, through the action of aliens, so Vonnegut wounds no sensitivities while maintaining his sardonic attitude towards all humans. As he says in *Timequake*, "[I] would never allow myself to be funny at the cost of making somebody else feel like something the cat drug in" (121).

Vonnegut's achievement lies in the communication of his disparaging and depressing viewpoint. Story and character remain minimal, often just pro-forma conventions. Idea is pursued largely to the point of its failure or manifest inadequacy in the face of his minimalist presuppositions. Futility and loneliness pervade the whole. If this were truly the core experience, then Vonnegut would never have found so many readers. What gives the novels their power is their humor and the friendly relationship that grows up between the reader and author, with his wry gentleness and melancholy sensibility.

NOTES

1. R. S. Crane makes this neo-Aristotelian distinction in his famous essay, "The Concept of Plot and the Plot of *Tom Jones*," *Critics and Criticism: Ancient and Modern*, ed. R. S. Crane. (University of Chicago Press, 1952), 616–647. In *Timequake* (London: Jonathan Cape, 1997), Vonnegut claims to create caricatures, not characters (63).

2. William E. H. Meyer, Jr., identifies Vonnegut's project (at least for novels since *Slaughterhouse-Five*) as "the impossibility of *verbalizing* the good/evil 'essence' of the New World, the cold-blooded murder of the social Word by the solitary Eye" (95). In this goal, he links Vonnegut to most of the major writers of American literature. See "Kurt Vonnegut: The Man with Nothing to Say," *Critique* 29.2 (1988): 95–109.

3. *Galápagos* (New York: Delacorte Press, 1985), 148.

4. See Hume, "Vonnegut's Self-Projections: Symbolic Characters and Symbolic Fiction," *The Journal of Narrative Technique* 12.3 (1982): 177–190.

5. *Player Piano* (1952; New York: Avon, 1967), 300.

6. Donald Morse makes this point in "Kurt Vonnegut's *Jailbird* and *Deadeye Dick*: Two Studies of Defeat," *Hungarian Studies in English* 22 (1991): 109–119. See also chapter six of his book, *Kurt Vonnegut* (Mercer Island, WA: Starmont House, 1992).

7. Lawrence Broer analyzes Vonnegut's war with machines in "Pilgrim's Progress: Is Kurt Vonnegut, Jr., Winning his War with Machines?" *Clockwork*

Worlds: Mechanized Environments in SF, ed. Richard D. Erlich and Thomas P. Dunn (Westport, CT: Greenwood Press, 1983), 137–161.

8. Fourier makes the dirt-loving children the collectors of trash, and he further rewards them by having the trash collectors ride ponies and be licensed to make lots of loud noise when performing their social function. Insofar as Vonnegut wants solutions to his problems and tries to supply them, he is definitely working in a utopian vein. John R. May argues that Vonnegut limits hope of doing anything in his novels to strictly encompassable actions, and feels that Vonnegut sees any utopian approach as dangerous. "Vonnegut's Humor and the Limits of Hope," *The Critical Response to Kurt Vonnegut*, ed. Leonard Mustazza. (Westport, CT: Greenwood Press, 1994), 123–133. However, Kermit Vanderbilt describes his utopian strain in "Kurt Vonnegut's American Nightmares and Utopias," *The Utopian Vision: Seven Essays on the Quincentennial of Sir Thomas More*, ed. E. D. S. Sullivan (San Diego State University Press 1983) 137–173 and Tunnell sees him as a preacher of redemption in "Kesey and Vonnegut: Preachers of Redemption," 1972; rpt. In *A Casebook on Ken Kesey's* One Flew Over the Cuckoo's Nest, ed. George J. Searles (University of New Mexico Press, 1992), 127–133.

9. *Timequake* (London: Jonathan Cape, 1997), 146.

10. For an analysis of this joining as the healing of a long-standing split in his self see Lawrence Broer's *Sanity Plea: Schizophrenia in the Novels of Kurt Vonnegut* (1989; revised edn. University of Alabama Press 1994). The moderately optimistic air of Vonnegut's later work is discussed by David Cowart, "Culture and Anarchy: Vonnegut's Later Career," *Critical Essays on Kurt Vonnegut*, ed. Robert Merrill (Boston: G. K. Hall, 1990), 170–188.

11. *Cat's Cradle* (1963; New York: Dell, 1970), 11.

12. For the reuse of such names, see Hume, "The Heraclitean Cosmos of Kurt Vonnegut," *Papers on Language and Literature* 18.2 (1982): 208–224.

13. As Leonard Mustazza points out in his book, the novels also use allusions to Genesis to project their sense of man's having lost paradise. *Forever Pursuing Genesis: The Myth of Eden in the Novels of Kurt Vonnegut* (Bucknell University Press, 1990).

14. *Breakfast of Champions: or Goodbye Blue Monday!* (New York: Delta, 1973), 8.

OLIVER W. FERGUSON

History and Story:
Leon Trout's Double Narrative in Galápagos

"How much can you get away with in a book?" (Allen, *Conversations* 251). Kurt Vonnegut posed that question in reference to the unorthodox narrative strategy he devised to solve an "enormous" technical problem that he faced in writing his novel *Galápagos:* how to relate, from the perspective of a narrator of our own time, a story extending from 1986 to one million years into the future.

Galápagos portrays humankind in the year 1,001,986 A.D. and recounts the circumstances that have led to its condition. As the result of certain events occurring in the last decades of the twentieth century—worldwide economic collapse, a destructive war waged by Peru on Ecuador, the global spread of a bacteria that sterilized human females—the only specimens of humanity in existence are the descendants of a handful of people whose errant luxury liner ran aground in 1986 on Santa Rosalia, one of the Galápagos Islands. Thanks to the remoteness of that island, the adaptability of the small group, and the ingenuity of one of them, humankind escaped the manmade and natural disasters that eventually destroyed human life everywhere else; and over time, through the inexorable process of natural selection, the inhabitants of Santa Rosalia underwent physiological and behavioral modifications that brought them into perfect harmony with their environment:

Critique: Studies in Contemporary Fiction Volume 40, Number 3 (Spring 1999): pp. 230–238.
Copyright © 1999 Heldref Publications.

19

It was the best fisherfolk who survived in the greatest numbers
in the watery environment of the Galápagos Archipelago. Those
with hands and feet most like flippers were the best swimmers.
Prognathous jaws were better at catching and holding fish than
hands could ever be. And any fisherperson, spending more and more
time underwater, could surely catch more fish if he or she were more
streamlined, more bulletlike—had a smaller skull. (291)

That evolutionary process had other consequences. Because the raison
d'être of the Santa Rosalians of a million years hence is to further Nature's
goal of ensuring the survival of the species through reproduction, "men and
women now become helplessly interested in each other [. . .] only twice a
year—or in times of fish shortages, only once a year" (226). And because of
their limited cranial capacity, they are not troubled with the "big brains" (the
phrase is ubiquitous and unvaryingly sardonic) responsible for the complex
totality of human achievement as we know it. In the society of the latter-day
Santa Rosalians "nobody [. . .] is going to write Beethoven's Ninth Symphony—or tell a lie, or start a Third World War" (259).

That Darwinian version of the combined New Eden and Noah's Ark
myths not only required a plot that unfolded over a million years, but Vonnegut also had to provide a credible point of view for the novel. "The problem
was," he remarked in an interview, "who's going to watch for a million years?"
(Allen, *Conversations* 291). He solved the problem by creating an omniscient
narrator who informs the reader that he is a ghost with the power to assume invisibility and to enter the minds and thereby learn the thoughts and
histories of whomever he chooses. Because he is, as he puts it, "Nature's experiment with insatiable voyeurism" (82), he has elected to stay on Earth as a
ghost for a million years so that he can see how Nature's experiment with the
Santa Rosalians turns out.

The narrator of Vonnegut's evolutionary fable is Leon Trotsky Trout,
son of Kilgore Trout, an eccentric writer of science fiction whom readers will
recall from some of Vonnegut's earlier novels. Leon is a Vietnam veteran and
deserter from the United States Marines who was granted political asylum
in Sweden. There, he relates, "I became a welder in a shipyard, [. . . where] I
was painlessly decapitated one day by a falling sheet of steel while working
[. . . on] the *Bahía de Darwin*" (219), the vessel that would take the first set-
tlers to Santa Rosalia.

A recent critic has praised Leon as "the perfect vehicle" for the novel,
noting that "Vonnegut's boldest experiments in fiction have always been with
narrative strategy" (Berryman 198, 195). A one-million-year-old ghost as
narrator is undeniably a bold contrivance. I suggest that Vonnegut's experiment with narrative strategy in *Galápagos* may be even more interesting—and

no less bold—than is generally supposed. All of the analyses of the novel with which I am familiar take Leon's assertion of his ghostly nature at face value, tacitly allowing Vonnegut to "get away with" a supernatural solution to his problem. Although such a reading by no means diminishes the impact of the novel, there is another way to regard Vonnegut's narrator, one that relates Leon more intimately to the events in *Galápagos* and that makes him both a more realistic and a more subtly conceived character than the one he professes to be.

***

Galápagos comprises two narratives: Leon's story—the comparatively detailed record of the Santa Rosalians—and Leon's history—the much briefer, seemingly haphazard account of his life before his metamorphosis. In narrating his history, Leon concentrates on two crucial experiences: his relationship with his family and his military service in Vietnam. Those two experiences are causally related. Leon's parents had diametrically opposed temperaments and attitudes toward life. In their son's succinct characterizations, "my father was Nature's experiment with cynicism, and my mother was Nature's experiment with optimism" (82). Young Leon's naive belief that his father was a great writer led him to become "co-conspirator [. . .] in jeering along with him at Mother," eventually "driving [. . . her] away forever" (255). When he was sixteen he realized that Kilgore Trout was "a repellent failure," a writer of total and deserved obscurity, "an insult to life itself" (256). With that rejection of his remaining parent, Leon also left home, to embark on a fruitless quest to find his mother—and, subconsciously, the father he admired before his disillusionment. His aimless drifting ultimately led him to the Marines and Vietnam.

There is also a significant emotional parallel between Leon's childhood and Vietnam experiences. Each is characterized by enormous feelings of guilt resulting from a traumatic episode. The episode of his childhood is his mother's abandonment of her husband and son and Leon's subsequent rejection of his father; in Vietnam, it is his shooting a Vietnamese grandmother who had killed his best friend with a hand grenade. His emotional response to each is identical. After he shot the Vietnamese woman, he rejected his life as "a meaningless nightmare," wishing he were "a stone at the service of the Natural Order" (127). "The most terrible part of the experience to me," he recalls, "was that I hadn't felt much of anything. [. . .] I hadn't come close to crying. [. . .] I wasn't much for crying even before the Marine Corps made a man out of me. I hadn't even cried when my [. . .] mother had walked out on Father and me" (294).

That confession is made to a Swedish doctor who was treating him for syphilis contracted in Saigon. From Saigon, where Leon was hospitalized for the "nervous exhaustion" he suffered after he killed the old woman, he was sent on furlough to Bangkok. There the doctor (eventually responsible for Leon's flight to Sweden) astonished him by asking if he was related to "the wonderful science-fiction writer Kilgore Trout." The discovery "that in the eyes of one person, anyway, my desperately scribbling father had not lived in vain," moved Leon to "cry like a baby—at last, at last" (295, 294). With the re-establishment of the emotional bond with his father, he now *felt* something.

The effect of that emotional release was more profound than Leon realizes: "Father," he explains, "had published more than a hundred books and a thousand short stories, but in all my travels I met only one person who had ever heard of him. Encountering such a person after so long a search was so confusing to me emotionally, that *I think I actually went crazy for a little while*" (256; my italics). Leon did not go crazy simply "for a little while." With the return of the emotions repressed since childhood also came the reawakened consciousness of guilt. To escape the horrors of the present, Leon took refuge in Sweden; but he could not leave behind his past—with its accumulated guilt. Unable to cope rationally with his tortured history, he took refuge in his imagination. Acting not as a stone but as a ghost at the service of the Natural Order, he denied his corporeal existence and created a story that envisioned a species to which not only familial life and human affections but also the common ills of twentieth-century society—domestic discord, economic free-booting, environmental despoliation, and war—were unknown.[1]

After completing his lunatic construct, he saw that it was good: "I have now described almost all of the events and circumstances crucial [...] to the miraculous survival of humankind to the present day. I remember them as though they were queerly shaped keys to many locked doors, the final door opening on perfect happiness" (270). That uncritical approval of the life Leon imagines for the Santa Rosalians—an existence devoid of all the humanizing aspects of society—is, like Kilgore Trout's wasted career, "an insult to life itself." And he resembles Kilgore Trout in yet another way:

> And now I catch myself remembering my father when he was still alive. [...] He was always hoping to sell something to the movies. [...] but no matter how much he might yearn for a movie sale, the crucial scenes in every one of his stories and books were events *which nobody in his right mind* would ever want to put into a movie. [...] So now I myself am telling a story whose crucial scene could never have been included in a popular movie of a million years ago. (267; my italics)

Leon is not the only character in *Galápagos* who is not "in his right mind." Varying degrees of mental deterioration affect some of the peripheral characters of his story: Roy Hepburn's dementia, Siegfried von Kleist's Huntington's Chorea, and, especially, Giraldo Delgado's paranoia. Significantly, Leon draws a suggestive parallel between himself and that homicidal Ecuadorian soldier: "As to how a person as crazy as Delgado got into the army in the first place: He looked all right and he acted all right when he talked to the recruiting officer, just as I did when I enlisted in the United States Marines" (150).[2]

Readers familiar with Vonnegut will recognize that recurrent motif of mental instability. The two characters from earlier novels who most interestingly resemble Leon are Billy Pilgrim (*Slaughterhouse-Five*) and Eliot Rosewater (*God Bless You, Mr. Rosewater*). Like Leon, they have suffered breakdowns because of traumatic wartime experiences. (The three have an additional point of contact: in *Slaughterhouse-Five* Billy and Eliot meet in a veterans' hospital, where Eliot introduces his fellow-patient to the novels of Kilgore Trout.) The most suggestive similarity between Eliot and Leon is the comparable double burden of guilt that each carries: Leon for rejecting his mother and for shooting the Vietnamese grandmother; Eliot for believing himself responsible for his mother's accidental drowning and for bayoneting a fourteen-year-old German boy.

There is an even more striking parallel between Leon and Billy Pilgrim. One critic has described Billy as "an innocent, sensitive man who encounters so much death and so much evidence of hostility to the human individual [. . .] that he takes refuge in an *intense fantasy life*" (Tanner 126; my italics). Leon is not the innocent that Billy is (because after World War II innocence is impossible?) and his fantasizing is constant, whereas Billy's is intermittent. For both, however, fantasy is a refuge, a means by which they attempt to cope with a tormented past and an unbearable present. To do that, each performs a radical, though unconscious, manipulation of time.

At random intervals throughout *Slaughterhouse-Five*, Billy comes "unstuck in time." In that mode he is moved arbitrarily from the present moment, "through the full arc of his life" (43), either to a vividly relived episode from his past or to an equally vivid hallucination of a future event. His first experience with that time warp occurred during the war. Later, under the influence of Kilgore Trout's fiction, he comes to believe that he has been kidnapped by aliens from the planet Tralfamadore, where he now lives, making occasional visits to Earth by means of time-travel. That elaboration of his fantasy is Billy's way of providing a philosophical rationale for his time-traveling and of making his remembered past bearable. To the Tralfamadorians, past, present, and future exist simultaneously. As his captor explains, "[We see] all time as you might see a stretch of the Rocky Mountains. All time is all time. It does not change. [...] It simply *is*" (85–86). Hence, "When a person dies he only *appears* to die. He is still very much alive in the past" (26). That conception of time enables Billy not only to endure the memory of the fire-bombing of Dresden but also to deny death its role as a basic fact of the human condition: "Now, when I myself hear that somebody is dead, I simply shrug and say what the Tralfamadorians say about dead people, which is, 'So it goes'" (27).

Leon's time-travel, unlike Billy's, is unidirectional. His fantasy enables him to know the pasts of the various characters in his story, but after he "comes unstuck in time" in 1986, his concern is with the future—by implication even beyond the year 1,001,986: "Thanks to certain modifications in the design of human beings, I see no reason why the earthling part of the clock-work can't go on ticking forever the way it is ticking now" (291).

Through their manipulation of time, Billy and Leon are able to accept the conditions of their existence. Billy accepts the events of "all-time." Although Leon does not come to terms with the past—his history—quite so satisfactorily, his fantasy—his story—enables him to accommodate to it. By the end of the book, he acknowledges that Nature's successful experiment on Santa Rosalia "almost made me love people just as they were back then, big brains and all" (273).

***

In his essay on *King Lear*, Harley Granville-Barker observed of the scene in which Lear divides his kingdom, "Its probabilities are neither here nor there. A [... writer] may postulate any situation he has the means to interpret, if he will abide by the logic of it after" (I, 271–272). In following the logic of the postulate that informs *Galápagos*, Vonnegut has provided two equally plausible solutions to the problem of how to contrive a credible plot that must span a million years: the unambiguously supernatural one of Leon as ghost, and the less fanciful but no less ingenious one of him as madman.

Asked how he would grade *Galápagos* (as he had done his previous books in *Palm Sunday* [311–312]), Vonnegut replied, "In terms of technique I think it's A+. I think technically what I undertook was impossible. I think I solved the technical problems, and it was miraculous to me that I was able to do that" (Allen, *Conversations* 259). Vonnegut was understandably pleased with his employment of Leon Trout as the narrator of *Galápagos*. Not only is the problem of point of view obviated, but Leon is also useful in other ways. The flashbacks and foreshadowings—as he moves between his story and his history—determine the novel's structure, and his narrative style establishes its tone. And, whether madman or ghost, Leon is the conduit for Vonnegut's criticism of twentieth-century society.

That last function raises the question of the degree to which the narrator of *Galápagos* should be identified with his creator. There are compelling points of resemblance between the two. Both have a common distrust of the benefits of human intelligence: "The human brain," Vonnegut remarked in a 1973 interview, "is too high-powered to have many practical uses in this particular universe," a sentiment echoed by Leon a dozen years later: "The brain is much too big to be practical" (Allen, *Conversations* 81; *Galápagos* 81). Parallels for Leon's mordant observations on contemporary society can be found throughout Vonnegut's fiction; and in the 1973 interview Vonnegut anticipated Leon's brave new world on Santa Rosalia. Deploring the rootlessness and isolation of present-day social structures, he described his "sunny little dream [. . .] of a happier mankind," a dream of the kind of community once found in primitive societies: "I couldn't survive my own pessimism if I didn't have some kind of sunny little dream. [. . .] I want to be with people who don't think at all, so I won't have to think, either. I'm very tired of thinking. It doesn't seem to help very much. [. . .] I'd like to live with alligators, think like an alligator" (Allen, *Conversations* 80–81).

Those strong similarities, however, do not warrant reading Leon as Vonnegut's alter ego. As the only reporter of the events of the novel and as an unequivocal critic of contemporary society, Leon necessarily reflects Vonnegut's disapproval of much in that society. As for Vonnegut's yearning for a saurian utopia, we should not be too ready to take it at face value. Hyperbole comes easily for Vonnegut. "You understand, of course, that everything I say is horseshit," he cautioned in the interview (77). Like his sunny little dream of a life among the alligators, his description of the Santa Rosalian seals is the hyperbolic expression of his anger and despair over the current state of affairs. Leon, it is important to note, is not given to hyperbole. As *Galápagos* abundantly illustrates, his preferred rhetorical figure is meiosis. His approval of the society he describes on Santa Rosalia is consistent and serious. Vonnegut's first novel, *Player Piano*, depicts a nightmarish superstate of the future in which the worship of technology has all but extinguished the human spirit. In the foreword, Vonnegut characterizes it as "not a book about what is, but a book about what could be." Though he probably did not regard *Galápagos* as a book about what could be, he assuredly did not intend it to represent a way of life that should be.

One critic, who argues that Vonnegut's ostensible desire for a species of humanity unencumbered by a big brain is ironic, compares *Galápagos* to Swift's *Modest Proposal*.[3] A more telling Swiftian parallel is with the fourth book of *Gulliver's Travels*. To satirize the human animal Swift conceived of the houyhnhnms, an equine race of superior beings with none of the vices of mankind. And to maximize the impact of his satire, he employed a naive agent, Lemuel Gulliver, who rejects his own kind and accepts the houyhnhnms as "the perfection of nature." Vonnegut, to express his disgust at the "murderous twentieth-century catastrophes which [. . .] originated entirely in human brains" (*Galápagos* 25), constructed a fable in which homo sapiens evolves into a race of seal-like creatures incapable of thought, creativity, or mutual destruction. And to intensify the force of his indictment of modern society, he employed Leon Trout, who rejects everything associated with human culture and enthusiastically characterizes the life that has evolved on Santa Rosalia as a condition of "perfect happiness."

Leon is an effective instrument of satire, but his reliability, like Gulliver's, is limited. Both characters have to some extent the qualities they condemn in others. Because of his indiscriminate loathing of humanity, Gulliver is ungrateful to Captain Mendez, his altogether admirable benefactor, and on his return to England treats his wife and children with brutal indifference. Leon's behavior is not so extreme, but he has the besetting folly that he abhors in mankind, "Nature's experiment with [. . .] voyeurism": He chooses to remain a ghost on Earth for a million years to satisfy his curiosity (259). And though he does not become, as Gulliver does, an object of ridicule, his attitude toward Mary Hepburn's experiment is ridiculously muddled. Mary's "soul," he writes, "[felt] that it would be a tragedy if a child were born" into the inhospitable environment of Santa Rosalia; "but her big brain began to wonder, idly, so as not to spook her," whether the experiment with artificial insemination might possibly work (265). She did not realize, Leon concludes, that her big brain

> would make her life a hell until she had actually performed that experiment. [. . .] That [. . .] was the most diabolical aspect of those old-time big brains: They would tell their owners, in effect, "Here is a crazy thing we could actually do, probably, but we would never do it, of course. It's just fun to think about." And then, as though in trances, the people would really do it—have slaves fight each other to the death in the Coliseum, or burn people alive in the public square for holding opinions which were locally unpopular, or build factories whose only purpose was to kill people in industrial quantities, or to blow up whole cities, and on and on. (266)

In his deluded admiration for the supposed utopia on Santa Rosalia, Leon is indifferent to the fact that it is the product of humankind's big brain, the origin of everything about modernity that he hates.

In another important way *Galápagos* invites comparison with *Gulliver's Travels*. By separating themselves from the extreme views of their respective narrators, Swift and Vonnegut can achieve the effectiveness of an exaggerated attack on the object of their satire. They can also suggest the possibility of some positive values as a corrective. In the fourth book of *Gulliver's Travels* that hint of something better than Gulliver's distorted vision of humanity is Captain Mendez. In *Galápagos* it is Leon's mother. Leaving her negating husband and son was an act of affirmation. Her favorite quotation (which Leon chooses as the epigraph for his book) is from Anne Frank's diary: "In spite of everything, I still believe people are really good at heart." But because satire is essentially noncelebratory and because Swift and Vonnegut have the temperamental bias toward a pessimistic view of affairs characteristic of the writers of moral satire, those hints of something better are overshadowed. Mendez makes too brief an appearance to offset the terrible yahoos and Gulliver's relentless misanthropy. Anne Frank's poignant expression of faith is vitiated by Leon's complacent application of it to the Santa Rosalians' pointless existence that he so admires: "Mother was right: Even in the darkest times, there really was still hope for humankind" (259). And the symbolic value of Leon's mother—"Nature's experiment with optimism"—is undercut by the bitter ironies of his history: that after a lifetime of searching he never found her; and of his story: that ultimately he comes to identify with his father, Nature's experiment with cynicism: "By golly if I haven't now become a writer, too, scribbling away like Father, without the slightest hint that there might actually be a reader somewhere" (257).

Galápagos, like *Gulliver's Travels,* recognizes the complexity of the human situation. A civilization capable both of producing Beethoven's Ninth Symphony and of destroying itself in a Third World War cannot be dismissed in Leon's simplistic way. That is one part of Vonnegut's message. The other is his unflinching diagnosis of the mortal peril in which humanity finds itself. To convey that, Leon Trout—the mad narrator writing "insubstantially, with air on air" (290), his desperate fantasy created and made credible by the pressures of his history—is indeed the perfect vehicle for Vonnegut's bleak fable.

NOTES

1. In his mad imaginings, Leon has conceived an equally bizarre notion to account for his ability to become a ghost. Normally, he explains, at the moment of death a person enters "the blue tunnel into the Afterlife" (135). Once Leon's curiosity about the outcome of Nature's experiment with the Santa Rosalians has been satisfied ("Nothing ever happens around here anymore that I haven't seen or heard so many times before" [259]) and his story has been completed, he is ready to enter the blue tunnel when it next appears.

2. In the critical studies of *Galápagos* that I have read, only that by Lawrence Broer suggests that Leon's story may be the product of dementia: "[. . .] bouts with syphilis, drugs, alcohol, followed by crying jags and psychiatric treatment, created escapist fantasies of putting down his weapons and becoming [a] fisherman, a desire for eternal sleep not unlike the narrator's dystopian vision of life on earth in One Million A.D., which may in fact be only the hallucinated vision of a very sick ex-soldier [. . .]" (157). That suggestion, however, is unelaborated, and everywhere else in his discussion of the novel Broer accepts the events described in Leon's story

as actual—for example, "With the benefit of nearly a million years of hindsight, the narrator's ghost, which has survived from the year 1986 to the year One Million A.D. [. . .]" (152); and "Leon chooses to haunt the earth for a million years" (160). Further, as my argument makes clear, I do not share Broer's view that Leon becomes an integrated personality.

    3. Allen, *Understanding Kurt Vonnegut*, p. 157. For a discussion of Swiftian techniques in some of Vonnegut's earlier novels, especially *Slaughterhouse-Five*, see Wymer.

WORKS CITED

Allen, William Rodney, ed. *Conversations with Kurt Vonnegut*. Jackson and London: University Press of Mississippi, 1988.

————. *Understanding Kurt Vonnegut*. Columbia: University of South Carolina Press, 1991.

Berryman, Charles. "Vonnegut and Evolution: *Galápagos*." *Critical Essays on Kurt Vonnegut*. Ed. Robert Merrill. Boston: Hall, 1990. 188–199.

Broer, Lawrence R. *Sanity Plea: Schizophrenia in the Novels of Kurt Vonnegut*. Revised ed. Tuscaloosa and London: University of Alabama Press, 1994.

Granville-Barker, Harley. *"King Lear." Prefaces to Shakespeare*. London: Batsford, 1958.

Tanner, Tony, "The Uncertain Messenger: A Reading of *Slaughterhouse-Five*." *Critical Essays on Kurt Vonnegut*. 125–130.

Vonnegut, Kurt, *Galápagos*. New York: Delacorte, 1985.

————. *Palm Sunday*. New York: Delacorte, 1981.

————. *Player Piano*. New York: Avon, 1971.

————. *Slaughterhouse-Five*. New York: Delacorte, 1969.

Wymer, Thomas L. "The Swiftian Satire of Kurt Vonnegut, Jr." *Voices for the Future*. Ed. Thomas D. Clareson. Bowling Green, OH: Bowling Green University Popular Press, 1976. 238–262.

DONALD E. MORSE

Sensational Implications:
Kurt Vonnegut's Player Piano *(1952)*[1]

I like Utopian talk, speculation about what our planet should be, anger
about what our planet is.

—Kurt Vonnegut

Kurt Vonnegut's *Player Piano* falls within one of the longest and strongest
suits in twentieth-century science fiction. "From H. G. Wells to Samuel
Delany, science fiction is full of utopias, dystopias, ambiguous utopias, and
'heterotopias.'"[2] As Kermit Vanderbilt observes, "*Player Piano* is astonishing
for the richness of utopian and dystopian matter in this first major outing of
the writer who would soon own the best utopian imagination in American
literature since World War Two."[3]

In *Player Piano*, the world, having passed through the First Revolution
where machines took over man's manual labour, and the Second Revolution
where machines took over all human routine work, is now about to undergo a
Third Revolution where machines will do all the thinking. The huge computer,
EPICAC XIV—the one the president of the United States with not the slightest trace of irony refers to as "the greatest individual in history"—sits in the
Carlsbad Caverns in Colorado determining all of the country's needs from
the number of refrigerators to be manufactured this month, to the kinds of
books people should read, to the types of educational degrees universities may

The AnaChronist (2000): pp. 303–314. Copyright © 2000 *The AnaChronist*.

offer.[4] Vonnegut used as his model for the all-wise, all-powerful machine the first digital computer, the "Electronic Numerical Integrator and Calculator" or ENIAC. Developed at the University of Pennsylvania's Moore School of Electrical Engineering from a proposal by John Presper Eckert and John W. Mauchly and weighing in at thirty tons with eighteen thousand vacuum tubes, the first public demonstration of ENIAC occurred on February 14, 1946. It was followed by a series of lectures at a conference in Philadelphia, summer of 1946, which led in turn to the widespread adoption of stored-program which eventuated in the modern electronic computer. Only a few short years later, Vonnegut extrapolates from these events to create EPICAC XIV. In *Player Piano* the United States has become a planned society run by corporations for profit.[5] But this governing by computer results predictably in an increasingly sterile American society—a society with no real place or need for humans. As Norbert Wiener, who is often referred to as "the father of cybernetics," caustically observed in his popular book, *Cybernetics: Control and Communication in the Animal and the Machine,* "the average human being of mediocre attainments or less has nothing to sell that it is worth anyone's money to buy."[6] In *Player Piano,* a discerning visitor from another culture, the Shah of Bratpuhr, the spiritual leader of six million people, correctly identifies all the citizens of this new ideal United States as "Takaru" or slaves.

The power and wealth of the United States, which grew through the nineteenth and twentieth centuries in large measure thanks to an amazing outburst of creative technology and invention, remains almost synonymous with the machine. The machine may take the form of the car that provides the famous American mobility while contributing heavily to American personal isolation. Or it may take the form of the telegraph/telephone, or more recently, the "net" that tied the country together through instant communications. Or it may be the various electronic media machines (radio, movies, and television) that shifted the emphasis from news to instant event. Or it may be any of the vast array of technics that transformed agriculture into agribusiness, the company into the multinational corporation, or the sleepy stock market into that behemoth of arbitrage, leveraged buy-out, and institutional investment of the new turn of the century.

> Instead of building temples, we build laboratories;
> Instead of offering sacrifices, we perform experiments;
> Instead of reciting prayers, we note pointer-readings;
> Our lives are no longer erratic but efficient.[7]

Lewis Mumford as early as 1934 stated in his prescient study, *Technics and Civilization:*

Mechanization and regimentation are not new phenomena in history: what is new is the fact that these functions have been projected and embodied in organized forms which dominate every aspect of our existence. Other civilizations reached a high degree of technical proficiency without apparently, being profoundly influenced by methods and aims of technics.[8]

In the United States of *Player Piano* and especially in Vonnegut's Ilium, where Paul Proteus tries but does not really succeed in becoming his own person, a "free man" remains squarely within and controlled by a society dominated by such technics. The novel thus satirises both the over-dependence on technology and the over-reliance on the expertise of technocrats.

Sheppeard contends that "because technology is inextricable from twentieth-century man's life and has profoundly changed him, Vonnegut cannot reflect upon contemporary man's metaphysical anguish without also commenting upon his technology."[9] But the reverse may be even truer in that Vonnegut cannot reflect upon the role of technology in the twentieth century without also reflecting on human metaphysical anguish, especially as exemplified in Paul Proteus.

Proteus's flailing about, trying to be at home in Homestead, buying a farm that he cannot run, and attempting to be the Messiah of the saboteurs all reflect his blind desire to become a conscious being, to become fully human. The corporation, on the other hand, wants him to be its ideal manager—bright, but completely within the corporate mould. His wife, in her turn, wants him to be her ideal husband—loving but totally dedicated to succeeding in the corporation. The revolutionary Ghost Shirts want him to be their ideal leader—famous, but selflessly dedicated to their cause. None of these—the corporation, his wife, the Ghost Shirts—wants him simply to be or to be for himself alone. Needless to say, no one ever asks what he wants. The wonder is that he does not become like his fellow workers: alcoholics, dropouts, or flunkies—the hollow shells of wasted men, "Leaning together / Headpiece filled with straw."[10] When the corporation or his wife is not using Paul, then the revolutionaries are. The latter write letters in his name, issue manifestos he does not know if he agrees or disagrees with, and act generally as if he were their Messiah—a role he definitely does not wish to play. If he does not really know what he wants to be or become, Paul at least knows that he does not want to be a lone human manager overseeing machines.

Vonnegut's book is a plea for human beings to be what they are able to be best: human—which is, frail and strong, thick-headed and intelligent, cruel and kind, failing and succeeding, hating and loving. This belief in the humanness of human beings will become a constant in all of Vonnegut's later novels and stories. It is also his warning against that ancient human desire for perfection, especially perfection in society which all too often, as in this novel, leads simply to sterility. Aldous Huxley, similarly worried, chose for the epigraph to *Brave New World* a telling quotation from Nicolas Berdiaeff's *Slavery and Freedom: "Les utopies apparaissent comme bien plus réalisables qu'on ne le croyait autrefois. Et nous nous trouvons actuellement devant une question bien autrement agoissante: Comment éviter leur réalisation définitive?"*[11]

In *Player Piano*, the corporation, working to establish its notion of utopia here on earth actively opposes any belief in the importance of variety in humans and their experience. All in the name of making everything as easy as possible for everyone and granting everyone a far greater degree of certainty than is usually possible in a non-planned, unregulated, free society. The good life in *Player Piano* will be achieved thanks to the corporation responsible for running everything in Ilium, which, in return, demands complete loyalty and service. Such loyalty and service are, however, not just expected, they are required. Vonnegut satirises the kind of husband-wife working relationships that may and often do result from such expectations in the meaningless conversations which take place daily between Paul and Anita. Proteus proves the upwardly mobile, aspiring young husband, while his wife, Anita—"Ilium's Lady of the Manor" (12)—dutifully spends all her time and energy plotting ways to boost him up the corporate ladder. Vonnegut's sharp satiric eye neatly skewers his target as Anita dresses Paul for success by buying him clothing identical with that of those who appear just a bit higher up the ladder. She then coaches him on how to behave at meetings, how to effectively deliver speeches, and how to conduct himself on various social occasions. Anita and Paul's juvenile relationship reflects the price of the certitude promised by an EPICAC XIV-run society. The theologian, Paul Tillich, observed that "men will quickly commit themselves to any cause that promises certainty in their existence."[12] The all-knowing computer in *Player Piano* not only promises but delivers such certainty but at some cost. The Shah several times points to an obvious cost when he "equates American society with the noxious materialism suggested by the nephew's name [. . .] Khashdrahr ('cash drawer') Miasma."[13] Another but not quite so apparent cost of this utopia lies in what is absent from the world of *Player Piano* and what is often overlooked in creating such a good life in a perfect world. The noted Irish writer, Francis Stuart pinpointed this lack when he wrote "Where everything is seen as making life easier for all, there is no room for grief, pain and doubt, in which are the roots of a thriving organic consciousness."[14] Stuart's prescription holds true for individuals but it also proves important for fiction. As Kevin Alexander Boon emphasises, "Vonnegut's fiction [especially in *Player Piano*] points to the confluent boundary between the morbid and the sublime where humor and grief are inevitably conflated."[15]

In extrapolating from the present to create his future utopian society, Vonnegut includes a satiric, highly amused look at the morés of the corporate world as he had observed them while working for the General Electric Company. One of his prime satiric targets—on which he scored a direct hit—was the North Woods summer festival where General Electric executives had to go and play the silly games described in hilarious detail in *Player Piano* (see especially 181–194). "The island was shut down after the book came out," Vonnegut boasts in various interviews.[16] "So, you can't say that my writing hasn't made any contribution to Western civilization."[17]

Juxtaposed to the corporate world in *Player Piano* lies Homestead where ex-workers and those with minimal jobs live and where revolt may be incipient but life itself is as dead as it is at the top of the corporate organisation chart.[18] Here there is no dignity in labour, no virtue in an honest day's wages, no reward for exceeding expectations. Instead, people realise that the corporate world wishes to use their labour as cheaply as possible and will replace them with more reliable machines whenever and wherever possible, not stopping to count or even acknowledge the human cost of those dismissed, fired, or forced to quit. This point becomes clear early in the novel when Bud Calhoun is fired because he had invented a machine to replace him and so made himself redundant (62–65). Much of Vonnegut's theme of the exploitation of human workers and of machines that make people redundant leaving behind a pile of human rubble with little or nothing to do appears familiar from some nineteenth- and many twentieth-century British and American writers. John Ruskin, Thomas Hardy, D. H. Lawrence, E. M. Forster, and J. R. R. Tolkien, and American writers from Mark Twain through the muckrakers and after—all attacked the human waste caused by technology and Big Business. Like the best of these writers, Vonnegut goes beyond speculation and like most of them, describes both the atmosphere of the corporation and the ethos and values it promulgated based upon careful observation. "It was a genuine concern that drove me to write my first book," he claims.[19]

While working at General Electric, he recalls

One day I came across an engineer who had developed a milling machine that could be run by punch cards. Now at the time, milling machine operators were among the best paid machinists in the world, and yet this damned machine was able to do as good a job as most of the machinists ever could. I looked around, then, and found looms and spinning machines and a number of textile devices all being run the same way and, well, the implications were sensational.[20]

These sensational implications are realised in *Player Piano* as this future, electronically run society places the good of the corporation and the *full employment of machines* ahead of human needs and desires, including the human necessity for meaningful work. "[T]he only safeguard of order and discipline in the modern world is a standardized worker with interchangeable parts. That would solve the entire problem of management," says The President in *The Madwoman of Chaillot* by Jean Giraudoux[21]—a sentiment echoed and re-echoed throughout this novel. In *The Sirens of Titan* (1959), Vonnegut explores this issue further through the ultimate machine-run civilisation of Tralfamadore, whose people originally made machines in order to free human beings from work:

> *This left the creatures free to serve higher purposes. But whenever they found a higher purpose, the purpose still wasn't high enough.*
> *So machines were made to serve higher purposes, too.*
> *And the machines did everything so expertly that they were finally given the job of finding out what the highest purpose of the creatures [humans] could be.*
> *The machines reported in all honesty that the creatures couldn't really be said to have any purpose at all.*
> *The creatures thereupon began slaying each other [. . .] And they discovered that they weren't even very good at slaying. So they turned that job over to the machines, too. And the machines finished up the job in less time than it takes to say, "Tralfamadore."*[22]

As Zoltán Abádi-Nagy notes "Tralfamadore turns out to be a dehumanized planet with a machine civilization: what they can teach man is that man should not learn from them."[23]

Against nineteenth century popular belief, Ralph Waldo Emerson vigorously and correctly maintained that "society never advances,"[24] yet there are always those, such as the twentieth-century behaviourist psychologist, B. F. Skinner, who promise societal advancement in return for merely surrendering unwanted human dignity and unneeded individual freedoms. As the Shah of Bratpuhr keenly observes in *Player Piano* surrendering such freedoms in the name of "progress" or comfort or efficiency reduces people from their once proud status as free citizens in a democracy to "takaru" or slaves. But those who believe and belong to the Skinnerian utopia, *Walden Two* (1948) "entertain no nonsense about democracy." "This is a totally planned society, structured so that a self-perpetuating elite shapes to their specifications the inhabitants of the world they control,"[25] and those inhabitants should be grateful. John Pierce invented an excellent term for this kind of thinking. He called it "the hubris of altruism;" that is, the "blind pride in seemingly benevolent ideals," which must be imposed on humanity "for its own good."[26] From a wealth of historical examples of this kind of utopia Pierce selects John Calvin's Geneva and Pol Pot's Democratic Kampucheatwo where "the practical consequences of the hubris of altruism" were much in evidence. "It is important," Pierce adds, "to remember that both might still be regarded as noble ideas had they not succeeded so thoroughly."[27] Hence the imposition of Skinnerian values and techniques on a population essentially not consulted either about the values themselves or about participating in such a noble experiment. Had they been so consulted, there might have appeared that lone individual or even a group who like Bartleby would "prefer not to" participate in the noble experiment. It is against this kind of planned society dedicated to a certain set of values however benign or well meaning, that anti-utopian literature, such as *Player Piano* is often written. Vonnegut, in contrast to Skinner but much like Emerson, remains a non-believer when it comes to societal progress or the necessity for controlling society.

If Vonnegut continues very much aware of the almost absolute centrality of machines for late twentieth-century American society, he also insists on their right use. In his view, machines are both a proper and a necessary subject for the contemporary American writer. "Machinery is important. We must write about it," he affirmed in one of many interviews.[28] But Vonnegut's point in *Player Piano* so familiar from American history, philosophy, theology, politics, and literature is that machines and technology are or should be the means by which humans gain—not lose—their freedom. Machines are not now nor should they ever become simply ends in themselves. Ralph Barton Perry argued that "even ideas and skills do not suffice unless they are linked with the purposes for which they are used, or the feelings which give them value." He continues, "It is necessary, furthermore, that these purposes and feelings should be shared, in order that they may afford a basis of reciprocal action. When thus socialized and charged with emotion, durable ideas constitute the essence of culture and of civililation."[29] Machines, therefore, do not need to be "preserved from dissolution" only their "essential formulas and aptitudes should be remembered, in order to be re-embodied in new machines."[30] Not any specific machine itself then but *the idea* of that machine should remain paramount. At the end of *Player Piano,* for instance, bitter irony resides in Bud Calhoun's immediate repairing of the orange soda machine. Those repairs, made as the revolution has barely concluded, become Vonnegut's sharply etched image of the failure of this individual and all like him to distinguish between the means and ends for which this machine and every machine was invented. He is about to do himself out of a job once more by preserving this specific machine rather than internalising his knowledge of it. Bud has become a true *takaru* or the slave of the machine. As such, he exemplifies Lewis Mumford's contention that Europe and America became unlike other cultures that "had machines; but […] did not develop 'the machine.' It remained for the peoples of Western Europe to carry the physical sciences and the exact arts to a point no other culture had reached, and to adapt the whole mode of life to the pace and capacities of the machine."[31] In Ilium this process reached its zenith in the machine-run society.

The novel's title, *Player Piano,* derives appropriately from a machine, the player piano, invented in the nineteenth century and perfected in the twentieth. The late Tony Tanner most succinctly summarised the ominous quality of this symbol for the novel. "A piano player is a man consciously using a machine to produce aesthetically pleasing patterns of his own making. A player piano is a machine which has been programmed to produce music on its own, thus making the human presence redundant."[32] In an early chapter of the novel someone observes that "watching them keys go up and down […] You can almost see a ghost sitting there playing his heart out" (28). David Hughes, in developing the player piano as an ideal image and symbol for Vonnegut's satire, discovered that "the heart of a player piano, the perforated music sheet, was invented in 1842 […] and by about 1890 it was brought to perfection in the United States." He concludes that this image "affords Vonnegut the blend he wants of nostalgia, technical proficiency, and corporealization of the spiritual world."[33] This blend will reappear even more poignantly in *Galápagos* (1985) when Zenji Hiroguchi programs Mandrax, the super computer, to reproduce the intricacies of ikebana, the Japanese art of flower arranging which his wife, Hisako teaches. Hisako loses not only her pride but also her very reason for existence. "Her self-respect has been severely crippled by the discovery that a little black box could not only teach what she taught, but could do so in a thousand different tongues […] ikebana turned out to be as easily codified as the practice of modern medicine."[34] Vonnegut thus makes crucial to *Galápagos* his argument and its consequences about the uselessness of human beings first outlined in *Player Piano* and which later became central to several short stories as well as *God Bless You, Mr. Rosewater* (1965).[35] The Shah in *Player Piano* wishes to pose a simple question to the giant computer, "What people are for?" (277). What indeed are humans for if machines can duplicate not only their music and work, but also their arts and sports?[36] This question haunts all of Vonnegut's fiction from *Player Piano* to *Timequake* (1998). But for Vonnegut there is no going back on technology, unless nature itself, deciding it has had enough of human destruction should enter the picture as it does in *Galápagos.* In *Player Piano,* perhaps more acutely than elsewhere in Vonnegut's fiction, this issue of the right role of machines and their right relation to people illustrates the difficulty American society has often shown in identifying clearly right means to achieve good ends. *Player Piano* as a mid-century anti-utopia, illustrates, albeit negatively, the right role of technology and machinery within the goals and values of human civilisation while at the same time arguing passionately for the sacredness of human beings.

Robert Elliott contends that after World War II, the Bomb, and the holocaust "we will never again be able to create imaginative utopias with the easy confidence of the nineteenth century; the terror to which the eschatological vision applied to human affairs has led in our time forecloses that possibility."[37] Yet at the end of the twentieth century the American public and its leaders still fall prey to imagining that society or its organisation can be perfected. Many still believe naively in that recurring human delusion which the poet, e. e. cummings so graphically called: "the foetal grave / called progress."[38] "[T]he dystopia in *Player Piano* looks much more ominous to us in the 1990s than the ones in Huxley and Orwell."[39]

In the second half of the twentieth, as in the first years of the new twenty-first century American society appears dominated by the multinational corporation, "the only social unit of which our age is capable,"[40] and clearly needs to heed the warning embedded in *Player Piano*'s extrapolation from current trends and values. Not to do so may well mean being condemned to live in a city much like Vonnegut's Ilium—something that appears an all-too-real prospect for millions of Americans. *Player Piano* thus remains Vonnegut's plea for bringing into being an American society composed of individuals who have discovered shared purposes and feelings, who distinguish clearly between means and ends, who affirm the truth that American culture is neither true nor utopian, but partial and imperfect. Above all, this society must be run not by corporations or by machines but by and for free citizens.[41] These themes emerge again and again in Vonnegut's later novels and stories, as they will preoccupy Vonnegut for the rest of his writing career.

NOTES

1. An earlier version of this essay will appear in the 1999 Conference proceedings of the International Conference in the Fantastic in the Arts. All references to *Player Piano*. 1952. New York: Dell, 1980 will be given parenthetically in the text.

2. Brian Attebery. "Fantasy as an Anti-Utopian Mode." *Reflections on the Fantastic*. Ed. Michael Collings. Westport, CT: Greenwood Press, 1986, p. 5. Krishan Kumar maintains that utopias are in decline in the twentieth century, but as Barbara Goodwin points out "he does this only by discounting a healthy number of recent science fiction and feminist utopias." ("The Perfect and the Perfected." Review of Krishan Kumar, *Utopia and Anti-Utopia in Modern Times*. Oxford: Blackwell, n. d., *Times Literary Supplement*, 24 July 1987: 786). Vonnegut's book is one of dozens within the science fiction and/or fantastic mode.

3. Kermit Vanderbilt. "Kurt Vonnegut's American Nightmares and Utopias." *The Utopian Vision: Seven Essays on the Quincentenniel of Sir Thomas More*. San Diego: San Diego State University Press, 1983, 137–173, pp. 139–140. Vanderbilt

lists the typical elements of a utopian novel—all, of which, he claims, are present in *Player Piano*. "The new post-industrial civilization will be, customarily, a socialistic commonwealth of rational men and women, with wisely planned urban communities, maximum individual freedom, socially oriented education, material abundance (with wise conservation of natural resources), non-alienating and non-competitive day labor and professional life, self-transcending leisure time for recreation and the arts, effortless virtue, dynamic social stability, permanent peace, and gratifying love" (p. 140).

4. The computer's name, EPICAC is awfully close to Ipecac, the children's medicine used to induce vomiting, as several commentators have noted.

5. Vonnegut's economics in *Player Piano* are intriguing. He postulates private socialism where the corporations, not needing to compete because of being monopolies, nevertheless are government regulated. Although there are no taxes on things, there is a heavy tax on machine labour.

6. Quoted in Hugh Kenner. *Dublin's Joyce*. Bloomington, IN: Indiana University Press, 1956, p. 163. Vonnegut was well aware of Wiener's work borrowing his first name for the "crass medical genius," Dr. Norbert Frankenstein in his play *Fortitude* (Kurt Vonnegut. *Wampeters, Foma & Granfaloons*. New York: Delacorte Press, 1976, pp. 43–64) and quoting from his work both in interviews and in *Player Piano* (13). Hughes believes that "Vonnegut appears indebted not to Wiener's 1948 monograph *Cybernetics, or the Control and Communications in the Animal and the Machine*. 1948. New York: Massachusetts Institute of Technology (MIT) Press and Wiley, 1961, but to its popularization, *The Human Use of Human Beings* (Cambridge, Mass: Riverside Press, 1950). The latter was revised and toned down in the second edition (1954) after *Player Piano* was published. No mere catalog of borrowings can reveal Vonnegut's assimilation of the 1950 edition . . . " (David Y. Hughes. "The Ghost in the Machine: the Theme of *Player Piano*." *America as Utopia*. Ed. Kenneth M. Roemer. New York: Burt Franklin, 1981, p. 113, n. 4).

7. W. H. Auden. "For the Time Being." *W. H. Auden: Collected Poems*. Ed. Edward Mendelson. New York: Random House, 1976, p. 287.

8. Lewis Mumford. *Technics and Civilization*. New York: Harcourt, Brace, 1934, p. 4.

9. Sallye J. Sheppeard. "Kurt Vonnegut and the Myth of Scientific Progress." *Journal of the American Studies Association of Texas* 16 (1985) 14–19, p. 15.

10. T. S. Eliot. "The Hollow Men." *The Collected Poetry of T. S. Eliot*. New York: Harcourt, Brace, 1952, pp. 56–59, ll. 3–4.

11. [In a rough translation: "Utopias appear far more realisable than we had formerly believed. And now we find ourselves facing a question equally painful in a new kind of way: How to avoid their actual realisation?"] Quoted in Aldous Huxley. *Brave New World*. 1932. Harmondsworth, MS: Penguin, 1955, p. 5. Vonnegut "borrowed" the familiar utopian plot from *Brave New World*, as Huxley, Vonnegut claims, had in his turn "ripped [it] from Eugene Samiatan's *We*" (*Wampeters, Foma & Granfaloons*, p. 261). The publishing history of *Player Piano* reflects Vonnegut's fortunes as an author since of the original hardcover edition "less than a third of its first printing of 7600 copies was purchased (and most of these, Vonnegut insists, in Schenectady). The next year, however, the Doubleday Book Club prepared a cheap edition of 15,000 copies, which sold very quickly to its subscribers; a second printing of 5000 was soon ordered. And in 1954 came the book's greatest success [. . .] Outfitted with a luridly futuristic cover and re-titled *Utopia-14*, the

Bantam paperback [. . .] hit the stands in numbers exceeding 248,000" (Jerome Klinkowitz. *Kurt Vonnegut*. New York: Methuen, 1982, p. 40).

12. Paul Tillich. "Critique and Justification of Utopia." *Utopias and Utopian Thought*. Ed. Frank Manuel. Boston: Houghton Mifflin, 1966, p. 307.

13. Sallye J. Sheppeard. "Signposts in a Chaotic World: Naming Devices in Kurt Vonnegut's Dresden Books." *The McNeese Review* 312 (1986) 14–22, pp. 18–19.

14. Francis Stuart. *The Abandoned Snail Shell*. Dublin: The Raven Arts Press, 1987, p. 19.

15. Kevin A. Boon. *Chaos Theory and the Interpretation of Literary Texts: The Case of Kurt Vonnegut*. Lewiston, New York: Mellen Press, 1997, p. 111, n. 86.

16. Kurt Vonnegut. "A Talk with Kurt Vonnegut, Jr." with Robert Scholes. *The Vonnegut Statement*. Ed. Jerome Klinkowitz and John Somer. New York: Dell Publishing, 1973. 90–118. Reprinted in William Rodney Allen. *Conversations with Kurt Vonnegut*. Jackson, MS: University Press of Mississippi, 1981, p. 113.

17. Vonnegut, Kurt. "Two Conversations with Kurt Vonnegut" with Charlie Reilly, *College Literature*. 7 (1980) 1–29. Reprinted in Allen, p. 199. Vonnegut was chosen Man-of-the-Year on the 25th anniversary of the GE Alumni Association which is composed of people like himself who worked for GE then went on to other professions (Kurt Vonnegut. "A Skull Session with Kurt Vonnegut." Interview with Hank Nuwer. *South Carolina Review*. 19 (1987) 2–23. Reprinted in Allen. 240–264, p. 247). Paul Keating, in *Lamps for a Brighter America* (New York: McGraw Hill, 1954), claims that General Electric's Association Island, the model for Vonnegut's The Meadows was used extensively between 1910 and 1930, but by the 1950s was no longer in use (see David Y. Hughes, p. 110). Whatever the historical facts, Vonnegut's satire on corporate culture and its excesses succeeds admirably.

18. While there is no evidence Vonnegut is echoing Emily Dickinson in using "Homestead" ironically as the name for a lost Eden, their use is strikingly similar: "The Bible is an antique Volume— / Written by faded Men / At the suggestion of Holy Spectres— / Subjects—Bethlehem— / Eden—the ancient Homestead . . . " (Emily Dickinson. "The Bible is an antique Volume—." *The Poems of Emily Dickinson*. Ed. Thomas H. Johnson. [Vol. 1–3] Cambridge: Harvard University Press, 1958, Vol. 1, pp. 1065–1067, ll. 1–5).

19. Kurt Vonnegut, "Two Conversations," p. 4.

20. Kurt Vonnegut, "Two Conversations," p. 200; cf. *Wampeters, Foma & Granfaloons*, p. 261.

21. Jean Giraudoux. *The Madwoman of Chaillot*. Trans. Maurice Valency. In *Jean Giraudoux: Four Plays, Adapted, and with an Introduction by Maurice Valency*. New York: Hill and Wang, 1958, p. 17.

22. Kurt Vonnegut. *The Sirens of Titan*. New York: Dell, 1959, pp. 274–275.

23. Zoltán Abádi-Nagy. "Ironic Historicism in the American Novel of the Sixties." *John O'Hara Journal* 5.1&2 (N.D.) 83–89, p. 87).

24. Ralph Waldo Emerson. "Self-Reliance." *Ralph Waldo Emerson: Essays & Lectures*. New York: Library of America, 1983, p. 279.

25. Robert C. Elliott. *The Shape of Utopia: Studies in a Literary Genre*. Chicago: University of Chicago Press, 1970, p. 150. All references to *Walden Two* are to Skinner, B. F. *Walden Two*. New York: Macmillan, 1948.

26. John J. Pierce. *Foundations of Science Fiction: A Study in Imagination and Evolution*. Westport, CT: Greenwood Press, 1987, p. 168.

27. John J. Pierce, p. 168.

28. Kurt Vonnegut. "Kurt Vonnegut, Jr." Interview with John Casey and Joe David Bellamy. *The New Fiction: Interviews with Innovative American Writers.* Ed. Joe David Bellamy. Urbana: University of Illinois Press, 1974. 194–207. Reprinted in Allen. 156–165, p. 157.

29. Ralph Barton Perry. *Puritanism and Democracy.* New York: Harper, 1944, p. 27.

30. Ralph Barton Perry, p. 27.

31. Lewis Mumford, p. 4.

32. Tony Tanner. *City of Words. American Fiction, 1950–1970.* New York: Harper & Row, 1971, p. 182.

33. David Y. Hughes, p. 114, n. 20.

34. Kurt Vonnegut. *Galápagos.* New York: Dell, 1985, pp. 68–69.

35. Kurt Vonnegut. *God Bless You, Mr. Rosewater.* 1965. New York: Dell, 1970, see especially pp. 21–22.

36. Kurt Vonnegut, *Galápagos,* p. 71.

37. Robert C. Elliott, p. 101.

38. e. e. cummings. "you shall above all things be glad and young." *Poems 1923–1954.* New York: Harcourt, Brace, 1954, p. 345, lines 12–13.

39. David Rampton. "Into the Secret Chamber: Art and the Artist in Kurt Vonnegut's *Bluebeard*" *Critique* 35 (1993) 16–26, pp. 24–25.

40. Jean Giraudoux, p. 17.

41. Yet, as his introduction to *Slaughterhouse-Five* some fifteen years after *Player Piano* makes abundantly clear, Vonnegut cannot be overly optimistic about the prospects for American society and culture. "[. . .] I crossed the Delaware River where George Washington had crossed it [. . .] went to the New York World's Fair, saw what the past had been like, according to the Ford Motor Car Company and Walt Disney, saw what the future would be like, according to General Motors" (Kurt Vonnegut. *Slaughterhouse-Five.* New York: Dell, 1969, p. 18).

DONALD E. MORSE

The "Black Frost" Reception of Kurt Vonnegut's Fantastic Novel Breakfast of Champions (1973)

It appears to me [that] I'm wildly experimental.
—Kurt Vonnegut

Of all Kurt Vonnegut's novels to date, none has provoked such strong and diverse reactions as *Breakfast of Champions* (1973). A novel some critics love to hate so much that they devote a disproportionate amount of space to denigrating it and pointing out its "weaknesses." "To read *Breakfast of Champions* a decade after its publication," writes one with qualified disdain, "is to be somewhat put off by the author's crabbiness, effrontery, self-indulgence, and admissions of mental instability" (Cowart 173). Others remain comfortable discussing the novel using critical clichés, such as "no matter how assertively or repetitiously the claim is made, there is no 'I' that means an author outside the text" (Greer 317).[1] Still others appear content to belabor the obvious as a result of believing that "Vonnegut has taken a fictional cul-de-sac" (Messent 113–114), while an unwary few take *Breakfast of Champions*' narrator's assessments at face value as those of Vonnegut himself with unfortunate critical results. "Vonnegut describes himself [sic] as 'programmed at fifty to perform childishly.' The style of the novel with its drawings of a light switch, a cow, and a hamburger is so apparently childish that perhaps Vonnegut should be taken at his word. [. . .] *Breakfast of Champions* [. . .] mixed critical reception

Journal of the Fantastic in the Arts, Volume 11, Number 2 (2000): pp. 143–153. Copyright © 2000 Florida Atlantic University.

41

is therefore no surprise" (Berryman, "After the Fall" 101).[2] But it is. As Peter Reed contends, *Breakfast of Champions* "is perhaps the most obviously experimental of all of his novels, forthrightly downgrading traditional novelistic preoccupations such as character motivation and plot development. The author appears—as author and as character—in the fiction and notes the fictionality of the other characters" (534). Other novelists may have downgraded one or another of the various techniques of fiction. Some have eliminated the narrator or made the narrator almost completely unreliable, while still others have included drawings, diagrams, pictures, or even more outrageously left a page blank for readers to fill in with their own description of the ideal heroine. Yet when Vonnegut innovates in such or similar ways with considerable skill and art in *Breakfast of Champions*, critics pounce. What are Vonnegut's literary offenses in this wonderfully self-reflexive, post-modern, fantastic comic novel that so infuriated critics and reviewers?

Vonnegut's literary progenitor in American literature, Mark Twain also had a predilection for offending the literary establishment of his day. In what proved his most memorable offense, Twain in December 1877 gave an after-dinner speech commemorating the seventieth birthday of John Greenleaf Whittier. In the audience were such dignitaries as Henry Wadsworth Longfellow, Ralph Waldo Emerson, and Oliver Wendell Holmes—each of whom Twain parodied in the talk. The parodies involved satiric versions of their verse including misattribution, comic speech, comic action, and even physical comedy, all set in a miner's cabin in the Far West. The piece concludes with Twain assuring the poor beleaguered miner that "these were not the gracious singers to whom we & the world pay loving reverence & homage: these were impostors." To which the miner replies: "Ah—impostors, were they? are you?" (294). This speech, including its postmodern conclusion, was entirely satiric and meant to be wildly comic. Instead, it produced a prolonged silence and, what Twain later described as, "a sort of black frost."

Almost one hundred years later—and, I believe, for quite similar reasons—Vonnegut's *Breakfast of Champions* met with a similar black frost reception. Twain and Vonnegut both gore some sacred cows and pay for it with poor reviews. Twain's belonged, of course, to the Boston Brahmins, the literary establishment of his day, while Vonnegut's sacred cows are the darlings of some of the most fashionable literary critics who form the literary establishment of his day. *Breakfast of Champions'* offense lies first and foremost in Vonnegut's parodying the postmodern novel. The novel successfully laughs at several postmodern fictional devices, especially that of the self-reflexive author who trespasses the boundaries of his own work. Charles Berryman correctly concludes, "if the author becomes a naive character, bewildered and lost in his own novel, the result is comedy and satire. No one has presented this aspect of postmodern fiction with more comic delight than Kurt Vonnegut in *Breakfast of Champions*"

("Comic Persona" 162). But what offends many critics is that this comic delight arises, in part, from Vonnegut's satire of the very device itself.[3] Vonnegut's bungling and inept author loses control of his fiction, not only "performing childishly," but also foolishly and often ineptly. When Flann O'Brien in *At Swim-Two-Birds* (1939) had the characters of his fictional author revolt against him, because he, as author, insisted on writing inappropriate, childish, and often immoral actions for them as characters to perform, the result was a clear parody of the convention of the omniscient author. O'Brien's author modeled on James Joyce, having established his fictional world, then attempted unsuccessfully to remove himself from it in order to pare his fingernails. Rather than stage a character revolt like O'Brien's with its emphasis on the fictional author's inability to control his characters, Vonnegut focuses instead on his fictional author's inability to perform as an omniscient, omnipotent deity. Not only can he not control his characters, but he also has difficulties with elements of the setting and even with some of his own actions within the story. "Vonnegut's narrator has very limited power to create or destroy. He is trapped and victimized in the world of his own characters. Any attempt to assume godlike power leads quickly to a pratfall" (Berryman, "Comic Persona" 167).

Perhaps to compensate for such limitations, the narrator of *Breakfast of Champions* adopts a pose of innocent, uninvolved objectivity—"I just got here myself," might sum up his attitude—and uses it to point out the lunacy of much of what he sees. The most obvious example is that of people manufacturing poisons or taking other similar actions to destroy the earth. The narrator details America's willingness to despoil the planet in order to produce waste from "Kleenex tissues, and newspapers and soot" (83) and "wash day products, catfood, pop" (84). The results may be seen in the "poisoned marshes and meadows of New Jersey" through which the truck rolls (84). Apparently having only a rudimentary comprehension of English, the narrator speaks as if deciphering activities and feelings for a visitor from another galaxy. For instance, when the truck driver confesses that "It broke his heart when he imagined what the marshes and meadows had been like only a hundred years before," the narrator observes "He had a point. The planet was being destroyed by manufacturing processes, and what was being manufactured was lousy, by and large" (84). Later, the driver perceptively remarks that "he knew that his truck was turning the atmosphere into poison gas, and that the planet was being turned into pavement so his truck could go anywhere." "So I'm committing suicide," he concluded (85).

The narrator's disingenuously naive style also proves well matched to his indiscriminate interest in everything on this peculiar planet from the Architectonic Plate Theory of the earth (143), the identity and biography of St. Anthony (211–212), the diagram of a plastic molecule (227), to the famous Nelson Rockefeller greeting and handshake. He is so impressed with "a

Mexican beetle which could make a blank-cartridge gun out of its rear end. It could detonate its own farts and knock over other bugs with shock waves" (160) that he includes a felt tip pen drawing of a beetle. This deadpan, always-willing-to-explain-even-the-obvious pose reflects the narrator's objectivity, while also emphasizing how removed he is attempting to be from the novel's action. Yet his remarks often lead to social criticism by way of the comedian's stock-in-trade, the "double-take." For example, he describes Kilgore Trout's hitching a ride on that destructive truck going from New York City to Midland City, Ohio:

> He crossed the island of Manhattan from east to west in the company of Kleenex tissues and newspapers and soot.
> He got a ride in a truck. It was hauling seventy-eight thousand pounds of Spanish olives. It picked him up at the mouth of the Lincoln Tunnel, which was named in honor of a man who had had the courage and imagination to make human slavery against the law in the United States of America. This was a recent innovation.
> The slaves were simply turned loose without any property. They were easily recognizable. They were black. They were suddenly free to go exploring. (83)

Of the nine sentences quoted, eight are simple declarative sentences: subject, verb, object; and very few of the words have more than two syllables. It is as if the narrator is explaining something to a child. Ostensibly, he clarifies the tunnel's name, but more subtly he asserts the origins and continuation of America's racism, with its failure to provide for the newly freed slaves, its continuing failure to offer work and opportunity to black people.

This flat naïve style has a secondary effect as well. Although some critics have argued that Vonnegut's "stylistic approach basically fails and comes close at times to mere childishness" (Messent 113–114), a closer analysis of the text of *Breakfast of Champions* reveals that this naive style, this so-called "childishness," actually helps defamiliarize what we have come to accept as ordinary everyday truth. For example, there is often an inherent, if rarely remarked upon, contradiction in phrases and name brands, such as "Pyramid Trucking Company." Their fleet of trucks are ironically named for "buildings which haven't moved an eighth of an inch since Christ was born" (*Breakfast of Champions* 109, Hume's example 210). Vonnegut's technique of "digging the literal out of what have become dead metaphors" (Hume, "Heraclitean" 210) often startles the reader. Moreover, the over-all satiric effect of this childishness, naivete, and simplicity arises from the increasing comic dislocation. Addressing his apparently extra-terrestrial audience, for instance, the narrator patiently explains all too simply the logic behind the Vietnam War.

"Viet Nam was a country where America was trying to make people stop being communists by dropping things on them from airplanes. The chemicals [. . .] were intended to kill all the foliage, so it would be harder for communists to hide from airplanes" (85–86). The notion of changing a people's political beliefs "by dropping things on them from airplanes" is worthy of Jonathan Swift or Mark Twain. People who are being bombed rarely regard those who bomb them as friends nor do they see the bombing as part of an educative or persuasive process, but rather as one designed solely to achieve their own destruction. Here, logic has gone haywire since the means used (bombs) almost guarantee that the end they were designed to achieve (ending communism in Vietnam) can not, will not be achieved. The satire and comedy work by taking the political and moral justification for the Vietnam War—saving that part of the world from communism—and juxtaposing it to the means used—bombs and, worse, napalm and defoliants. This becomes yet another example of what Kathryn Hume calls, "the interrelating of disparities" ("Heraclitean" 211). The over-all artistic effect has been described trenchantly by one critic as "choice little epiphanies of reduction demonstrating the American penchant for the grotesquely asinine" (McGinnis 7).

Finally, the narrator of *Breakfast of Champions* is himself the butt of satire and parody. Nowhere in Vonnegut's fiction is there precedent, except as parody or satire, for this narrator's pretentious assertion that "I was on a par with the Creator of the Universe there in the dark in the cocktail lounge" (200). Yet as creator, the narrator is not personally very remarkable. Yes, it is true that in the words used to described the comic book hero, Superman, he can "leap completely over an automobile" (289) with a single bound, but meanwhile one of his characters breaks his toe and a dog from another version of the novel almost bites him! Not exactly an outstanding record. Yes, he can foretell the future, but whenever he does so what he says is truly trivial and ultimately not very revealing, as seen clearly in his predicting that a character will get a new set of radial tires! Seemingly unable to really manipulate his characters, this narrator discovers that once he creates them they have a life of their own which he is not free to violate.

If "Pride goeth before a fall," then this narrator is headed for a very big pratfall indeed. Charles Berryman is exactly right when he advises: "We should laugh at the vanity of the narrator" ("Comic Persona" 168).

Once the narrator of *Breakfast of Champions* is viewed as a naive storyteller, the many conversations in the novel about the very process of writing are understandable in a new context. When the narrator says to himself, "this is a very bad book you're writing," we should hear the comic despair of Philboyd Studge unable to live up to the standards of the Houyhnhnms. If the dissatisfaction were Vonnegut's, there would be no excuse for publishing the book = ("Comic Persona" 167).

Still, several critics insist on equating the author with his persona or narrator in ways somewhat similar to those of readers, such as Queen Anne of England who famously misread Swift's "An Argument Against Abolishing Christianity." But the Vonnegut who narrates *Breakfast of Champions* this fictitious character with all his "crabbiness, effrontery, self-indulgence, and admissions of mental instability" (Cowart 173) clearly bears little or no relation to Kurt Vonnegut, the author of numerous novels, stories, and plays.[4]

The narrator does not merely narrate the book he also cannot avoid playing a substantial role in it. He often comes perilously close to what Will Kaufman has described as "oily, devious, flattering, and two-faced as Mephistopheles or Tartuffe—and cruel as well [. . .]. By calling attention to his own confidence game as an artist and comedian, he warns that escapism into art may assist adaptation, but it may also amount to self-deception with dangerous consequences" (32). Vonnegut, as author, meanwhile continuously undercuts such perilous consequences by holding the narrator also named "Vonnegut" up to ridicule whenever he boasts of his omniscience or omnipotence. "Anticipating an audience now ready to chip away at his new fame and fortune [after the critical and commercial success of *Slaughterhouse-Five*], Vonnegut presents a comic image of the author dissatisfied with his own work and then attacked by a ravenous dog at the end of the book. The writer appears as a character in his own novel, not merely to conduct a dialogue with himself about the relationship of art and life, but also to deflect the charges of his audience" (Berryman, "Comic Persona" 164). Both as narrator and as character this "Vonnegut" simply fails to accomplish much, if anything. Perhaps the best, clearest example of his ineffectiveness occurs close to the novel's end when the narrator as all-powerful author in pursuit of his character Kilgore Trout attempts to turn on the dome light of his rented car and instead turns on the windshield wipers. While this error is a common enough, if mildly embarrassing experience of anyone who's rented an unfamiliar car, it becomes devastating for this particular narrator. For this narrator claims to be not just anyone, but Someone who is both Omnipotent and Omniscient. Similarly, when this narrator issues his pompous, god-like, pronouncement, "Arise, Mr. Trout, you are free, you are free" (294), he is immediately confronted not by a grateful Trout, but by the image of Vonnegut's father who, like the vicious dog that bites the fumbling narrator, is another rejected character from another unfinished novel (*Jailbird* 13–15).[5]

The narrator of *Breakfast of Champions* appears not surprisingly far removed from the successful, accomplished author, Kurt Vonnegut and perilously close to the failed author, Kilgore Trout. Trout emerges in *Breakfast of Champions* not only as a central character but also as the exemplary failed author. As character, Trout spins improbable and half-thought-out plots that allow Vonnegut to introduce ideas, motifs, characters, and situations without committing to them fictionally or having them as an integral part of the story. As the failed author primer *inter pares* he fails in every sense, not just in one or two. He fails commercially, being published in sleazy porn magazines as filler between the lurid, graphic pictures. He fails critically, having never been reviewed or acknowledged by any reader, reviewer, or critic, except Eliot Rosewater who has enough money to make Trout famous. He fails artistically, producing only hackwork, trivia, and ill-considered potboilers. (All of that makes him a perfect foil for Vonnegut's own carefully formed and crafted work.)

Trout as failure plays a key role in the climax of *Breakfast of Champions* where the pompous narrator, makes his long-awaited announcement about setting his characters "free." Confronting Trout as his creator, he announces:

> "I am approaching my fiftieth birthday, Mr. Trout," I said. "I am cleansing and renewing myself for the very different sorts of years to come. Under similar spiritual conditions, Count Tolstoy freed his serfs. Thomas Jefferson freed his slaves. I am going to set at liberty all the literary characters who have served me so loyally during my writing career." (293)[6]

"The paradox, of course, is that by setting him free, Vonnegut reveals his character's unfreedom. This is a paradigmatic postmodernist moment of ontological short-circuit," as Brian McHale observes (214). And Trout, who as the novel progresses has come more and more to resemble Vonnegut's father, answers in a voice which is also that of Vonnegut's father, "Make me young, make me young, make me young!" (295). Trout dreams of returning to his youth, dreams of magically receiving a second chance from his creator—as do many people, but with the difference that this creator, as novelist, can make such fantasies come true by simply typing a new page. Yet even here, Vonnegut makes an ironic joke at Trout's expense, for, like the famous sibyl of Cumae, Trout makes the mistake of asking for youth and no more. The fumbling narrator of *Breakfast of Champions* is powerless to grant his wish since he is, like all of Vonnegut's narrators, a single-book author. But Vonnegut, the author and creator of Kilgore Trout, can and does willingly oblige him. In *Jailbird* he does make Trout young again, but puts him in jail serving a life sentence! As the Latin satirist wryly remarked, "When the gods want to punish us, they answer our prayers!"

Breakfast of Champions is, itself, much like Trout's wish for youth; that is, the novel projects a fantasy of returning to lost innocence.[7] Set first in the bleak landscape of New York City, then in the psychotically disturbed one of Midland City, the book projects an air of innocence throughout—even when discussing pornography, pollution, and crime. In part, this viewpoint reflects the narrator treating everything and everyone equally, so that nothing surprises and nothing stands out—not even himself as creator. There may well be echoes of the "duty dance with death" of *Slaughterhouse-Five* in the discussion of suicide (192) and in the certain knowledge of mortality shared by all the characters including the narrator. The narrator at the beginning of the novel describes himself as feeling "as though having ascended one slope" of a roof and now finding himself "crossing the spine" (4). But unlike in *Slaughterhouse-Five,* all such considerations of the duty dance with death in *Breakfast of Champions* become linked with the book's antic comedy and playfulness. Resisting "the seduction of fatalism," Vonnegut suggests that if "we cannot make ourselves young again, [. . .] we can make ourselves more humane" (Merrill 160).

Besides the dream of personal eternal youth externalized in Trout's crie de coeur—"Make me young, make me young, make me young!" (295)—there lies behind *Breakfast of Champions* a second, similar all-encompassing dream of regaining the lost innocence of the United States. Once a green and pleasant land, America is now in great danger of being destroyed by greed, lust, and stupidity. Once there was the promise of America, "the last and greatest of all human dreams," as F. Scott Fitzgerald phrased it in *The Great Gatsby.* As *Breakfast of Champions* demonstrates, that promise disappeared on the anonymous Interstate, in the drab motel, in the polluting washing powder and tissues and waste, and in the ubiquitous advertising for these and other ephemeral products. "What passes for a culture in my head is really a bunch of commercials, and this is intolerable," lamented Vonnegut in *Wampeters, Foma & Granfaloons* (281) and so wrote this satiric novel about the lack of a true culture in the United States. The false culture may be seen in the book's title, "Breakfast of Champions" and subtitle, "Goodbye Blue Monday" which represent two of over five to six thousand ads which an average American sees every single day. And, what then becomes of the parallel equally naïve dream of the young child staring at the cereal box with its advertising slogan liberally dipped in hope—"Breakfast of Champions?" That motto promised the child that she, too, could be a winner, a "champion." But even that dream disappeared, trivialized, turned into the consumerism of American sports. In its place, there appears the pornographic dream of male dominance parodied in *Breakfast of Champions* by the significantly large dimensions of the narrator's penis (284). (Of course, even his sizable organ fades to insignificance when compared to that of the blue whale! [147].)

Moreover, all the characters in *Breakfast of Champions* together with the bumbling narrator and "—including Vonnegut himself—are stranded in a stagnant, indifferent American present with no promise of a viable future. [. . .] Death is pitted against the life of America itself, a nation deceived by the impression of its own glory and moral supremacy, slowly suffering from the crumbling of its very foundation, the spirit of its people" (Kaufman 24,

25). Some critics misinterpret this picture of "a stagnant, indifferent American present" as "signs of tiredness" in the author rather than as a satiric, critical portrait. Some go so far as to patronize Vonnegut by citing *Breakfast of Champions* as clear evidence of Vonnegut's being mentally and emotionally drained by the efforts required to write *Slaughterhouse-Five* (Messent 104).[8] Still others view Vonnegut's fiction after *Slaughterhouse-Five*, beginning with *Breakfast of Champions*, as a descent from the peak of Billy Pilgrim's story. Such vistas and views are, however, more likely to be in the eye of the reader than in the fiction itself.

In the exuberant comic dislocation of *Breakfast of Champions* Vonnegut "plays" in a serious way with the nature of narrative and with his role as a writer. These innovations in narrative and point of view, help enable Vonnegut to discuss large social issues, such as ecocide, racism, drug addiction, and economic inequality.[9] Having dealt in his first six novels with such imponderable questions as why evil appears ubiquitous and how there can be such unmotivated human suffering in the world, the antic comedy of *Breakfast of Champions* must have come as a kind of relief. In *Breakfast of Champions*, he shares with his reader both the exhilaration that comes with "crossing the spine" of the roof—including the attendant danger of being so far above the ground—and the speculation possible when viewing the human comedy from such a height. The flux of human life must be accepted as permanent, suggests *Breakfast of Champions*, as *Slaughterhouse-Five* stressed the necessity of accepting the inevitability of suffering in human experience. Vonnegut "has explored this flux as madness, as the product of evil, as the result of man's consuming greed, and as the result of natural forces," writes Hume.

> He has looked anthropologically at man's defenses against the instability, and he has explored man's ways of keeping the tides of change at bay. More important, Vonnegut has found his own way of anchoring his perceptions amidst the flow. What he can accept as fixed may be very limited, but he has found some stabilities—human consciousness, helpfulness, decency—and from these he is beginning to build further fictions. ("Heraclitean" 224)

These "stabilities" form the normative base from which Vonnegut launches his elaborate satire of the post-modern self-reflexive novel. Unable to recognize his satiric intent or sometimes unable simply to accept his considerable artistic success, some critics have ignored when they have not out-rightly disparaged *Breakfast of Champions*. While this most experimental of all Vonnegut's novels may have produced a black frost of critical reception, it has also proven one of his most complex, most accomplished of fantastic fictions in its post-modern comic self-reflexivity.

Notes

1. Greer maintains that "in a schizophrenic text [. . .] every time you try to settle the problem of who is real, the problem itself becomes unsettled because the terms that define the problem become indistinct. *Breakfast of Champions* argues the impossibility of the real/unreal dichotomy" (Greer 315). Fair enough, but Greer's essay proves impossibly ponderous often belaboring the obvious, such as the fact that Vonnegut did not write *Venus on the Half-Shell* but Phillip José Farmer did as part of his Fictional Authors Series. (Surely it is time to lay to rest that controversy so well documented in interviews and writing by both authors.)

2. Berryman apparently had a change of mind some years after writing this essay, since his later essay "Vonnegut's Comic Persona" (1990) lavishly praises *Breakfast of Champions*.

3. For a discussion of Vonnegut's satire in general exclusive of *Breakfast of Champions*, see Morse, "Once and Future."

4. For a contrast with the parodies in *Breakfast of Champions* of Vonnegut's values and incidents in his life, see *Timequake* (1997) a novel that seriously reflects upon events in Vonnegut's life and fiction writing.

5. This unfinished novel takes place in heaven, where to the narrator's dismay, his "father [. . .] chose to be only nine years old." And from there on his father torments him extensively. "It insisted on being a very unfriendly story, so I quit writing it" (*Jailbird* 13, 15).

6. There is an irony here at the expense of the narrator since Jefferson, when he went to free his slaves, found he could not because they were too heavily mortgaged. As for Vonnegut freeing Kilgore Trout, John Leonard accurately observes, "readers hate this, which is why Conan Doyle had to bring back Sherlock Holmes [. . .]" (302) and Vonnegut had to bring back Trout albeit with an alias as early as *Jailbird*.

7. For a discussion of Vonnegut's uses of the techniques of the fantastic, see Morse, "Gaudi."

8. Vonnegut once commented that "*Slaughterhouse-Five* and *Breakfast of Champions* used to be one book. But they just separated completely. [. . .] I was able to decant *Slaughterhouse-Five,* and what was left was *Breakfast of Champions*" (*Wampeters, Foma & Granfaloons* 281). A somewhat similar process occurs with *Timequake* and *Timequake One.*

9. Berryman claims that Vonnegut withheld *Breakfast of Champions* from publication for several years fearing that his audience would expect a sequel to *Slaughterhouse-Five* ("Comic Persona" 163–164). Unfortunately, given the radical nature of *Breakfast of Champions* I doubt most publishers would consider publishing it as a first novel by an unknown writer.

Works Cited

Berryman, Charles. "After the Fall: Kurt Vonnegut." *Critique* 26 (1985): 96–102.
———. "Vonnegut's Comic Persona." In Merrill, *Critical Essays.* 162–170.
Cowart, David. "Culture and Anarchy: Vonnegut's Later Career." In Merrill, *Critical Essays.* 170–188.
Fitzgerald, F. Scott. *The Great Gatsby.* 1926. New York: Penguin, 1950.
Greer, Creed. "Kurt Vonnegut and the Character of Words." *Journal of Narrative Technique* 19 (1989): 312–330.

Hume, Kathryn. "The Heraclitean Cosmos of Kurt Vonnegut." *Papers on Language &*
Literature 18 (1982): 208–224. Reprinted in Merrill, *Essays*. 216–230.

———. "Kurt Vonnegut and the Myths and Symbols of Meaning." *Texas Studies in Literature*
and Language 24 (1982): 429–447. Reprinted in Merrill, *Essays*. 201–216.

Kaufman, Will. "Vonnegut's *Breakfast of Champions:* A Comedian's Primer" *Thalia: Studies in*
Literary Humor 13 (1993): 22–33.

Klinkowitz, Jerome. "Vonnegut in America." *Vonnegut in America*. Ed. Jerome Klinkowitz
and Donald L. Lawler. New York: Delacorte Press, 1977. 7–36.

Leonard, John. "Black Magic." Review of *Hocus Pocus*. *The Nation* 15 (October 1990:
421–425). Reprinted in Mustazza, Leonard, ed. *The Critical Response to Kurt Vonnegut*,
Westport, CT: Greenwood Press, 1994. 301–307.

McGinnis, Wayne D. "Vonnegut's *Breakfast of Champions:* A Reductive Success." *Notes on*
Contemporary Literature 5 (1975): 6–9.

McHale, Brian. *Postmodernist Fiction*. New York: Routledge, 1987.

Merrill, Robert, ed. *Critical Essays on Kurt Vonnegut*. Boston: Hall, 1990.

———. "Vonnegut's *Breakfast of Champions:* The Conversion of Helliogabalus." *Critique* 18
(1979): 99–109. Reprinted in Merrill, *Critical Essays*. 153–161.

Messent, Peter B. "*Breakfast of Champions:* The Direction of Kurt Vonnegut's Fiction." *Journal*
of American Studies 8 (1974): 101–114.

Morse, Donald E. "Kurt Vonnegut: the Antonio Gaudi of Fantastic Fiction." *The Centennial*
Review 42.1 (1998): 173–183.

———. "Kurt Vonnegut: the Once and Future Satirist." *The Dark Fantastic: Selected Essays*
from the Ninth International Conference on the Fantastic in the Arts. Ed. C. W. Sullivan
III. Westport, CT: Greenwood Press, 1997. 161–169.

O'Brien, Flann [Brian O'Nolan]. *At Swim-Two-Birds*. 1939. New York: New American
Library, 1976.

Reed, Peter J. "Kurt Vonnegut (1922–)." *Postmodern Fiction: a Bio-Bibliographic Guide*. Ed.
Larry McCaffery. Westport, CT: Greenwood Press, 1986. 533–535.

Twain, Mark [Samuel Clemens]. "Whittier Birthday Dinner Speech." *Anthology of American*
Literature: II. Realism to the Present. Ed. George McMichael. New York: Macmillan,
1974. 2.290–294.

Vonnegut, Kurt. *Breakfast of Champions*. 1973. New York: Dell, 1991.

———. *Fates Worse Than Death: An Autobiographical Collage of the 1980s*. 1991. New York:
Vintage, 1992.

———. *God Bless You, Mr. Rosewater*. 1965. New York: Dell, 1970.

———. *Jailbird*. New York: Dell Publishing, 1979.

———. *Palm Sunday: An Autobiographical Collage*. 1981. New York: Dell, 1984.

———. *Slaughterhouse-Five*. New York: Dell, 1969.

———. *Timequake*. New York: Putnam, 1997.

———. *Wampeters, Foma & Granfaloons*. New York: Delacorte Press, 1976.

———. "Interview with Kurt Vonnegut." *Writer's Workshop*. SCTV, Public Broadcast Service,
1980.

———. "Two Conversations with Kurt Vonnegut" with Charlie Reilly, *College Literature* 7
(1980): 1–29. Reprinted in Allen, William Rodney. *Conversations with Kurt Vonnegut*.
Jackson, MS: University Press of Mississippi, 1981. 196–229.

MÓNICA CALVO PASCUAL

Kurt Vonnegut's The Sirens of Titan: Human Will in a Newtonian Narrative Gone Chaotic

Every pattern may in fact be part of a larger pattern outside its control, [...] the spectacle of the plotter plotted [...]. Can the binary opposition of fixity/ fluidity be mediated by some third state or term? (Tanner 1979: 183, 19)

This paper intends to explore the notion of human identity in its relation with the much-debated issue of free will as portrayed by Kurt Vonnegut's 1959 novel *The Sirens of Titan*. The key point in my proposal shall be the idea that, written at the very threshold of the postmodernist period, *The Sirens of Titan* invites a shift of perspective in the interpretation of "reality"—namely, a transition from the modern Newtonian to a postmodernist chaotic scientific paradigm. Thus, I shall try to unravel how there is in the novel an implicit counter-message parallel to and subtly undermining its apparent affirmation of determinism. For this purpose, I shall focus on the way some passages in the novel reflect some of the major theories about the chaotic behavior of molecular systems as developed by thermodynamicist Ilya Prigogine and thermodynamicist, philosopher and historian of science Isabelle Stengers, basically temporal irreversibility and the combination of chance and necessity in molecular creative processes. Finally, I shall analyze the metaphysical macrocosmic implications of Vonnegut's novel—first, as an answer to the individuals' felt inability to find their identity through

Miscelánea: A Journal of English and American Studies, Volume 24 (2001): pp. 53–63. Copyright © 2001 University of Zaragoza.

decision-making; and second, as a way out of constraining, totalizing explanations of the world and of the collective paranoia which the search for those explanations may bring about.

In the sci-fi guise through which *The Sirens of Titan* is presented, the novel can be read as a landmark in *scientific* fiction inasfar as it forces a shift in the readers' views of the universe and human experience that will enable them to handle the apparent inner contradictions of the novel's implied premises.

Some critics assert that *The Sirens of Titan* centres on the conflict between the belief in free will and a deterministic understanding of the world and of human "progress", in which it is the latter, they agree, that gets the upper-hand (cf. Silver 2000; Klein 1998; Lundquist 1980: 29; Mayo 1977: 18–19). At first sight, indeed, the novel looks like a bleak but definitive affirmation of a deterministic universe ruled by some sort of unknowable external forces. These forces apparently control and manipulate every human being's actions and thoughts for their own mean purposes. And this human inescapability from a "destiny" which one cannot even understand is represented in the novel as having two possible consequences: either apathy and self-abandonment to those mysterious forces, or engagement in a personal quest to discover the meaning of one's role in the universal design.

Both attitudes find expression in *The Sirens of Titan*. The first is encouraged by Winston Niles Rumfoord's Tralfamadorian, deterministic view of events, epitomized in the motto he repeats in almost the same wording: "everything that ever has been always will be, and everything that ever will be has been" (1996: 19–20, 201). The second attitude clearly stems from a centuries-long mechanistic Newtonian interpretation of the world: the need of human reason to account for everything that happens and exists by means of the law of cause and effect. Every event and experience must have a reason or come about as the consequence of some previous thing for the "Enlightened" mind to feel in charge of what is outside itself. In fact, the human need to rationalize not only the workings of the self but also everything different from it seems to be an inevitable result of the nature of human beings as symbolic animals. According to Robert Nadeau (1981: 5), the acquisition of symbolic language by human beings resulted in the separation of their individuality from the rest of the world, while external "reality" became fragmented into multiple separate categories. And the only way for those symbolic beings to relate to those categories and make sense of them was, paradoxically, by creating patterns in which those categories could fit by means of the symbolic language which had estranged and fractured human experience.

Hayden White describes the human tendency to narrativize isolated events in order to make them meaningful as the outcome of "a desire to have real events display the coherence, integrity, fullness, and closure of an image of life that *is and can only be imaginary*" (1981: 23; emphasis added). It is this need to find or create patterns, Jerome Klinkowitz argues, that defines Vonnegut's characters and plots. Indeed, he goes on, the novelist's training as both anthropologist and fictionist has taught him that "men and women [...] are the only creatures in nature whose lives seemed bedeviled by having to find a purpose for things, a meaning for existence that in natural terms would rather follow its own rhythms of being" (1998: 8). This need for a global explanation of human affairs may have, in turn, two distinct consequences: for one, the individuals may unconsciously *project* an invented, conveniently meaningful narrative in which all the pieces fit together. Or they may be infected by one of the more common diseases of the current American ethos, as Tony Tanner suggests:

> There is [...] an abiding American dread that someone else is patterning your life, that there are all sorts of invisible plots afoot to rob you of your autonomy of thought and action, that conditioning is ubiquitous. [...] The possible nightmare of being totally controlled by unseen agencies and powers is never far away in contemporary American fiction. [...] Confronted with this, American hero and author alike tend to react with a somewhat paranoid worry about who or what implanted those "underlying patterns" which programme their responses (1979: 15, 421).

These two possibilities are differently embodied in *The Sirens of Titan* and constitute the basic pillars of its structure. The first one is activated by Malachi Constant's initial belief that, given the meaning of his name ("faithful messenger" (14)), he was to be gifted with "a single message that was sufficiently dignified and important to merit his carrying it humbly between two points. [...] What Constant had in mind, presumably, was a first-class message from God to someone equally distinguished" (14). This character's attitude represents not only the people's need to make "purposeful" sense of their lives, as conventionally understood, but also their wish that the "purpose" involved be outstanding and that they be the protagonists.

The two possibilities fuse most conspicuously in the figure of Winston Niles Rumfoord. Being "chrono-synclastic infundibulated" (11) and therefore able to see all temporal dimensions—past, present and future—simultaneously, he jumps to the conclusion that everything in the history of humankind follows a pre-established order programmed by some extraterrestrial robots from "Tralfamadore" to serve their own ends (190–191). Rumfoord is both "plotter" and "plotted", to use Tanner's terms (1979: 183): enjoying a global view of time, he "plots" or imposes a totalizing "meaningful" pattern to what he sees (his conviction that history is governed by Tralfamadorians), while feeling "plotted" in it (he believes the accident by which he became chrono-synclastic infundibulated was just another Tralfamadorian maneuver to achieve their ends through his aid). Rumfoord, therefore, unconsciously gets trapped in the pattern of meaning he himself imposes, becoming a paranoid victim of his own forceful projections.

From the start, the reader tends to identify with this character insofar as they share the knowledge of what the whole succession of events eventually amounts to and this viewpoint places them in a superior, ironic position with respect to the other characters in the novel. Consequently, the reader is forced to adopt in a straightforward manner the bleak, deterministic view of the universe that the novel seems to present. However, this view turns out to be nothing but a reflection of Rumfoord's paranoid machinations. Rumfoord is clearly depicted as a selfish, blinded man who consciously and deliberately manipulates hundreds of people so that everything fits into the scheme he has elaborated. This forcing of events inevitably brings about a suspicion that "destiny" may be not so inevitable after all and that there may be some place for free will in the world. This initial little fracture in the identification reader/character is supposed to widen the more as the reader realizes how contradictory Rumfoord's ideology is. On the one hand, he expounds the creed that human beings are just the victims of a series of accidents (161). But, on the other, he seems to ignore the *chance* aspect inherent in accidents and interprets them as part of the extraterrestrials' deterministic plan for the universe—with the paradoxical result that, as Stanley Schatt has stated, "he creates the Church of God the Utterly Indifferent because he cannot tolerate the thought that he does not control his own destiny" (1976: 39). That is to say, he cannot even face the ideological implications of his order-imposing activities.

The fact that such a goal-oriented man suffers from this inner conflict raises the issue of the relationship between *free will*, or the capacity to decide one's destiny, and *human-ness* itself (cf. Mayo 1977: 51; Schatt 1976: 32). For, if human beings are relegated to the position of mere pawns in a superior entity's prearranged game, they immediately lose their human dignity and status, and become little more than flesh-and-blood automata. On these assumptions, *The Sirens of Titan* has been frequently interpreted as "an expression of the belief that we are imprisoned in a universe that lacks meaning and that there is no way to make sense of the human condition [...] by showing everything as meaningless, [...] a statement of human absurdity" (Lundquist 1980: 29). My point here is to argue how this kind of limiting approach to Vonnegut's novel is caused by a failure to recognize the *shift of scientific paradigm* that underlies the logic of the story: the conflict between a *Newtonian* and a *chaotic* reading of "reality". As Prigogine and Stengers put it, Newton sought "a vision of nature that would be universal, deterministic, and objective inasmuch as it contains no reference to the observer, complete inasmuch as it attains a level of description that escapes the clutches of time" (1985: 213). The transcendence of this dependence on time can be fully appreciated in the figure of Laplace's demon—a creature who, interestingly and by no means accidentally, bears a strong resemblance to Winston Niles Rumfoord. According to Eric Charles White, Laplace's demon is "that creature of Newtonian science who, once apprised of the position and motion of all masses in the universe, could both predict the future and retrodict the past. [...] 'For it [Laplace wrote], nothing would be uncertain and the future, as the past, would thus constitute a simultaneity in the mind of this entity'" (1990: 103). White goes on to explain how

> Prigogine and Stengers suggest that the deterministic universe of *classical physics,* in which past and future are merely attributes of a theoretically graspable present totality, offers *spiritual consolation and relief from anxiety* by discovering an *imaginatively* satisfying *design* in nature. That is to say, Newtonian mechanics supports an essentially cosmic vision of the universe as an ordered, harmonious whole (1990: 103; emphasis added).

It is the influence of this Newtonian frame of mind that positions readers and critics on Rumfoord's side, who thereby see the novel's plot as the character sees the plot of history. Yet, they seem to forget that, having precise knowledge of what the future will be like, he interprets it *retrospectively,* which allows him to impose patterns that transform accidental isolated events into meaningful and purposeful ones. At the same time, critics also seem to ignore the fact that Rumfoord is forcing some of those events to happen the way he has "fore-seen" them—which implies some fear on his part that they would not really take place without his help. It is also worth noticing that the contextualization of his "task" as the engine motivating those events involves the use of traditional science-fiction motifs: antennas implanted in humans' skulls, extraterrestrial robots; spaceships or life on other planets, to mention a few. This fact makes it even harder to take Rumfoord seriously as bearer of the novel's "message" or as the author's spokesman.

Even though what seems to dominate in the novel is the characters' yearning for a totalizing grand narrative that may account for everything that happens, there are many hints in the text that point in a different direction. There is a straightforward statement by Rumfoord whose possible implications critics have systematically ignored—perhaps to avoid the contradictions it reveals at the core of his attitude. Yet, it leaves no room for doubt about the scientific frame of mind which the novel is demanding from the reader: "Things fly this way and that, my boy, [...] with or without messages. *It's chaos,* and no mistake, for the Universe is just being born. It's the great *becoming* that makes the light and the heat and the motion, and bangs you from hither to yon" (28; emphasis added).

The explicit allusion to "chaos" directs the reader's attention to the field of research in which studies on chaos theory were born, thermodynamics, inviting a parallelism between molecular and macrocosmic systems. As Prigogine and Stengers point out, before colliding, molecules behave *independently* of one another, and it is only the outcome of their collisions that creates a harmonious, coherent pattern (1985: 246):

> A system far from equilibrium may be described as *organized not because it realizes a plan alien* to elementary activities, or transcending them, but, on the contrary, because the amplification of a microscopic fluctuation occurring at the "right moment" resulted in favoring one reaction path over a number of equally possible paths. Under certain circumstances, therefore, *the role played by individual behavior can he decisive* (176; emphasis added).

The *free* actions of each individual in the universe—like a single molecule in a system—can therefore have the power to change the overall development of the structure. Nevertheless, it is not total anarchy at the hands of human beings that rules the cosmic sphere. As Eugene Debs Hartke, the protagonist of Kurt Vonnegut's *Hocus Pocus* puts it, "[. . .] all you can do is play the cards they deal you" (1990: 292)—but you *can* play them anyway. To use Prigogine and Stengers' terms once more:

> The "overall" behavior cannot in general be taken as dominating in any way the elementary processes constituting it. Self-organization processes in far-from-equilibrium conditions correspond to a delicate interplay between chance and necessity, between fluctuations and deterministic laws. We expect that near a bifurcation, fluctuations or random elements would play an important role, while between bifurcations the deterministic aspects would become dominant (1985: 176).

This interplay of necessity and chance (or time and luck) as the ruler of the universe is a recurrent theme in Vonnegut's oeuvre. It is clear, for instance, in the "prayer" Billy Pilgrim, the protagonist of *Slaughterhouse-5* has framed in his office wall and which is engraved on his lover's locket as well: "God grant me the serenity to accept the things I cannot change, courage to change the things I can, and wisdom always to tell the difference" (1991: 44, 153). Likewise, this is one of the central notions in the revision of the Book of Genesis Kilgore Trout (Vonnegut's alter ego) makes in Vonnegut's latest novel, *Timequake*, and which he explains as follows: "I hate to tell you this, friends and neighbors, but we are teensy-weensy implications in an enormous implication" (1997: 28).

This "order out of chaos" view is notably metaphorized by the narrator's description of the Rumfoord estate garden when Constant first enters it—a passage that becomes an utterly self-conscious epitome of what the whole book is about:

> The turns in the path were many, and the visibility was short. Constant was following a damp green path the width of a lawn mower—what was in fact the swath of a lawn mower. Rising on both sides of the path were the green walls of the jungle the gardens had become.
> The mower's swath skirted a dry fountain. The man who ran the mower had become creative at this point, had made the path fork. Constant could choose the side of the fountain on which he preferred to pass. Constant stopped at the fork, looked up [...]. Impulsively, Constant chose neither one fork nor the other, but climbed the fountain itself. He climbed from bowl to bowl, intending when he got to the top to see whence he had come and whither he was bound (13).

On the one hand, this passage is an overt metaphor for a free conception of a "creative" universe insofar as the path that leads to the destination (the Rumfoord mansion) *bifurcates*, forcing the pedestrian to *choose* one way or another around the fountain. This combination of *necessity* (there is one single path) and *chance* (it forks and he must choose) is inherent to the process of collisions and consequent expansion that characterizes molecular systems in far-from-equilibrium conditions. The parallelism is in turn reinforced by the fact that "the visibility was short": following the arrow of time, human beings can never predict what the future will be like, as we can only see what lies ahead up to the next bifurcation point. On the other hand, the scene also epitomizes the Newtonian attitude towards complex systems: Malachi "looks up" as if for instructions from The Grand Designer, and decides to avoid any chance element by choosing neither bifurcation. Instead, Malachi creates a *third* path in this manner: he climbs the fountain so as to get a *global* perspective of past and future: where he has come from and where he will arrive.

In addition, the fact that Constant has to follow a lawn mower swath to cross the jungle that the garden has become indicates that it is the human subject who "mows" his or her own path across the jungle of life—a clear recognition of the power of the individuals' capacity to create their own destiny. The passage might be interpreted, as well, as a reminder that everybody impersonates the role they created for themselves in the narrative they built to come to terms with their apparently meaningless lives. As Thomas R. Holland explains, human predicament in Vonnegut's work is that "man attempts to make order out of chaos. The universe is absurd, unintelligible, but man must pretend that he understands it and must try to exert control over it" (1995: 54).

> Another significant issue raised by studies in thermodynamics is what Eddington has called the "arrow of time" (cf. Prigogine and Stengers 1985: xix): time can only flow towards the future, never turn backwards toward the past. This "irreversibility plays an essential role in nature and lies at the origin of most processes of self-organization" in molecular—as well as in macrocosmic—reactions (8): it is "a manifestation of the fact that the future is not given, that, as the French poet Paul Valéry emphasized, 'time is construction'" (16).

This change in perspective as regards the nature of time, flowing always toward the future according to the thermodynamic "order out of chaos" paradigm, in opposition to the Newtonian notion that past, present and future fuse in a static whole which Laplace's demon was able to transcend, is the key for bringing to light what is ultimately wrong in—and the cause of—Rumfoord's deterministic interpretation of universal development: he violates the arrow of time—something that cannot actually be done—and, consequently, he can observe the "chaotic" behavior of the cosmos backwards[1] and thus consider it determined in advance.

The inadequacy of Rumfoord's perspective is suggested in the novel through the use of "spirals", a recurrent term in the heterodiegetic narrator's accounts: "Titan describes [. . .] a spiral around the sun. [. . .] Winston Niles Rumfoord and his dog Kazak were wave phenomena—pulsing in distorted spirals [. . .]. For reasons as yet mysterious, the spirals of Rumfoord, Kazak and Titan coincided exactly" (187), and Chrono's good luck piece is a fragment of a spiral of steel strapping that *accidentally* snarls around a worker's ankle in a school tour to a factory (102). This motif connects again with chaos theory, which has demonstrated how the *becoming matter* that results from particle collisions appears in photographs as "graceful, spiraling lines" (Nadeau 1981: 18). Yet, the narrator says that Rumfoord's spiral is "distorted" (11, 187). It is compared to the white staircase in his mansion, which is described as "a *counter-clockwise* spiral" (29; emphasis added) and dearly points to his mistaken point of view. Thus, if Rumfoord—and the reader with him—were a man of the thermodynamic age instead of a Newtonian one, he would have realized how everything was just a series of *accidents* whose succession led to Salo's accidental reception of the piece he needed to repair his spaceship—not an inevitable sequence of extraterrestrial manipulations of world history to achieve his personal ends.

The shift in scientific paradigm may in turn be read as a correlate of the evolution from the modernist to the postmodernist ideological set-up taking place at the time *The Sirens of Titan* was written. Vonnegut's novel launches a satiric comment on the modernist ethos and its failure to provide an answer to the epistemological questions it raised. The modernist writers' beliefs in the coming of a revelation or "moment of truth" are parodied by recurrent allusions (34, 168) coupled to the eternal deferral of that moment and the harmful—paranoid—effects this frustrated quest for a vision of integrated illumination can lead to.

In contrast, chaos theory, like postmodernism, "shifts attention to those aspects of reality that characterize today's accelerated social change: disorder, instability, diversity, disequilibrium, nonlinear relationships (in which small inputs can trigger massive consequences) and temporality—a heightened sensitivity to the flows of time" (Toffler in Prigogine and Stengers 1985: xiv–xv). What is more important, not only do postmodernism and chaos theory alike focus on diversity and multiplicity; they do so by paying attention to the individual aspects of a multi-vocal "reality" in fragmentation: the different scales at which "molecules" go on colliding and creating larger scales of signification and *lateral* patterns of complexity are to be observed independently, shattering the old hierarchies that stem from integrative discourses.

Looking at one of those scales, the novel seems to suggest how moral values like love and friendship can make individuals' lives meaningful by themselves, with no need for transcendence or larger-scope narratives (cf. Vit 1997; Huber 1999). This message is explicit in Constant's late discovery that "a purpose of human life, no matter who is controlling it, is to love whoever is around to be loved" (220) and in the character's final reunion in heaven with his best friend, Stoney Stevenson (222). This emphasis on the importance of human communion is reinforced by the possibility of communication, which was reduced to scarce, fruitless attempts when people became victims of their search for a transcendent purpose in human existence: the soldiers on Mars who had an antenna implanted in their skulls according to Rumfoord's plan were allowed a few times "to look around and to send messages with their eyes, *if they had messages and could find receivers*" (71; emphasis added).

As a final remark, it is worth noting how the sense of closure provided by this belief in the power of love and communication emerges as a *tour de force* imposed upon the narrative structure to somehow lessen the overall bleakness of the plot, despite its connection with the narrator's retrospective statement in the first line of the novel that "EVERYONE now knows how to find the meaning of life within himself. But mankind wasn't always so lucky" (7). Yet, however skeptic about the coherence of this paradoxical "happy ending" the reader may be—or, more precisely, because of that very paradoxical quality—, the moral ending can be recognized as the novel's last attack on the validity of any closed, self-contained and coherent explanations—a glimpse of the post-modernist ethos which, as I have tried to demonstrate, reveals the ultimate intent of the text. As Linda Hutcheon puts it, "the paradoxes of postmodern-ism work to instruct us in the inadequacies of totalizing systems and of fixed institutionalized boundaries (epistemological and ontological)" (1988: 224). And, as she points out taking on David Caute's views on metafictional works, "if art wants to make us question the 'world', it must question and expose *itself* first" (36; emphasis in the original).

To sum up, the vision of human identity and the role of free will in the development of human affairs in *The Sirens of Titan* can be fully understood only when the reader accepts the novel's invitation to interpret the universe not as a static entity outside the clutches of time but as an eternal process of becoming or self-generation. This change of perspective results from a shift of scientific paradigm that goes hand in hand with the cultural and ideo-logical evolution that was being consolidated at the moment of the novel's publication in 1959—from the modernist obsession with the discourse of integrative "revelation" to a postmodernist reaction against the excesses of narrative totalization.

NOTE

1. The same conception of the development of human and cosmic affairs is beautifully reworked in *Timequake,* where the whole universe moves a ten-year step backward "making everybody a robot of their own past" (1997: 111), unable to change the least bit of what the past during that lapse of time had been. If reversibility is possible, the novel suggests, it is so only to demonstrate that it is not. However, this step back is by no means deterministic, as *free will* "kicks in again" everywhere when the moment in which the timequake had taken place is reached for the second time.

WORKS CITED

Holland, Thomas R. 1995. *Cliffs Notes on Vonnegut's Major Works.* Lincoln: Cliffs Notes, Inc.

Huber, Chris. 1999. 'The Vonnegut Web: *The Sirens of Titan.* 1959.' In http://www.duke.edo/crh4/vonnegut/sot.html.

Hutcheon, Linda. 1988. *A Poetics of Postmodernism: History, Theory, Fiction.* New York: Routledge.

Klein, Herbert G. 1998. 'Kurt Vonnegut's *The Sirens of Titan* and the Question of Genre.' In http://www.ph-erfurt.de/neumann/esse/artic99/klein2/5_99.html.

Klinkowitz, Jerome. 1998. *Vonnegut In Fact: The Public Spokesmanship of Personal Fiction.* South Carolina: University of South Carolina Press.

Lundquist, James. 1980 (1977). *Kurt Vonnegut.* New York: Frederick Ungar Publishing Co.

Mayo, Clark. 1977. *Kurt Vonnegut: The Gospel from Outer Space (or, Yes We Have No Nirvanas)*. San Bernardino, CA: The Borgo Press.

Nadeau, Robert. 1981. *Readings from the New Book on Nature: Physics and Metaphysics in the Modern Novel*. Amherst: University of Massachusetts Press.

Prigogine, Ilya and Isabelle Stengers. 1985 (1984). *Order out of Chaos: Man's New Dialogue with Nature*. London: Flamingo.

Schatt, Stanley. 1976. *Kurt Vonnegut, Jr.* Boston: G. K. Hall & Co.

Silver, Steven. 2000. 'Steven Silver's Reviews: *The Sirens of Titan* by Kurt Vonnegut.' In http://www.sfsite.com/silverag/Vonnegut.html.

Tanner, Tony. 1979 (1971). *City of Words. A Study of American Fiction in the Mid-Twentieth Century*. London: Jonathan Cape Paperback.

Vit, Marek. 1997. 'Kurt Vonnegut's Corner: Kurt Vonnegut Jr., *The Sirens of Titan*.' In http://www.geocities.com/Hollywood/4953/kv_titan.html.

Vonnegut, Kurt. 1990. *Hocus Pocus or Perpetual Motion. A Novel*. New York: Putnam.

———. 1991 (1969). *Slaughterhouse-5*. London: Vintage Books.

———. 1996 (1959). *The Sirens of Titan*. London: Indigo.

———. 1997. *Timequake*. New York: Putnam.

White, Eric Charles. 1990. 'Contemporary Cosmology and Narrative Theory.' In Peterfreund, Stuart (ed.). *Literature and Science: Theory and Practice*. Boston: Northeastern University Press: 91–111.

White, Hayden. 1981. 'The Value of Narrativity in the Representation of Real Events.' In Mitchell, W. J. T. (ed.). *On Narrative*. Chicago: University of Chicago Press: 1–23.

TAMÁS BÉNYEI

Leakings: Reappropriating Science Fiction —The Case of Kurt Vonnegut

There is an anecdote in Kurt Vonnegut's *Breakfast of Champions* that can be read as a little parable about the paradoxes of the critical reappropriation of science fiction for what is sometimes called high literature. The faltering and tentative madness of Dwayne Hoover finally gets its direction and content from a science fiction novel. Hoover takes seriously the absurd idea in one of Kilgore Trout's novels that except for him (the reader of the novel) everybody else is a robot. Hoover's interpretation of the book clearly defies Trout's authorial intention, for "Trout did not expect to be believed. He put the bad ideas into a science fiction novel, and that was where Dwayne found them. [. . .] It was a *tour de force*. It was a *jeu d'esprit*" (24). When Trout realizes the extent of the disaster caused by the misreading of his innocuous novel, he

> became a fanatic on the importance of ideas as causes and cures for diseases. But nobody listened to him. He was a dirty old man in the wilderness, crying out among the trees and underbrush, "Ideas or the lack of them can cause disease!"
> Kilgore Trout became a pioneer in the field of mental health. He advanced his theories disguised as science fiction. (24)

Journal of the Fantastic in the Arts, Volume 11, Number 4 (2001): pp. 432–453. Copyright © 2001 Florida Atlantic University.

Within a very limited space, Kilgore Trout incarnates two models (critical constructions) of science fiction, and these two models might be read as allusions to the difference—and the impossibility of distinguishing—between elite and pulp science fiction. He starts out as a nondescript pulp science fiction writer, at least in the sense that he does not really want to say (communicate) anything in his works; his machine/robot metaphor is not intended to be taken seriously, that is, it asks to be read as just that, a metaphor (if a rather heavy-handed one; so perhaps there is a message after all). His novels do not offer messages that can be translated into any language other than that of the metaphorical text of the novels, yet one among them at least is misread by Dwayne and the interpretative error leads to existential tragedy. Read as a general comment on the genre, the lesson to be drawn from the case is at least partly poetical: one should not take seriously what science fiction novels say. The dire consequences of Dwayne's literal reading of the fanciful metaphor suggest that science fiction is not *about* the world in any relevant way.

Yet it is exactly as a result of this realization that Kilgore Trout comes to assume a radically different position, the position that is so often the guarantee of the possible redemption of science fiction and its elevation into high culture (a guarantee, I should add, that rests on moral rather than on aesthetic assumptions): the science fiction writer is redeemable inasmuch as he is a prophet writer. The trope of the prophet is what often stands behind the possibility of co-opting science fiction into high literature in critical discourse. Ironically, this critical discourse, which claims to have left Romantic delusions behind, finds itself having to resurrect an "obsolete" Romantic and Modernist metaphor of art and the figure of the artist in order to be able to salvage science fiction. Vonnegut's frequent and playful use of the rhetorical position of the prophet in many of his novels (from the cautionary, dystopian tone of *Player Piano* to novels like *Cat's Cradle, Slapstick,* and *Galapagos,* where, naturalizing prophetic knowledge, he uses narrators speaking from a moment in the future) might be read in the light of this metacritical dilemma. The above possibility is especially evident in *Breakfast of Champions,* where the device of narrating from the future is used with an explicitly metafictional intention. Here, the only object of future knowledge is the present of the narrated world: between the narrated time and the time of narration there is no future the knowledge of which would require an extrapolated narrative position in the future. What we learn about the future (the time between the narrated present and the future of the narration) is quite simply *not relevant* at all. This in turn suggests that the device of future narration (the only rhetorical residue of science fiction in the novel) is here primarily a metacritical commentary, a prophetic position without message, a rhetorical device working away "emptily."

It is as a prophet writer that Kilgore Trout is admitted into high culture—all the time writing novels which are probably no different from his earlier pulp novels. His later works are thus "serious" texts that can be reclaimed for or appropriated by high culture *in the mode of the parable*. Paradoxically, the early Trout is an unwitting (and very probably undeserving) apostle of "pure art" in the sense that his texts deny any extra-textual relevance for themselves; yet, he is considered a pulp writer because he subscribes to this aesthetic credo *within* science fiction. "Late Trout" shifts away from the ideal of pure art and uses science fiction to promote his noble sentiments (the irony is enhanced by the fact that the serious message of the later novels is precisely the denial of any seriousness to texts exactly like the ones in which the denial appears). It seems that science fiction, to qualify as the proper object of serious critical discourse, has to be depoeticized first, purged of "science fiction." This anecdote, exploring the parabolic interpretability of science fiction and the critical paradoxes entailed by such a critical stance, indicates Vonnegut's awareness of the problem as well as his double or duplicitous position regarding it.

The name of Kurt Vonnegut will inevitably appear in any discussion of the problematic relationship between science fiction and "high literature." Vonnegut's name, however, is not so much an answer to the questions raised by this relationship as part of the uncertainties and undecidabilities that are introduced by them. The vicissitudes of the critical appreciation of Vonnegut are an index of this problematic relationship. A single, very banal example will suffice here, a sentence from the blurb off the Hungarian edition of *Slapstick:* "The author, well known for his science fiction novels, and displaying a scientific imagination in his 'proper' novels as well [the Hungarian equivalent of science fiction is 'science fantasy'], has come out with yet another of his absurd-ironical-bitter apocalyptic fantasies." The sentence is structured around several dichotomies: it begins by distinguishing two Vonneguts, one a science fiction writer (he is, of course, the famous, popular author) and the other the lesser known "proper" artist, but the contrast is established only to be questioned in at least two ways. First, if Vonnegut is drawing upon his "scientific" imagination also in his "proper" novels, what is the difference? Are Vonnegut's science fiction novels simply the ones that are not successful enough to qualify as items in the oeuvre of the "proper/real" Vonnegut? Or—and the answer to this question is clearly in the negative—is it that in his more serious novels Vonnegut uses his scientific imagination to explore weightier and more worthy matters? My interrogation of the dichotomy is in a sense quite unnecessary, for it is already challenged by the obligatory (perhaps self-mocking) scare quotes accompanying the adjective "proper," initiating a potentially endless series of chiasmic reversals: is the adjective "proper" equipped with quotation marks only as a tribute to the difficulty or trickiness of Vonnegut's particular case or do the quotes indicate a general difficulty? If the latter is the case, is it because after writers like Vonnegut such adjectives, referring to the difference between the two kinds of literature, may only be used with quotation marks? And therefore the adjective could not appear in any other way because of the rest of the sentence? Or, if the quotation marks are an indication of the special case of Vonnegut, are they there perhaps because we never can tell with him, the duplicitous author of science fiction novels as well as "proper" ones, and therefore no longer an entirely serious or respectable writer, and it is better to be on the safe side and use the adjective in quotation marks (that is, revoke it)? And isn't the laborious characterization of this "proper" Vonnegut novel as an "absurd-ironical-bitter apocalyptic fantasy" the reiteration of an age-old topos of science fiction (with an ill-assorted cluster of adjectives clearly unable to bear the burden of a serious critical distinction)?

The clearest sign of the undecidability pervading the sentence is that, having read the sentence, constructed around clear-cut dichotomies and inspired by a noble desire to clarify, one still does not know quite what *Slapstick* is supposed to be. The dichotomies that were invoked to assist in clarification and categorization have broken down into endless and infertile series of reversals. Perhaps this is the basic formula for reading Vonnegut and the fate of any critical language that wishes to discuss the relationship between science fiction and high literature.

In this essay, after outlining four of the interfaces between serious literature and science fiction produced by critical discourse, I shall look at some of Kurt Vonnegut's texts as metacritical commentaries on these critical interfaces and their own location within these critically produced "common places." A few cursory remarks on *The Sirens of Titan* and *Slaughterhouse-Five* will be followed by a more detailed reading *Breakfast of Champions,* where I believe this theme receives its fullest and most "systematic" fictional treatment. I read science fiction in Vonnegut's fiction as a metacritical trope of the difference of this fiction from a vaguely defined ("realist" and occasionally modernist) poetics of fiction. Obviously this is only one, fairly limited, way of reading the presence of science fiction elements in Vonnegut (I shall be bracketing, for instance, the ontological and moral perspectives); nevertheless, I think it is a legitimate one.

Interfaces

The very fact that this relationship could become the object of serious critical discourse, that scare quotes and undecidabilities have made their appearance, is no doubt the result of what is sometimes referred to as the postmodern blurring or breakdown of boundaries between high and popular culture. It is in the work of some theoreticians of the postmodern that these interfaces or discursive zones of encounter have been produced.

The first model of this interface promotes science fiction as the most adequate expression of contemporary experience, primarily because the post-humanist future so often extrapolated in science fiction is already with us. According to Leslie Fiedler, the repeated retelling of the "myth of science fiction" is the most urgent, most typical feature of the new generation.[1] Thus, the difference between the present generation and the preceding ones can be described only with metaphors familiar from science fiction: the scale of their difference is genetic (the difference of genetic mutants) or cosmic (the difference of extraterrestrials). In this model, science fiction appears as a kind of "new realism" as well as a version of the fantastic that is attuned to the con-temporary experience with particular sensitivity and, as such, the authentic self-expression of the psychedelic generation.

In a book that is not without a certain prophetic zeal, Robert Scholes (my second interface) declares that "the most appropriate kind of fiction that can be written in the present or the immediate future is fiction that takes place in future time" (17). Projected into the future, argues Scholes, the prob-lems of realism and fantasy both vanish, for "all future projection is obviously model-making, poiesis not mimesis" (18). For all its naivete, this suggestion could provide a framework for an examination of the critical rehabilitation of science fiction with poetically relevant elements. In Scholes' view, science fiction by definition does not, cannot, create the illusion that it is the verbal rendering of the actual world; thus, on the basis of his suggestion, one could say that science fiction might be co-opted into high literature as a mode that accepts and even asserts ontological pluralism, having abandoned the illusion of referentiality in the moment of its inception: a mode that is neces-sarily postmodern in its most un-self-reflexive state. Such a claim, however, would obviously be wide of the mark, primarily because of what a Hungarian critic calls the "poetical paradox" of science fiction: in most texts belonging to this mode "imaginary formations are combined 19th-century—primarily realist—narrative structures" (H. Nagy 129). One could go even further than that, following the arguments of Christine Brooke-Rose in *A Rhetoric of the Unreal* and Christopher Nash in *World Games.*

Taking his cue from Yuri Lotman and Brooke-Rose, Nash concludes his investigation of fantastic literature with the tentative rule of thumb that the narrative formations which violate the rule of probability (science fiction, fantasy fiction) tend to follow the representational traditions of realism in all other respects: although they present an imaginary world, this created world is then treated from the start as if it were really there (that is, such narratives follow not simply the realist tradition but the much broader referential as-sumption underlying most of European narrative tradition). Science fiction texts are seen to subscribe to a mimetic, referential logic, containing nothing that would indicate an awareness of the linguistic turn or turns that have changed the face of postmodern literature. In their desire to enjoy their licence in abandoning the code of probability, science fiction texts would not even think of breaching other representational strategies of narrative fiction. In Brooke-Rose's formulation: "the freer the paradigmatic axis, the more rigid the syntagmatic, and vice versa" (362; cf. Nash 80). A literature that is transgressive in its handling of language and representation, claims Nash, will not as a rule create alternative worlds and imaginary creatures, reserving its energies for linguistic experimentation (his examples include Robbe-Grillet, Beckett, and Cortázar's *Hopscotch* [78]).

For all the neatness and symmetry of this system of reversed proportionality, this rule is obviously not universally applicable. On the one hand, technical experiment does not at all preclude imaginary formations (as testified by Nabokov's *Ada*, Arno Schmidt's *Republic of Scientists*, the work of William Burroughs, or surrealist prose); on the other hand, the characterization of science fiction as an entirely unreflexive mode that continues to produce fantasies in blissful unawareness of the linguistic turn, although an adequate description of more than ninety percent of the genre, is still not wholly accurate.

The third critical interface is precisely the proposition that science fiction has been able to create, as it were, an internal elite. The mode has simply come of age, producing those classics that need to be taken seriously by everyone. At this point, however, the possible argument might fork and run in at least two directions. On the one hand, it might lead to a notion of a science fiction elite that satisfies the vaguely defined standards (including things like "depth of characterization") of high literature—that is, a set of works that satisfy the demands of realist (or later, modernist) poetics. These novels, thus, are "serious" only by virtue of the elements that distinguish them from run-of-the-mill science fiction, the contamination of the latter made acceptable (in fact, invisible) only by the other, serious features of the book. Science fiction is thus generously forgiven, excised or defused in the process of the critical appropriation into high literature, the co-opted novels becoming canonized as normal novels with a little exotic thematic coloring.[2] In fact, such critical acceptance of some science fiction amounts to describing the eligible works as having borrowed elements of high literature (cf. Greenland 172, 202); their elevation or promotion is thus the return of high cultural elements after a detour in popular culture: what is accepted is precisely what returns (what has always been inside). Instead of encouraging the rethinking of certain critical prejudices and boundaries, the generous co-opting of science fiction along these lines entails a retrenchment, an implicit confirmation of existing categories.

On the other hand, as in Brian McHale's model of interface (59–72), one may conceive of an experimental, postmodern science fiction that has been able to bring about the "postmodernization" of the mode by drawing upon its internal resources. Instead of a mere borrowing of the linguistic concerns of high literature, this internally produced postmodernity would thus be a specifically "science fiction postmodern" that could have a beneficial influence on high literature not only through the smuggling in of a new kind of thematics but also in some other, unspecified but poetically relevant way. McHale does seem to detect parallels between the postmodernization of high literature and the postmodernization of science fiction, claiming that the two processes tend to converge, inasmuch as the postmodernization of high literature consists, for him, in the foregrounding of ontological pluralism. It is difficult to see in McHale's rather rigid system just what the specifically science fiction elements of the postmodernization of science fiction are supposed to be: he mentions Samuel Delany and J. G. Ballard, but his only criterion appears to be the growing emphasis on ontological concerns, which, apart from being difficult to interpret in a poetical/metacritical context, fails to distinguish between science fiction and a more general sense of the fantastic.

It is possible to imagine the creation of a critical interface between science fiction and high literature "from above"; such an approach would be based on attempts by "serious" novelists to appropriate elements of science fiction.[3] At this point, however, the argument once again splices itself and continues in several directions. One such direction is that of parody, which seems to leave the clearcut boundaries unscathed, although what a thorough investigation of parody invariably reveals is precisely the disruption and destabilization of the boundaries (inside and outside) that would seem to be reasserted by its very practice. Going one step further, it is possible that such writing self-reflexively uses science fiction elements in order to interrogate alien and incompatible types of discourses by juxtaposing them or grafting one upon the other, where the implied contrasts (high/low, inside/outside) are made problematic by the disturbing liminal position of science fiction: like classical detective fiction, science fiction is the elite of popular culture, often resorted to by consumers of high culture as a kind of civilized entertainment, not to be confused with "proper" art, of course, but providing a reasonable amount of intellectual excitement and satisfaction (one thinks of writers like Asimov). This little quandary is only the manifestation of a more important and more disturbing dilemma: are the concerns of science fiction really so different from those of the high literature that uses science fiction elements? Science fiction may become (at least potentially) subversive precisely because its basic concerns have been present in elite culture, especially in the by no means underestimated or scorned utopian and dystopian traditions—let alone the equally respectable tradition of the speculative, philosophical fable (in the work of writers like Borges, Adolfo Bioy Casares, or Massimo Bontempelli). Science fiction (or at least serious science fiction, whatever that means) attached itself to traditions that are far from marginal in an intellectual and moral sense (in the 20th century, Zamyatin, Huxley, Orwell, Nabokov, Burgess, and many others). It is another question whether these highly prestigious, though linguistically unreflexive, traditions, which can be reinscribed into high culture in the modes of satire, allegory and parable, have contributed anything (apart from thematics) to postmodern fiction with its well-known resistance to monological, unreflexive, didactic discourses.

The quandaries raised by this last critical interface provide the most rewarding context for a discussion of the role of science fiction in Kurt Vonnegut's work. Vonnegut is an uneasy but inevitable inhabitant of all the critical models that try to account for the presence of science fiction in postmodernism (or one could say that all these models have been duly reproduced in the critical controversy over his work): he has been the cult writer of the flower generation, prophetically warning against the dangers of the machine age (Kilgore Trout is awarded, significantly, the medical instead of the literary Nobel Prize); he has been a kind of upstart science fiction writer who has managed, or almost, to extricate himself from the ghetto of science fiction (Klinkowitz 79–80, Crichton 107, 109–110); he has been seen as one of the key figures of the serendipitous encounter between science fiction and postmodernism (the chapter in MacHale I have referred to earlier concludes with a discussion of Vonnegut), and he has been cast as the postmodern experimental writer the object of whose self-reflexive textual games happens to be science fiction (that is how he is treated by Patricia Waugh [8, 22, 86]). Similarly debated is the existence, extent and proper nature of Vonnegut's parodistic attitude towards science fiction; Stanley Schatt, for instance, ingeniously divides science fiction into an elite and a pulp section in order to be able to position Vonnegut as a writer who, although parodying traditional elements of hardcore pulp science fiction, borrows the framework of future projection successfully used by the classics of science fiction (Schatt 35).

Vonnegut's interfaces

In what follows, I shall read three of Vonnegut's novels as metapoetical allegories "talking about" their ambiguous relationship with science fiction, as explorations of the possible metacritical/poetical relevance of the introduction of science fiction elements.[4] The uncertainties repeatedly reproduced in the critical discourse about Vonnegut are perhaps partly a result of the fact that the strategy of his metacritical allegory does not seem to be uniform—accordingly, different critical strategies have been applied in the attempts to redeem Vonnegut's novels by purging them of science fiction, by presenting it as something more than science fiction that, for specific purposes, masquerades as science fiction. For reasons of space, I shall discuss only one of the novels (*Breakfast of Champions*) in any detail, confining myself to a few cursory remarks on *The Sirens of Titan* and *Slaughterhouse-Five*. Nevertheless, certain important differences in the treatment of science fiction as a metacritical trope will be apparent even from my disproportionate treatment.

The depicted (diegetic) world of *The Sirens of Titan* is undeniably a science fiction world, complete with creatures from outer space, space travel, and space war. In this novel, the science fiction thematics can probably be reinscribed into the order of parable without major difficulties; that is, the novel seems to be recuperable for high literature by virtue of the serious questions it addresses. One of the science fiction-specific metacritical contributions of the novel is precisely here:[5] "serious" or "proper" questions are asked in an "unserious" or "improper" language or register, with the result that the very mode of posing the questions is inscribed into the questions themselves, and the metaphysical questions are allowed to appear only as already contaminated by the alien language, cultural baggage, and silt of science fiction. All this is, of course, a rethinking of the satirical strategy of the mock heroic, a rethinking that exploits the cultural inferiority or lowliness of science fiction (and therefore the target of the satire is not primarily science fiction), with consequences that appear at the text level rather than in the story proper. Science fiction may be said to be one discourse in the polyglossic textual universe of the novel; nevertheless, since the primary diegetic level is decidedly, self-mockingly an over-familiar science fiction universe, the other, culturally much more prestigious discourses appear as always already inserted into a larger "science fiction" discourse. In what can be seen as an interesting irony, science fiction seems to be doing the opposite of what it is supposed to do in McHale's model: instead of creating or revealing a multiplicity of universes and thereby fulfilling an ontologically subversive textual function, it collapses the multiplicity of words into a hackneyed, self-reflexive science fiction universe that is emphatically textual.

In *The Sirens of Titan*, several religious and metaphysical systems, inquiring into the ultimate questions of existence, are affected by the corrosive contamination of science fiction. The novel reverses the actualising tendencies of popular religion that tries to absorb "low culture" linguistic registers in order to make itself accessible; thus, simple contaminations, the likes of referring to the planet Earth as "God's space ship" (24), in the sermon of a probably fake television preacher, turn against themselves because they are inserted into a science fiction universe. The entire novel can be read as the thinking through to their logical end point of the consequences of similar contaminations: metaphysical perspective is absorbed or converted into science fiction perspective. Consequently, the possibility of mutual contaminations transforms the relationship between prestigious cultural/textual systems (religion, theology, philosophy, science) and science fiction from the incompatible and incommensurable difference of systems that are different in kind into a relation between lexicons and orders of metaphor, readily convertible into each other. Scientific discourse is by definition allied to science fiction that often appeals to science (for instance, paroxysms of highly technical language that deliberately turn into their opposite and end up as mystification) for its pseudo-legitimation; in *The Sirens of Titan*, the best-known example is probably the chronosynclastic infundibulum, which is both the science fiction version of the physical qualities of the Einsteinian universe and a parody of the theological or mystical concept of suprareality and infinity (cf. Sigman 28). The result of such contaminations is a consequence of Bakhtinian polyglossia: since words remember their uses in very diverse cultural/discursive systems, their use in a particular system is never unambiguous, burdened as it is with memories of incompatible usages. This is how prophetic discourse, one of the novel's fundamental discourses (the key trope of the text is the—among others prophetically conceived—*message*), becomes one particular subtype of the discourse of science fiction. The ultimate irony of this strategy is its potentially deflating absorption of the metaphysical thought structure of ultimate irony and deflation of human aspirations: in the well-known rewriting of human history (it is a message sent by a spaceship asking for a spare part), cosmic irony, an inherited topos of romantic metaphysics and aesthetics, is redeployed as truly cosmic, galactic, specifically science fiction irony, as well as the parody of the theological concept of Providence, as Joseph Sigman has noted (33–34), in such a way that, as a result of science fiction contamination, cosmic irony loses its romantic grandeur and pathos: the prestigious thought structure of deflation itself is deflated by means of its insertion into the discursive dynamics of Vonnegut's novel.

As a metacritical strategy, the use of science fiction in *The Sirens of Titan* may be said to create a polyglossic discursive field where prestigious discursive systems of high culture find themselves as examples of science fiction; science fiction functions as something like the lowest common textual denominator of textually imagining/producing the world. In this way, the text may be reinscribed into high culture as a mock heroic exposure of the vanity and futility of rivalling textual versions of the universe and the fate of human beings in it. This reading manages to survive even the deflating of romantic irony by recasting the novel as one more, textually more self-conscious, version of it.

In *Slaughterhouse-Five*, although science fiction becomes the agent of similar infiltrations and metaleptic switches, this is not the main direction of its reappropriation for high culture. The plot is based on one of the most hackneyed among all science fiction clichés: the Tralfamadorian contingent intrudes into an unproblematically realistic fictional world to kidnap Billy Pilgrim. As a result of its emphatically clichéd nature, the intrusion takes place on the level of plot and on that of the text simultaneously. In its second capacity, it has certain precedents: while convalescing after the war in a military hospital, Pilgrim read the works of Kilgore Trout, including a novel called *The Big Board* (133) that describes his story—but Billy realizes this only when his UFO adventure has already taken place. What happens is therefore not simply the intrusion of aliens into the fictional world but also the "coming true" of a science fiction novel through the person of Billy Pilgrim; in this way, the diegetic level (reality level) of the science fiction elements remains slightly dubious throughout the novel, since the suspicion of Billy's mild madness is never dispelled. This strategy leaves open the possibility of reinscribing the science fiction elements into the order of high literature as psychological reality, as the delusion or escape fantasy of a character who is unable to live with the reality overdose of the Dresden bombing. This assumption seems to be supported by the fact that the science fiction elements (the little green people "shaped like plumber's friends" [24], the classically rimmed and portholed flying saucer [55]) are clichéd to the point of self-mocking absurdity: there is always a chance that the science fiction elements are pulp science fiction clichés working subliminally in Billy's fantasy life—and, consequently, that the novel's attitude to science fiction is one of parody.[6]

For all these dismissive strategies of reading the science fiction elements, *Slaughterhouse-Five* remains a formally innovative text, not recuperable by any realist poetics, going beyond, or at least deciding not to choose, modernist association technique. The novel's long subtitle indicates or prefigures the fundamental change that I have already referred to in connection with the double nature of the intrusion of science fiction and that will become fully dominant in *Breakfast of Champions. Slaughterhouse-Five* is "a novel somewhat in the telegraphic schizophrenic manner of tales of the planet Tralfamadore" (frontispiece). That is, science fiction appears as an alternative style or representational strategy rather than as an alternative world: if in *The Sirens of Titan* science fiction was largely a matter of vocabulary, in this novel it is present on the level of narrative syntax. If we decide to take Vonnegut's textual experiments seriously and admit him into the postmodern canon (not an easy thing in the case of a sly cryptohumanist), then we could perhaps say that he uses science fiction as a metaphor of his own idiosyncratic mode of writing. What is new in his fiction from a poetical perspective is defined as the borrowing of Tralfamadorian style. While on the level of the fictional world the coming of the aliens is experienced as a rupture, an irruption, on the level of the text the Tralfamadorians are always already here. Tralfamador is not an alternative world (that is why the text needs nothing besides the science fiction clichés in order to make the aliens realistic) but an alternative conception of time and space, an alternative poetics of the novel.

Billy Pilgrim "has come unstuck in time" (23); his unique experience of
time coincides with the Tralfamadorian view of time, according to which "[a]ll
moments, past, present and future, always have existed, always will exist" (25).
At the same time it is quite clear that the Tralfamadorians have nothing to do
with Billy's new experience of time: all they can do is "give him insights into
what was really going on" (27). In a different language: Billy's coming unstuck
in time might be correlated with a new poetic principle of construction, but
it can become one only with the help of the Tralfamadorians. The Tralfamadorian telegraphic poetics of the novel reflects Billy's temporal experience:

> each clump of symbols is a brief, urgent message—describing a
> situation, a scene. We Tralfamadorians read them all at once, not
> one after the other. There isn't any particular relationship between
> all the messages, except that the author has chosen them carefully,
> so that, when all seen at once, they produce an image of life that
> is beautiful and surprising and deep. There is no beginning, no
> middle, no end, no suspense, no moral, no causes, no effects. What
> we love in our books are the depths of many marvelous moments
> seen all at one time. (63)

The Tralfamadorian poetics of the novel (largely, and significantly, a poetics of reading) resembles the experience of being unstuck in time, for it creates
the utopia of a text without the constraints of linearity, without the compul-
sion to write and read linearly. Vonnegut's novel, although it announces itself
as a Tralfamadorian text, is naturally unable to work in this way, to become a
Tralfamadorian novel; however, the extent of its anti-Aristotelianism is also the
extent of its Tralfamadorianness. Vonnegut does not attempt to do away with
narrativity for the sake of the wondrous and transcendental atemporality of the
moment; rather than insisting on the modernist-epiphanic strategy of valu-
ing the moment, his method of providing a novel experience of temporality is
through the fragmentation of the narrative into anecdotes. *Slaughterhouse-Five*
is constructed out of tiny scraps of story (and not epiphanic moments) where
the order of the scraps is immaterial. Or rather, this is what would happen if it
were a fully Tralfamadorian text; the fact that this is not the case indicates the
irreducible inhumanity of Tralfamadorian poetics; just as the extent of its Tralfamadorianness is the extent of its anti-Aristotelian stance, its failure to become
a Tralfamadorian text is the extent of its (and therefore Billy's) humanity. For all
this, the organization of the novel is Tralfamadorian enough for us to describe it
as such. The Tralfamadorian time technique has a double consequence: on the
one hand, the story is "degraded" to the level of anecdotes, on the other hand,
however, the process of reading and meaning-making immediately triggers off
a new, non-narrative reordering or redeployment of the fragments: elevated out

of the continuity of the story, anecdotes, in order to become meaningful and relevant, have to assume the status of parables. The result is a narrative formation without a centre (Dresden?), a formation that potentially transforms each of its units into parables (metatexts). Instead of being related causally, fragments are either entirely unrelated (but then this is not allowed by the process of reading) or reflect each other in a parabolic/metaphorical relationship.

This is a rather peculiar (anti-)narrative organization that enters the novel metaleptically: a world-view and representational strategy erupting into the world of the novel turn out to have been there always; in fact, it is precisely this novelistic strategy that organizes the novel we are reading. As a metacritical allegory, this might be seen as a comment on the role of "science fiction" in the narrative tradition: seen as an inferior outsider, an alien, science fiction (its themes, metaphors, strategies) has always been inside. Naturally, the Tralfamadorian experience of reading and writing (the self-reflexive science fiction element) can also be eliminated by a recuperative reading, to be duplicated once again: it can be seen as the site of the coming into being of absurd meaninglessness as "meaning" (the dissemination of Dresden over the entire surface of the novel) or as an utopian space of being and reading. Read in these terms, the entire poetic construction is easily recuperated for a psychological reading (the reinscription of science fiction in the register of psychopathology): Tralfamadorian poetics and world-view are exactly what Billy Pilgrim would need, a temporality where Dresden is not more important than all the other moments of time, where death is not an end-point but one of the moments existing all the time. Tralfamadorian time (the novel's "alienness"), ultimately unacceptable for Billy or for the reader, is, on the psychological level, the detraumatization of traumatic time: instead of the eternal recurrence of the same, intolerably painful moment, the anaesthetising process of the unfolding of every single moment at the same time. The failure of the novel to become a truly Tralfamadorian novel is exactly the impossibility of absolute alienness.

Science fiction as poetics: *Breakfast of Champions*
I have tried to show how both *The Sirens of Titan* and *Slaughterhouse-Five* can be recuperated or retrieved for high culture (that is, the science fiction element is made to disappear by means of the attempt to transform into something that stands for something else): in the first case, the science fiction element is transmuted into satire (even if it is a metadiscursive satire), whereas in the second case it becomes a psychological allegory. In a sense, my reading of *Breakfast of Champions* is a similar attempt at critical recuperation by the removal or defusing of science fiction, or its transformation into something harmless. Seeing the science fiction element as metacritical allegory similarly makes it disappear from the text as a critical problem; on the

other hand, if *Breakfast of Champions* is seen as talking about its own poetic otherness in terms of science fiction, this reading leads to the rediscovery of the science fiction element in the text, to its problematic reinscription into the critical discourse about the novel.

Poetic transgression, metaphorized as science fiction, can be recuperated by a psychological reading also in *Breakfast of Champions* (the motif of the search for a father), but such recuperation makes much less sense than in the case of *Slaughterhouse-Five*. The novel's world is entirely plausible, all deviations from the codes of realism—as if the text wanted to demonstrate the truth of Nash's observation—occurring on the level of narrative discourse and organization (the most important among these being the overt, even ostentatious presence of metafictionality). *Breakfast of Champions* brings the process started in *Slaughterhouse-Five* to an exciting conclusion: the metapoetical relevance of science fiction is clear from the fact that it is present exclusively as *science fiction literature*, as the oeuvre of Kilgore Trout. There are no extraterrestrials or time travels, only science fiction novels that exist at a certain angle to the primary fictional world.

What exactly is the status of the brief summaries of Trout's work scattered in the novel (that is, the overtly textual presence of science fiction): are they "Shakespearean clowns" (see note 6), or do they have some additional poetical relevance in the texture of the novel? One possible direction of interpreting the science fiction elements, as in *Slaughterhouse-Five*, is clearly metacritical, with the difference that in the later text their metacritical implications are much more pervasive and multifunctional.

In *Breakfast of Champions,* science fiction cannot help being anything else than a textual tradition, most conspicuously present in the works of Kilgore Trout (although not all of his works belong to this mode). Due to the essentially metaleptic nature of the novel, the world of the Trout stories somehow leaks into the narrated world, infecting it in various ways, as in the case of Dwayne's madness or the Pluto gang (76–77). More interestingly, the discourse level is also contaminated; the most obvious case of the latter being precisely the curious metaphorical use of the word "leak." "Leak" is Kilgore Trout's word for "mirror": "it amused him to pretend that mirrors were holes between two universes" (27). This metaphor, like all similar metaphors in the novel, possesses a metacritical relevance or readability. By referring to mirrors as leaks, Trout takes the most traditional trope of the mimetic conception of art and transforms it into something else: if the mirror is defined as a hole between the two ("real" and "fictitious") universes, through which infiltration or contamination is possible, on the level of the metacritical allegory the mimetic, reflective, mirroring principle of construction is replaced by the metonymic principle of leaking, or infiltration. "Leak" has leaked from Trout's stories into the discourse of the novel: the narrator, speaking from the future, quite independently of the Trout summaries, also refers to mirrors and reflective surfaces as leaks.[7] The metaleptic logic means that the language which creates the narrated world creates this world using linguistic idiosyncrasies that are born within the narrated world itself. Local examples of such leaking (that is, when the vocabulary of a Trout novel contaminates its immediate textual environment) include the defamiliarizing description of the activity of walking, borrowed from Trout: "their feet sticking to the planet, coming unstuck, then sticking again" (74). The dominant man=robot/machine metaphor is also a leaking from the novel that poisoned Dwayne's mind (e.g. 200).[8]

The relationship between the stories of Trout (seventeen texts are referred to altogether) and the primary narrated world is not at all clear. Trout stories are mentioned and summed up randomly, usually because the given book turns up in the story as a physical object. As if a button were pushed, the narrator immediately and obligingly provides a summary of the particular Trout story which, sooner or later, enters into connection with the novel. This relationship *(the relationship between science fiction and "the world")* has to be, *is* the motivation, the *meaning* of the persistent presence of the Trout oeuvre. The reader's first reaction is to try and establish a parabolic, mirroring relationship, expecting the Trout stories to offer parabolic commentaries on the novel or parts of it. The stories, however, fail to generate a relevance that could be interpreted as parabolic: instead of the vertical principle of parable, the horizontal logic of leaking begins to prevail in the reading of the relationship. After reading all the plot summaries, some kind of relationship perhaps begins to take shape: the aggregate of stories functions as a narrative encyclopaedia intended to explain the entire narrated world. It seems that there is not a single element in the narrated world that is not included in a Trout story; even the privileged role of the clitoris in sexual intercourse (hardly a science fiction theme, incidentally) has, of course, been a subject of a fascinating tale by Trout (143–144), and the same applies to the making of alcohol and many other topics. It seems that "Kilgore was here": the entire narrated world has already been "covered" by Trout, and the narrator, whenever he feels like it, picks out an object and tells, with sublime irrelevance, the relevant Trout tale. It seems that the function of Trout summaries is primarily performative: the assertion of this watertight and all-inclusive coherence that, isomorphically, leaks into the narrated world on account of the prevailing metaleptic logic.

The fact that the metonymic logic of leaking rules in the text has in itself nothing to do with science fiction—but it might if we extend the relevance of science fiction as a metacritical metaphor and locate it in *Breakfast of Champions* as *perspective:* not only in the sense of a cosmic perspective that ironically dwarfs human ambition and achievement but also in the more strictly narratological sense of the word.

The very first sentence goes like this: "This is a tale of a meeting of two lonesome, skinny, fairly old white men on a planet which was dying fast" (17). Defining the setting like this at once places the narrative in the register of science fiction. The idiosyncrasies of the narrative voice are accounted for by the choice of perspective: the narrator is obviously talking to "extraterrestrials"—where extraterrestrial is a science fiction-inspired trope for the absolute unpredictability of the narratees. It is important that the defamiliarizing mode (the single most conspicuous strategy of the text) is determined by the perspective of the assumed reader rather than the limited knowledge or naivete of the speaker, and governed mainly by the assumed expository or explanatory mode of the narrator, as in *Gulliver's Travels*.[9] There is in *Breakfast of Champions,* however, a feature that destabilizes the linguistic world of the novel to an extent that is inconceivable in Swift. The defamiliarization coloring the explanatory rhetoric necessarily divides the narrated world as well as the narrating words into two categories: that of the things familiar to the listener and that of the things that still need to be explained. In texts that use a similar rhetorical strategy, the reader after a while becomes capable of predicting which elements will go into either category. In Vonnegut's novel, however, it seems that nearly every new definition (as well as each of the equally educational illustrations) inscribes the boundary between the two (linguistic) categories at a different place: words that are tagged with explanations are chosen without any apparent logic ("Nigger" [47]; "cooping" [58]). Most definitions laboriously clarify extremely basic things: these include cultural facts whose defamiliarized description or redefinition achieves a satirical effect (for instance, the discovery of America), but most of these definitions are attached to truly elementary and familiar things like apples, peas, guns and lambs; at the same time, much more difficult notions are allowed to go unexplained. The definitions use words and locutions that are much more difficult than the entity that is being defined: gunpowder, we are told, is a "mixture of potassium nitrate, charcoal, and sulphur" (21). Words are explained after they have already been used several times ("alcohol" 194). The set of defined words is totally random and cannot be penned into any single category. The outcome is a destabilization of the novel's verbal universe, not unlike Borges's famously heterocosmic encyclopaedia, where every category divides up the entire field according to a different principle, and therefore, in the lack of a unified grid that would have made meaning-making possible, the categories remain mutually immeasurable, with no possibility of any logical relationship between them. In Vonnegut's novel, every definition forgets and makes us forget all previous definitions, rewriting the boundary between the regions of the known and the unknown.

The basis of this destabilizing linguistic logic is perspective. The narrator does not know how much his listeners know. Science fiction is smuggled back here on the level of linguistic organization (or disorganization): in *Breakfast of Champions*, the extraterrestrial, the alien and unknown sphere is embodied in the implied listener or reader whose total and perfect alienness and unknowability make the text reproduce the boundary between the known and the unknown in every moment. We do not know, we cannot know, what the listener will know or understand, and this perfect alienness, this unmeasurable (not in the sense of unmeasurably long) distance of the listener entails the absolute and unqualified risking and restructuring of the entire narrative horizon. The apotheosis of science fiction conceived as perspective or horizon is the episode in the seedy New York porn movie where Kilgore Trout is involved in a conversation with God (in the novel's terminology: the Creator of the Universe), always uncertain how much God actually knows: "'The carpeting under my feet,' he signaled from the lobby, 'is springy and new. I think it must be some miracle fiber. It's blue. You know what I mean by *blue?*'" (69). He could ask the very same question after each word. Later: "I am headed for Forty-second Street now. How much do you already know about Forty-second Street?" (70) In Vonnegut, God had always been a popular and widely known subcategory of science fiction clichés; the perspectival structure of *Breakfast of Champions* (similarly to that of *The Sirens of Titan*) conflates theology and science fiction, with the crucial difference that in the later novel this conflation clearly takes place in the field of language use, entailing serious metacritical consequences. In Vonnegut, science fiction had always functioned as a horizon of defamiliarization (his characters are often called "Earthlings"); in *Breakfast of Champions*, however, it creates a defamiliarizing horizon that, through its radical alienness, makes the linguistic mode of the novel unpredictable and semantically aleatory.

This is brought out also by the illustrations, which fulfill a function similar to that of the definitions, but which also resemble the Trout summaries—at least in one respect. Ninety percent of the illustrations represent not an object but a *sign:* most of them feature letters, legends, symbols, that is, they reproduce or represent objects in the case of which mere graphic representation is clearly inadequate and irrelevant for, as semiotic objects, their meaning resides not in their outer shape but in their conventionally defined and encoded semiotic value. As a means of conveying information, these drawings are thus absolutely unnecessary. As a careful reading of the context will reveal, even many of the remaining, apparently purely "representational" illustrations turn out to be representations of a picture, like the flamingo (56), the clock (60), the mortarboard (61), and several others; many of the remaining illustrations are illustrations of the vehicle of a simile, representing not an element of the narrated world but a purely linguistic product that has no function whatsoever in the story (for instance, the drawing of lamb follows the phrase "He slept like a lamb" [82]).[10]

Another type of defamiliarization, resulting from the displaced presence of science fiction, works on the level of narrative grammar: connections between events are also defamiliarized. Causality, for instance, suffers on two levels: psychological causality (motivation) is absorbed into a pair of defamiliarizing science fiction metaphors or catachreses (one claims that human beings are machines, while the other maintains that human acts are the result of chemicals in our bodies). There is a further, overtly metafictional aspect of subverting motivation—a third, metafictional catachresis. Having discovered for himself Kilgore Trout's machine metaphor, the narrator, as it were, also goes berserk and begins to remote control his characters as if they were machines, transforming their motivational system into yet another defamiliarizing discourse: "And here Dwayne did something extraordinarily unnatural. He did it because I wanted him to. It was something I had ached to have a character do for years and years" (232).[11]

Causal-logical connections between events and entities are dissolved in the reign of coincidence. In *Breakfast of Champions,* coincidence loses its meaning (which is the making meaningful of accident, of a lack of meaning); the basic principle of narrative logic is the realization that every single element of the narrative can be related to every other element at one level or another. This logic considers the revelation of metonymic connections as the *production of meaning:* because their revelation is deemed important, because they are included in the text, metonymic relations are clearly meant to function as meaningful in the economy of the text. If, however, every connection is equally meaningful, relevant (that is, worth mentioning), then the hierarchy between more and less meaningful (relevant) connections is abolished. The transformation of coincidences into meaningful connections by rhetorical means ends up abolishing precisely that to which meaning, considered as relevance, owes its being: the multitudinous and chaotic background of meaningless coincidences.

The main source of energy in the linguistic economy of *Breakfast of Champions* is the process whereby the incessant, compulsive production of meaning is transformed into its opposite. To hold something up as *information* entails that this particular entity possesses meaning (relevance): information value is produced not by some inherent quality of an entity but by the communication process. Holding up every single element of the narrated world as information, however, will abolish the background of non-informative elements, the very condition of holding something up as information. In default of a hierarchy of information value and relevance, the logic of the text is taken over by irrelevance and redundancy.

Irrelevance and redundancy raise the possibility of global science fiction-inspired self-metaphors on the most elementary level of textual organization. Irrelevance, redundancy, and coincidence as narrative and textual principles create a world of functional homogeneity where "every person would be exactly as important as any other. All facts would also be given equal weightiness. Nothing would be left out. Let others bring order to chaos. I would bring chaos to order, instead, which I think I have done" (195). The textual economy of *Breakfast of Champions* could be described as the gradual transformation of entropy (in the sense in which it is used by information theory) into entropy in the thermodynamic sense. By transforming coincidence into its organizing principle, the text holds up every element, every textual event as information-laden, that is, as possessing high entropy. ("We consider as an event the occurrence of a given sign at a randomly chosen site of the text; such an event takes place with a given probability" [Andor 39]). Every sign possesses an equally high level of entropy, the amount of information possessed by a given sign (Andor 47). The entropy of information theory, however, depends on the frequency of the sign's uses rather than the frequency of the sign itself; thus it is a pragmatic feature determined by the communicative situation. By means of its rhetorical organization, Vonnegut's text displays every item (or event) as possessing high entropy, for it teases meaning out of contingency and accident. The outcome, however, is a message of uniformly high entropy, in which, since the signs are functionally levelled, "every sign will occur with equal probability" (Andor 48). The occurrence of any given sign cannot be predicted on the basis of the preceding signs, therefore the extent of the text's communicational disorder is maximal: "in maximal entropy, every sign has equal value and is entirely independent of all the other signs, and this situation indeed corresponds to what we ordinarily mean by disorder. One could also say that the average entropy is the level of uncertainty" (Andor 63–64).

 Breakfast of Champions is a text of maximum entropy—but then, it could also be seen as a text approaching that non-existent text or sign system of zero entropy which consists of the repetition of the same sign, itself of zero entropy (cf. Andor 48). This last formulation already evokes the thermodynamic notion of entropy: the textual organization of the novel might be said to resemble an energetic condition that could perhaps be likened to the rules governing the entropy of closed systems (cf. Davies 9–12, Feynman 120–121).

 Entropic textuality, "attacking" or affecting *Breakfast Champions* on the level of primary textual organization, can obviously be read as a global self-metaphor produced by the text as a result of science fiction contamination, a science fiction-inspired feature that clearly has poetical or metacritical relevance. In an attempt to account for the idiosyncratic narrative organization of the book in terms of the corrosive infiltration of science fiction elements, one could start out from different potential self-metaphors; for instance, the textual organization of the novel (this is obvious after having considered the consequences of the entropy metaphor) can indeed be conceived on the analogy of the polymer molecule graphically represented in the text (210): "The

molecule went on and on, repeating itself forever" (210): the same sign repeated endlessly where the repetition can begin or end anywhere. This molecule also embodies the other, cautionary version of the possible co-optation
of science fiction elements. It is the sole constituent of the industrial waste
that smothers the Miracle Cave in the novel, spreading slowly and threaten-
ingly in the narrated world. Cultural waste is an endlessly repeating polymer:
self-reflexive emblem of the satirical, referential, "serious" aspect of the novel,
as well as a self-metaphor that allegorically tells about the text's relationship
to tradition (including that of science fiction).

The novel—elaborating on one of its self-metaphors—functions as
a deposit of cultural rubbish, waste (15), or, viewed as a process, a kind of
"recycling" of material that is used, or useless, unnecessary. Far from being
illustrative, the illustrations function to remove semiotic rubbish. The text
"recycled"—"recycling" text—is able to construct itself only from the already
used external semiotic polymer (language), and only in the way that is already programmed in the molecule. This is obvious if we consider the recycled
character of the illustrations. The novel perpetuates itself by claiming to be
constructed entirely out of this recycled material: what is inside is outside,
what is outside is inside.

I hope it is clear that I do not claim to have found generally applicable
rules or principles of the co-opting of science fiction into postmodern fiction.
It seems that the introduction of science fiction elements can indeed have consequences that may become the object of a poetically minded critical discourse
(a new set of metaphors and self-metaphors, new—metacritical—lexicons, the
potentially subversive mixture of lexicons and registers, a defamiliarizing horizon, among others). In *Breakfast of Champions,* as in some other Vonnegut texts,
science fiction does function as a metacritical metaphor that allegorically speaks
about the critical quandaries around science fiction (including Vonnegut's own
position) and figuratively names the "postmodern" difference of Vonnegut's fiction. It is also clear for me, however, that this metacritical relevance is not acquired by science fiction elements in the same way even in Vonnegut's novels.
Every novel of his risks itself according to its own rules—most radically and
most excitingly, perhaps, *Breakfast of Champions.*

Notes

1. The myth, according to Fiedler, is that of the end of man, of the
disappearance of human functions or their appropriation by machines (382).

2. I feel that such co-optation took place in the case of books like *Solaris,
Martian Chronicles* or J. G. Ballard's early "inner space" fictions.

3. Such lists tend to include texts like Nabokov's *Ada,* Italo Calvino's short
stories, Doris Lessing's *Canopus in Argos* sequence, among others.

4. My rhetoric is of course questionable here, since, by talking about "introduction," I am establishing a hierarchy and an order of priority between "proper" literature and science fiction.

5. Another poetically relevant strategy that may be linked specifically to science fiction has to do with the plot structure. Joseph Sigman (36–37) convincingly argues that the fate of the major characters is "shaped" by means of quantum leaps; that is, a physical principle, in the present case the rules of the movements of subatomic particles, is transformed into a plot device.

6. One suspects that this readily available interpretation, involving the discarding of the science fiction element, could be one of the factors behind the relatively easy canonization of this particular Vonnegut novel. To a certain extent, this reading is confirmed by Vonnegut's well-known comment:

> And the science-fiction passages in *Slaughterhouse-Five* are just like the clowns in Shakespeare. When Shakespeare figured the audience had had enough of the heavy stuff, he'd let up a little, bring on a clown or a foolish innkeeper or something like that, before he'd become serious again. And trips to other planets, science fiction of an obviously kidding sort, is equivalent to bringing on the clowns every so often to lighten things up. (*Wampeters* 235)

7. This little detail confirms my earlier suggestion that the role of prophetic narration in the novel is chiefly metacritical: prophetic narration is working, as it were, as an empty emblem of science fiction. Its future perspective appears as a set of linguistic idiosyncrasies rather than as a certain amount of knowledge about the present that is only visible or understandable in the light of future developments.

8. This metaphor also appears in *Slaughterhouse-Five*, naturally as a Tralfamadorian insight (104).

9. The narrator is omniscient, omnipotent even. His omniscience, however, is put to a rather unorthodox use: instead of revealing the depth of the characters' minds, he offers insiders' tidbits and curiosities, providing information concerning certain elements of the narrated world in a gossipy, erratic, anecdotal manner. In an incisive analysis, Ágnes Pelyvás explores the micro-level workings of the defamiliarizing technique in the novel: the arbitrary transfer of certain phenomena from one cognitive model into another, the insertion of certain objects into a new and alien semantic row (for instance, referring to the young waitress unexpectedly as a "mammal" [130]), the suppression of generally well-known "institutional facts," the description of certain objects purely on the basis of their physical outlook (cf. Pelyvás 11ff.).

10. In the Hungarian translation, "lamb" is replaced by a "furcoat", adapting to the appropriate idiomatic simile ("to sleep like a furcoat"); this little fact also indicates the irrelevance of the illustrations to the story. Further similar examples include the drawings of the dinosaur and the pea (both 118) or the apple (119).

11. It should be noted that I do not consider the science fiction-based defamiliarization of motivation as ultimately simply the metaphor of metafictional, self-reflexive defamiliarization, that is, I don't mean to imply that the final referent of defamiliarizing techniques is necessarily metacritical. The various kinds of defamiliarization (machine, chemicals, author) work parallelly with each other, without any hierarchy between them.

Works Cited

Andor, Csaba. *Jel—Kultúra—Kommunikáció* ["Sign—Culture—Communication"]. Budapest: Gondolat, 1980.

Brooke-Rose, Christine. *A Rhetoric of the Unreal*. Cambridge: Cambridge University Press, 1983.

Buck, Lynn. "Vonnegut's World of Comic Futility." Mustazza 151–164.

Crichton, J. Michael. "Sci-Fi and Vonnegut." Mustazza 107–112.

Davies, Paul. *The Last Three Minutes*. New York: Basic, 1994.

Feynman, Richard. *The Nature of Physical Laws*. Harmondsworth: Penguin, 1992.

Fiedler, Leslie. "The New Mutants." *Collected Essays 2*. New York: Stein, 1971. 391–408.

Greenland, Colin. *The Entropy Exhibition: Michael Moorcock and the British 'New Wave' in Science Fiction*. London: Routledge, 1983.

H. Nagy, Péter. "Imaginárium: Vázlat a science-fiction poétikájának töredékeiről" ["Imaginarium: a sketch about fragments of a poetics of science fiction"]. *Szép literatúrai ajándék* 1998. 2–3: 127–136.

Hollinger, Veronica. "Cybernetic Deconstructions: Cyberpunk and Postmodernism." McCaffery 203–218.

Klinkowitz, Jerome. "*Mother Night, Cat's Cradle,* and the Crimes of Our Time." Mustazza 79–90.

McCaffery, Larry. "Introduction: To the Desert of the Real." *Storming the Reality Studio: A Casebook of Cyberpunk and Postmodern Fiction*. Ed. Larry McCaffery. Durham: Duke University Press, 1991. 1–16.

McHale, Brian. *Postmodernist Fiction*. London: Routledge, 1991.

Mustazza, Leonard, ed. *The Critical Response to Kurt Vonnegut*. Westport, CT: Greenwood, 1994.

Nash, Christopher. *World-Games: The Tradition of Anti-Realist Revolt*. London: Methuen, 1987.

Pelyvás, Ágnes. "Defamiliarization as a Source of Irony in Kurt Vonnegut's *Breakfast of Champions*." Debrecen, 1998 (unpubl. ms).

Reed, Peter J., and Marc Leeds, eds. *The Vonnegut Chronicles: Interviews and Essays*. Westport, CT: Greenwood, 1996.

Schatt, Stanley. *Kurt Vonnegut, Jr.* Boston: Twayne, 1976.

Scholes, Robert. *Structural Fabulation: An Essay on the Fiction of the Future*. Notre Dame: University of Notre Dame Press, 1975.

Schriber, Mary Sue. "Bringing Chaos to Order: The Novel Tradition and Kurt Vonnegut, Jr." Mustazza 175–186.

Sigman, Joseph. "Science and Parody in Kurt Vonnegut's *The Sirens of Titan*." Mustazza 25–42.

Vonnegut, Kurt. *Breakfast of Champions*. 1973. London: Granada, 1981. [*Bajnokok reggelije*. Trans. Békés András. Budapest: Maecenas, 1988.

———. *The Sirens of Titan*. 1959. London: Hodder, 1979.

———. *Slaughterhouse-Five*. 1969. London: Granada, 1979.

———. *Wampeters, Foma & Granfalloons*. 1975. London: Granada, 1985.

———. *Börleszk* [*Slapstick*. 1976]. Trans. Borbás Mária. Budapest: Európa, 1981. [NY: Dell, 1985].

Waugh, Patricia. *Metafiction: The Theory and Practice of Self-Conscious Fiction*. London: Methuen, 1984.

PETER FREESE

Kurt Vonnegut's Player Piano; or, "Would You Ask EPICAC What People Are For?"

In May 1945, a twenty-two-year old brevet corporal from the American Midwest came home from the European theater of war, where he had been taken prisoner by the Germans and miraculously survived the Allied firebombing of Dresden as a POW in a subterranean meatlocker in the building No. 5 of the Dresden slaughterhouse. His name was Kurt Vonnegut, Jr., and marrying his childhood sweetheart Jane Marie Cox from Indianapolis, he moved to Chicago, where he earned his living as a police reporter for the City News Bureau while working on his master's thesis in anthropology at the University of Chicago. But when his thesis was rejected as "unprofessional" (*BSB* 6),[1] he left the university without a degree and moved to Schenectady, New York, to work there as a publicist for the General Electric Corporation and its famous Research Laboratory for $92 a week. Since he needed extra money to support his wife and his two children, he "started writing short stories at nights and on weekends" (*BSB* 6), and in February 1950 his first story, "Report on the Barnhouse Effect," was published in *Collier's*. When he succeeded in selling several other stories to such 'slick' magazines as *Cosmopolitan* and *Esquire, Ladies' Home Journal* and the *Saturday Evening Post*, he decided to become a full-time writer. Thus, in 1951 he quit his job at General Electric, moved with his family to Provincetown, Mass., embarked upon a longer narrative, and a year later published his apprentice novel, *Player Piano*, with Charles Scribner's Sons.

AAA: Arbeiten aus Anglistik and Amerikanistik, Volume 27 (2002): pp. 123–159. Copyright © 2002 Peter Freese.

The original hardcover edition was no commercial success, since less than a third of its first printing of 7,600 copies were sold, mostly to curious readers in Schenectady, but the scattered reviews were rather friendly. In the *Saturday Review*, Lee, who mistook Vonnegut to be "a graduate engineer," found the book "mordantly amusing" and understood it as asking whether the new phase of the Industrial Revolution "will be geared to the spiritual and intellectual growth of the American people or whether it will grind their dream into a kind of abundant discontent."[2] And in the *Library Journal*, Henderson described it as "an Orwellian vision-of-the-future first novel" and as "an important plea for reconsideration of human values, emphasizing that 'men, by their nature, seemingly, cannot be happy unless engaged in enterprises that make them feel useful.'"[3] In the following year, an inexpensive Doubleday Book Club edition sold about 20,000 copies, but the biggest success came in 1954, when Bantam re-edited the novel as a cheap paperback with the new title of *Utopia-14,* and when about a quarter of a million copies found avid readers.[4] In 1966, Rinehart & Winston brought out yet another hardcover edition, and Theodore Sturgeon, himself an established science-fiction writer, found it "a joy to behold" and described it as "blackly humorous, extraordinarily well-written, bitter, funny, and sharp."[5] In the *Saturday Review*, Armstrong praised Vonnegut as "sanity's secret weapon" and considered the novel's "subject—full automation and then what?—[. . .] especially fascinating in Vonnegut's hands."[6] And in the *Southern Review*, Franklin observed that in a technology-dominated world "science fiction no longer seems a fanciful escape from reality and realistic fiction is getting to look more and more like science fiction," argued that *Player Piano* "makes the short leap from realistic fiction to science fiction by extrapolating from the environment in which it was written to one that may quite conceivably evolve into being," and maintained that "its reissue in 1966 ha[d] made its prophecy seem more and more likely." But he also found "a radical flaw in the social criticism" and characterized "much of *Player Piano* [as] shallow and amateurish" because the novel is insufficiently "aware of the tradition of anti-utopia."[7]

Since Vonnegut has freely commented on his fictions and the complex processes which brought them into existence in many essays and interviews, the genesis of *Player Piano* can be precisely reconstructed. In his 1973 *Playboy* interview, Vonnegut stated that at the onset of his career he resorted to science-fiction formulae, although they were generally looked down upon, because "you were able to put an awful lot of keen ideas into circulation fast," and he reminisced:

> I was working for General Electric at the time, right after World War II, and I saw a milling machine for cutting the rotors on jet engines, gas turbines. This was a very expensive thing for a

machinist to do, to cut what is essentially one of those Brancusi forms. So they had a computer-operated milling machine built to cut the blades, and I was fascinated by that. This was in 1949 and the guys who were working on it were foreseeing all sorts of machines being run by little boxes and punched cards. *Player Piano* was my response to the implications of having everything run by little boxes. The idea of doing that, you know, made sense, perfect sense. To have a little clicking box make all the decisions wasn't a vicious thing to do. But it was too bad for the human beings who got their dignity from their jobs.

And when he was asked whether science fiction had really seemed "the best way" to write about that topic, Vonnegut answered: "There was no avoiding it, since the General Electric Company *was* science fiction. I cheerfully ripped off the plot of *Brave New World,* whose plot had been cheerfully ripped off from Eugene Zamiatin's *We*" (*CwKV* 93). Eight years earlier, however, in an essay about "Science Fiction" in the *New York Times Book Review,* he had still described his relationship to 'science fiction' in rather different terms by complaining:

> Years ago I was working in Schenectady for General Electric, completely surrounded by machines and ideas for machines, so I wrote a novel about people and machines, and machines frequently got the best of it, as machines will. (It was called *Player Piano,* and it was brought out again in both hard cover and paperback.) And I learned from the reviewers that I was a science-fiction writer. I didn't know that. I supposed that I was writing a novel about life, about things I could not avoid seeing and hearing in Schenectady, a very real town, awkwardly set in the gruesome now. I have been a soreheaded occupant of a file drawer labeled "science fiction" ever since, and I would like out, particularly since so many serious critics regularly mistake the drawer for a urinal. (*WFG* 1)

These self-assessments confirm that *Player Piano* belongs to the formulaic tradition of the anti-utopian or dystopian novel, that it is concerned with the threatening replacement of men by machines, and that, being an apprentice fiction, it owes quite a lot to its famous forerunners. It is not only literary sources, however, that helped to shape the make-up of Vonnegut's first novel, but also the personal experience of its creator. In a 1973 interview conducted by Scholes, Vonnegut ironically remembered that a central episode of his fictional extrapolation, that is, the chapters which take place at The Meadows, a remote island in the North Woods, on which the leading members of the company are assembled to develop the atavistic team spirit thought necessary for a strong corporate identity, had a real-life model, since there actually existed a place called Association Island, on which "a morale-building operation for General Electric" was staged annually and to which "deserving young men were sent [. . .] for a week and played golf and there were archery contests and baseball contests and swimming contests and plenty of free liquor, and so forth." That his public exhibition of these bizarre events had, in turn, some real-life effect becomes obvious when Vonnegut says: "*Player Piano* when it came out was not a widely read book except in Schenectady, New York, The island was shut down after the book came out." (*CwKV* 113)[8] And in his 1980 conversations with Reilly, Vonnegut mentioned yet another intriguing aspect of his prophetic narrative, when he answered the question of whether it was "the threat of automation that started [him] off" by pointing out that he had begun the book "before the word 'automation' had been coined by the Ford Motor Company" (*CwKV* 199).

But it is not as if *Player Piano* were Vonnegut's first comment on what he had learned from being close to the famous scientists working at the cutting edge of technology in one of the leading research laboratories in the country. In his well-known story "Epicac," he had already introduced the huge thinking machine which would reappear as EPICAC XIV in the novel, and had thereby created the fictional equivalent of ENIAC, the *E*lectronic *N*umerical *I*ntegrator and *C*omputer, the world's first electronic digital computer, which was completed in 1946 for military purposes. In his mildly critical "The Package," Vonnegut had dealt with the questionable promises of technological progress, and in "Poor Little Rich Town," he had satirically exposed the inhuman consequences of Taylorism. And in the light of what he said in 1999 about his rejected M.A. thesis, "which proved that similarities between the Cubist painters in Paris in 1907 and the leaders of Native American, or Injun, uprisings late in the nineteenth century could not be ignored" (*BSB* 6), it seems highly probable that it was his anthropological research that made him depict the secret Luddite organization in *Player Piano* as the Ghost Shirt Society and thus relate it to the Paiute Indian Wowoka's messianic religion, which used the Ghost Dance as the central ritual in its failed revolution against white oppression. *Player Piano*, then, is a first novel that translates a complex combination of personal experience, anthropological research, and earlier narratives into a conventionally presented tale which is firmly embedded in the venerable dystopian tradition, and whose major claim to fame is neither its still imperfect structural execution nor its not yet fully accomplished personal style, but its thematic depth and the first prophetic depiction of "tyranny by computer"[9] in American literature, which in 1952 was a highly speculative anticipation of coming developments but assumes a surprising topicality in our computer-governed times.

The action of *Player Piano* covers about six months in the life of its protagonist, Dr. Paul Proteus and takes place at some unspecified time in the not-too-far future. "The Last War" (241), which was the last of "the three most horrible wars in history" (284) and the one to end all wars, has made the U.S. not only the sole remaining superpower that dominates the rest of the world, but has also resulted in a hierarchically organized and computer-controlled society in which machines have gained dominance over human beings. During that long and terrible war, which America won due to her superior technology, "managers and engineers learned to get along without their men and women, who went to fight. It was the miracle that won the war—production with almost no manpower. [. . .] it was the know-how that won the war. Democracy owed its life to know-how." (9) But with the "golden age" (15; 126) of world peace securely established, the tendency to ever greater 'automation' has gone on, and "ten years after the war" (9) all the power lies in the hands of the privileged managers and engineers. "Industry is privately owned and managed, and co-ordinated—to prevent the waste of competition—by a committee of leaders from private industry, not politicians." (28) This "National Manufacturing Council" (45) with an all-powerful "National Industrial, Commercial, Communications, Foodstuffs, and Resources Director" (217) at its head decides about production and consumption, and the giant central computer EPICAC XIV, which fills several chambers of the Carlsbad Caverns and is "wholly free of reason-muddying emotions" and therefore "dead right about everything" (116), delivers all the data necessary for the smooth running of a tightly centralized society. Thus, economics has marginalized politics, and "just as religion and government had been split into disparate entities centuries before, now, thanks to the machines, politics and government lived side by side, but touched almost nowhere" (119). Consequently, the U.S. President is a powerless ham actor who has "gone directly from a three-hour television program to the White House" (118) and is a mere marionette called upon to deliver ghost-written speeches at official occasions.

The omnipotent computer, however, decides not only about production and consumption, but also about every citizen's individual life history. "Everyone's I.Q., as measured by the National Standard General Classification Test, [is] on public record—[. . .] at the police station" (90), and the results of the GCT are the sole criterion for anybody's career. Children with a good score move on to college or university and leave not only with a Ph.D. degree but also with a machine-administered "Achievement and Aptitude Profile," which, "when the graduate [is] taken into the economy, [is] translated into perforations on his personnel card" (77), and decides about the engineering or management job he or she will be assigned to. But all children with a lower I.Q. are reduced to the roles of Huxley's Gammas, Deltas and Epsilons or Orwell's Proles, since, with very few exceptions, all simpler jobs are done by machines. Thus for the majority of people there are only two options left: "any man who cannot support himself by doing a job better than a machine is employed by the government, either in the Army or in the Reconstruction and Reclamation Corps" (27), with the latter conjuring up memories of the Works Progress Administration and the Civilian Conservation Corps from the era of the New Deal. Joining the Army, whose members are not allowed to carry guns except when sent overseas, means twenty-five years of senseless drill before a discharge with a pension; and joining the RRC, popularly known as the "Reeks and Wrecks" (31), means partaking in an unending series of meaningless work-providing measures such as road repair. The only cash which both soldiers and RRC-members receive is pocket money, because deductions are made from their pay for rent, furniture and car and for the many insurances which make their lives secure from the cradle to the grave.

From the point of view of the managerial oligarchy, the new and rigorously stratified society is a veritable utopia, with the misery of the past victoriously overcome and with every citizen enjoying social security from birth to death, a safe and comfortable home to live in, and state-of-the-art technology ranging from television and central heating to "radar [cooking] range" and "ultrasonic dishwasher and clotheswasher" (158f.). Consequently, the managers are inordinately proud of the unheard-of degree of 'progress' which American civilization has made under their benevolent guidance. For the jobless multitudes, however, whom the machines have robbed of a self-determined existence and, even worse, deprived of pride and "the feeling of being needed on earth [. . .] *dignity*" (94), the world is not a 'golden age' but a golden cage, filled with an insuperable *tedium vitae*, and thus, under the deceptive surface of a well-ordered and smoothly functioning totalitarian technocracy, unrest, discontent, and despair are dangerously growing.

That Dr. Paul Proteus is vaguely aware of this conundrum becomes obvious when he talks to his secretary about a speech in which he defines "the First Industrial Revolution" as having "devalued muscle work" and "the Second Industrial Revolution" as having "devalued routine mental work" (21). When his secretary muses that both revolutions must have seemed quite inconceivable to the people concerned, he ruefully admits that this is true with regard "to the people who were going to be replaced by machines, maybe," and when she asks whether there will also be "a Third Industrial Revolution," he concedes that such a revolution, which, in turn, will "devaluate human thinking," has already "been going on for some time, if [she] mean[s] thinking machines" (22) like EPICAC XIV, and mentions in passing that "Norbert Wiener, a mathematician, said all that way back in the nineteen-forties" (22). This fleeting reference reveals that Wiener's popular book *The Human Use of Human Beings* (1950) must have been one of Vonnegut's major references. Wiener's influential treatise contains a chapter entitled "The First and the Second Industrial Revolution," in which the famous M.I.T. cyberneticist argues that what is generally known as the Industrial Revolution "concerned the machine purely as an alternative to human muscle," whereas "what we shall term The Second Industrial Revolution" will apply to "all labor performing judgments of a low level, in much the same way as the displaced labor of the earlier industrial revolution included every aspect of human power." And when he predicts that the automatic machine "will produce an unemployment situation, in comparison with which the present recession and even the depression of the thirties will seem a pleasant joke," and demands from "those responsible for management to see that the new modalities are used for the benefit of man, for increasing his leisure and enriching his spiritual life, rather than merely for profits and the worship of the machine as a new brazen calf,"[10] he defines the very problems which lie at the center of *Player Piano*. Wiener, however, not only offered the socio-critical background for Vonnegut's dystopian scenario, but might also have provided him with his title metaphor. Making a crucial distinction between the "know-how," of which it is said in the novel that "it was the know-how that won the war. Democracy owed its life to know-how" (9), and the "know-what," he defines the first as the ability to accomplish one's purposes and the second as the ability to define what those purposes are. He then ironically states that America has given too much thought to the first and not enough to the second, and "distinguish[es] between the two by the following example":

> Some years ago, a prominent American engineer bought an expensive player-piano. It became clear after a week or two that this purchase did not correspond to any particular interest in the music played by the piano but rather to the overwhelming interest in the piano mechanism. For this gentleman, the player-piano was not a means of producing music, but the means of giving some inventor the chance of showing how skillful he was at overcoming certain difficulties in the production of music. This is an estimable attitude in a second-year high-school student. How estimable it is in one of those on whom the whole cultural future of the country depends, I leave to the reader.[11]

***

The major place of action in Vonnegut's brave new world is Ilium, New York, and in the opening paragraph he has his narrator subtly foreshadow the future of this city and cleverly establish a wider referential horizon through intertextual allusions:

Ilium, New York, is divided into three parts.

In the northwest are the managers and engineers and civil servants and a few professional people; in the northeast are the machines; and in the south, across the Iroquois River, is the area known locally as Homestead, where almost all of the people live. (9)

The fictional "Ilium" with its fictional "Iroquois River" is Vonnegut's poetic equivalent of the real Schenectady with its real Mohawk River, and this mythically charged city will recur in such later novels as *Cat's Cradle* (1963), *Slaughterhouse-Five* (1969) and *Galápagos* (1985). Since "Ilium," the Latin version of Greek ιλιον, is another name for Troy, it conjures up the city immortalized in Homer's epic,[12] which not only endured one of the most famous sieges in human history, but was also the first city captured and destroyed by a 'machine,' the Trojan Horse.[13] Thus the very name of the novel's main place of action obliquely evokes the battle to come, and that the opening sentence—"Ilium, New York, is divided into three parts"—is an easily recognizable variation upon the "Gallia est omnis divisa in partes tres" in Caesar's *De Bello Gallico*, further underscores the unspoken suggestion that the events to follow will be martial confrontations. And these conflicts will occur between the three carefully divided parts, with the "managers and engineers" with their "machines" playing the role of the occupying Romans on the one side, and the unemployed and superfluous "people" in their "Homestead" assuming the role of the conquered natives on the other side of a Rubicon-like river, which is spanned by a bridge "not many people on either side have reasons other than curiosity for crossing" (9).

However, it is not only the spatial division of a rigidly zoned Ilium that is charged with a disruptive potential, but the city also looks back upon a long history of warfare, which is evoked when the protagonist looks out of a factory window towards the river and muses:

Here, in the basin of the river bend, the Mohawks had overpowered the Algonquins, the Dutch the Mohawks, the British the Dutch, the Americans the British. Now, over bones and rotten palings and cannon balls and arrowheads, there lay a triangle of steel and masonry buildings, a half-mile on each side—the Ilium Works. Where men had once howled and hacked at one another, and fought nip-and-tuck with nature as well, the machines hummed and whirred and clicked, and made parts for baby carriages and bottle caps, motorcycles and refrigerators, television sets and tricycles—the fruits of peace. (*PP* 11)

This brief historical summary makes it clear that the message about lasting peace having been finally accomplished after centuries of warfare is only true as regards a deceptive surface, whereas the subversive subtext underlying the novel's beginning insinuates the very opposite, namely that the old conflicts will soon erupt again.

The man who stands in the center of this conflict and will have to decide which side to take is Doctor Paul Proteus, who is the successful "manager of the Ilium Works, though only thirty-five" (9) years old. Holding the most prestigious job and having "the highest income in Ilium" (29), being happily married to the beautiful Anita, and enjoying the goodwill of his boss, Doctor Kroner, who is considering him for promotion to the much more important Pittsburgh Works, Paul Proteus should be more than satisfied with his brilliant career. But instead he is haunted by a vague sense of discontent and suffers from "periods of depression" (14). What disturbs him are his diffuse misgivings about the fact that the machines have made most humans obsolete, and since "his job, the system, and organizational politics" make him "variously annoyed, bored, or queasy" (15), he wonders "if he wouldn't have been more content in another period of history" (12). Therefore he repeatedly goes to the oldest part of the factory, namely "the original machine shop set up by Edison in 1886" (14),[14] where he searches for reassurance in "a vote of confidence from the past [. . .] where the past admitted how humble and shoddy it had been, where one could look from the old to the new and see that mankind really had come a long way" (14). On one of these trips to the old workshop he lovingly carries a "black cat" (9), which he has picked up near the golf course as "a mouser for the plant" (10), and he is deeply upset by having to watch first the fatal confrontation between this cat and a robot cleaning machine and then the death of the mangled cat on an electrically charged fence (20f.).

The hapless cat is the lonely embodiment of God-given and freedom-loving animal life in a standardized world of man-made and frighteningly anthropomorphized mechanical gadgets.[15] It conjures up the similar fates of "deer or steer, puma or porcupine or coyote, or the greedy turkey buzzards," which are electrocuted by the "high-tension wire fence" surrounding the Reservation in Huxley's *Brave New World*,[16] and it is equally reminiscent of the nature-technology dichotomy of the thrush singing in the countryside in spite of the "concealed microphones" of the secret police in Orwell's *1984*.[17] In *Player Piano*, this symbolically charged scene anticipates not only the novel's central conflict, namely, the eventual rebellion of a group of Luddite insurgents against the omnipresent machines which is as clearly doomed to fail as the cat's futile stand against the robot sweeper, but the poor animal's fate also serves as an ominous foreshadowing of Paul's personal future, since the cat's only means of escape from the electrically guarded world of the managers and engineers is death.

When Paul, on some illogical impulse, orders the dead cat to be brought to his office, the readers' suspicion is confirmed that the frustrated manager does not yet know what he really wants to do with his life and that he is torn between conflicting impulses, since he is both a dedicated engineer who "love[s] the machines [as] entertaining and delightful" (16) and a concerned human being who cares for "the people [...] replaced by machines" (22). The fact that he has not yet found himself is also announced by his programmatic name. This name not only implies that he will undergo an existential change from a Saul into a Paul, but it also refers to Proteus, the 'protean' old man of the sea in Greek mythology, who can change himself into any shape he pleases.[18] In the combination of these two references Hoffman sees yet another intriguing implication of the name as resulting from "the Latin definition of Paul ('little') and the change aspect implicit in Proteus. Since the plot of the book concludes with a revolution that has failed to alter the system, its messiah Paul Proteus—'little change'—is symbolic of the results, which seems to be a principal statement Vonnegut is making."[19] 'Proteus' might also refer to Charles *Proteus* Steinmetz, a mathematician who worked at General Electric and, like Vonnegut's protagonist, had certain socialist leanings. The most important intra-textual aspect, however, is the fact that *Paul Proteus* shares his initials with the novel's eponymous *Player Piano* and is thus obliquely related to an "old player piano" (32) in a dingy bar in Homestead, which gradually assumes a key metaphoric significance in the novel. As a piano played by machinery it stands not only for the soulless automation of what is one of the most advanced expressions of human creativity, namely the making of music, but, with its music being controlled by a paper strip with holes cut into it for the notes, it also serves as one of the earliest attempts at duplicating human movements and thus represents the punched card machines that have come to dominate the mechanized world of the novel.

When Paul's wife informs him that his fellow student and old friend Ed Finnerty, who is by now "a man of consequence, a member of the National Industrial Planning Board" (24) in Washington, has come to visit and that Paul, before coming home, has "to go to Homestead for some Irish whisky for him" (24), the daily routine of Paul's life is disrupted and the novel's action proper is set in motion by means of the venerable narrative device of 'enter mysterious stranger.' Looking forward to seeing after so many years "one of the few persons he had ever felt close to" (30), Paul embarks with mixed feelings on one of his rare forays into the strange world of Homestead. In his old car, in the glove compartment of which he keeps an illegal "rusty pistol" (39) from the days of the riots, he drives across the bridge, on which he has a brief encounter with a group of Reeks and Wrecks, and having entered the dingy bar that serves the unusual liquor, he tensely waits for the bartender to fetch the bottle, while leaning as inconspicuously as possible "against an old player piano" (32) in the corner and hoping not to be recognized as someone from 'the other side' by the hostile customers, who "had been the rioters, the smashers of machines" and who now "let him know that he had intruded where he was not liked" (35).

An old toothless man, however, identifies him as "young Doctor Proteus" (34), and in the ensuing dialogue this pitiable wreck turns out to be Rudy Hertz, whom many years ago Paul and Finnerty had selected as the most competent machinist "to have his motions immortalized on tape" (18). By measuring the movements of this master mechanic and having his "essence distilled" (18) on tape, they had awarded him the questionable honor of providing the endlessly copyable model for the automation process which has since put him and his fellows out of work. The senile old man, who is still childishly proud of having been selected for bringing about his own demise, insists on inviting Paul for a beer and celebrates their reunion by putting a nickel into the player piano. And while the tinny music clangs away, Hertz comments on the workings of "the antique instrument" (37) by observing: "Makes you feel kind of creepy, don't it, Doctor, watching them keys go up and down? You can almost see a ghost sitting there playing his heart out." (38) Together with the violent death of the cat brought about by a soulless robot and an electrically charged fence, Paul's seemingly innocuous encounter with the player piano embodies the novel's central concerns. The pitiful "old-timer" (18) Rudy Hertz, who was once a smart and proud machinist, personifies the loss of the 'good old days' in which humans were not yet ousted by machines, and his name not only refers to the German physicist in whose honor the unit of electromagnetic frequency was named, but it also obliquely signals how much the mechanization of his plant 'hurts' Paul.[20] And the player piano, whose mechanical movements conjure up "a ghost [. . .] playing his heart out," not only anticipates the fact that the revolutionaries will later call themselves the *Ghost* Shirt Society, but also serves as the potent "symbol of the machines that turn men into idle ghosts."[21] In this context it is anything but an accident that Finnerty, the revolutionary misfit, is "a top-flight pianist" (41) who will later be metonymically referred to as "the piano player" (256), and that in a revealing scene he sits "at the player piano, savagely improvising on the brassy, dissonant antique" (105), thus doing the very thing a programmed machine cannot do and thereby demonstrating that in a world of mechanical player pianos he is a human piano player.

Vonnegut makes sure that the meaning of the "ghost" conjured up by the mechanical piano is not overlooked by the reader, because at the beginning of the next chapter Paul, who is still being haunted by Rudy Hertz's unwittingly perceptive comment, is greeted by his caring wife with the exclamation "Darling, you look as though you've seen a *ghost* [my italics]" (38). And when she then hands Paul his homecoming cocktail and he thinks ruefully of "the image of his father" (38), the famous George Proteus, who had helped America win the war by uniting all manufacturing facilities, who had been "the nation's first National, Industrial, Commercial, Communications, Foodstuffs, and Resources Director" (10), and who, like another historical George before him, is still the unanimously revered founding father of the new era, one more 'ghost' is conjured up—one which, on the novel's psychological plane, will turn out to be of central significance for Paul's further development.

With Paul's charming wife Anita and his idiosyncratic old friend Finnerty, the representatives of the two opposing forces between which Paul will have to decide are introduced. Anita, who had been Paul's secretary during the war and whom he dutifully married when she told him that she was pregnant, has ironically turned out to be "barren" (10). She, whose name might conjure up "a 'man-eater,' besides being 'neater,'"[22] and who represents "the corrupt system in female form,"[23] is a staunch supporter of the system and the privileges she enjoys as the wife of the influential chief manager, and since she is "the only wife on the north side who had never been to college at all" (168), she not only looks down upon the people on the other side of the river, but her "contempt for those in Homestead [is] laced with active hatred" (168), which is easily explained by the fact that she is all too aware that "if [Paul] hadn't married her, this was where she'd be, what she'd be" (168). Being the scheming woman-behind-the-man, she lives her life by proxy and puts all her energy into supporting her husband's career. "The only grounds on which she met the world were those of her husband's rank. If he were to lose the rank it was frighteningly possible that she would lose touch with the world altogether, or, worse for Paul, leave him." (133)

Anita's approach to life is "disturbingly rational, systematic," her feelings are "shallow" (25), and she only "enjoy[s] the ritual attitudes of friendships, of which she ha[s] none" (24). The single proof of her alleged 'creativity' is her interior decoration of her fully electronic kitchen in mock colonial style, and this questionable feat has gained her the community's verdict that she is "*artistic*" (110). But Paul likes and needs her, because she possesses "a sexual genius that gave Paul his one unqualified enthusiasm in life" (134). When it is said about her that she "has the *mechanics* [my italics] of marriage down pat, even to the subtlest conventions" (25), the telling phrase reveals that with her the mechanization of the world has spilled over into her private life, and that the Paul-Anita relationship is 'mechanized' is underscored by the ritualized, and totally meaningless way in which they end all their dialogues—"I love you, Paul. I love *you*, Anita." Thus, it is a telling detail that Paul, when after his dismissal he sleeps with a prostitute, answers her mumble half-asleep with the "*automatic* [my italics] reply, 'And I love *you*, Anita'" (246). It is the clear-sighted Finnerty who brutally exposes Anita's human limitations when, enraged about her meddling with what he considers men's privacy, he threatens to have her replaced by a machine: "I'll design a machine that's everything you are [. . .] Stainless steel, covered with sponge rubber, and heated electrically to 98.9 degrees." (46) Later, Anita will turn this very threat against her husband by complaining that "all you need is something stainless steel, shaped like a woman, covered with sponge rubber, and heated to body temperature. [. . .] I'm sick of being treated like a machine!" (237) This woman, then, will do whatever she can to keep Paul a faithful servant of the system.

The "tall gaunt Irishman" (39) Edward Francis Finnerty, on the other hand, who lives up to the ethnic stereotype, is the very opposite of the immaculate but shallow Anita. This hard-drinking bachelor and "unsanitary-looking" man, about whom it is rumored that he is "a mutant, born of poor and stupid parents" (40) and who is "shockingly lax about his grooming" (39), leads a seemingly irrational life, which on closer scrutiny turns out to be "a studied and elaborate insult to the managers and engineers of Ilium, and to their immaculate wives" (40). But this maverick, who suffers from "the loneliness, the not belonging anywhere" and hates "this damn hierarchy that measures men against machines" (88), has the unbelievably high classification number E-022 (91), is exceptionally gifted and "could be anything he wanted to be, and be brilliant at it" (41). This solitary intellectual iconoclast, who casually informs the surprised Paul that he has quit his prestigious job in Washington and is not afraid to proclaim openly that "[his] sympathy's with any man up against a machine" (63), is a born misfit and outsider, and when Paul suggests that he should see a psychiatrist, he explains: "He'd pull me back into the center, and I want to stay as close to the edge as I can without going over. Out on the edge you see all kinds of things you can't see from the center. [. . .] Big, undreamed-of things—the people on the edge see them first." (86)

Whereas Anita tries to make Paul feel at home within the status quo, thereby personifying a future of stability and security for her faltering husband, Finnerty defects to the other side of the river—"At last I'm finding myself. Those dumb bastards across the river—they're *my* kind of people. They're real, Paul, real!" (139)—thereby embodying a future of change and risk for his friend. But these two people are not the only ones who will influence Paul in his search for "some sort of rebirth" (87) and a "fresh, strong identity" (102). There is also the spiteful Doctor Lawson Shepherd, who feels slighted by being only "second-in-command to Paul" (17) and is doing everything he can to denounce Paul with the powers that be, so that he might take over his job; and there is the Reverend James J. Lasher, cynical barfly, Protestant minister and anthropologist from across the river, who supplies Paul with the subversive insights and ideas which make him hate the system even more.

Doctor Lawson ("Dog-Eat-Dog") Shepherd is "a fine engineer, dull company, and doggedly master of his fate and *not* his brother's keeper" (54), whose name, together with the Biblical allusion, gives him away as a faithful 'son of the law,' who is not a 'shepherd' in the sense of a caring fellow-human, but a shepherd dog in the sense of jealously registering other people's smallest infringements of the rules. As an other-directed schemer who is "grimly respectful of the *mechanics* [my italics] of the competitive system" (54), he is a repulsive example of what the ruling system can make a man become, and he serves as a negative role model for Paul, repeatedly confronting him with the very mentality which Paul is afraid of developing himself. That this self-righteous organization man will later begin an affair with Anita, and that after Paul's defection Anita will triumphantly announce that she is "going to marry Doctor Lawson Shepherd as soon as she [can] get a divorce from Paul" (296) is the final confirmation of how perfectly the shallow upper-middle-class housewife from suburbia and the reckless careerist fit together in their mindless pursuit of success and social status.

It is, however, not Ed Finnerty, the disgruntled loner, but the RRC chaplain Reverend Lasher from across the river who provides the intellectual center of the novel, and this clear-sighted "anthropologist with a master's degree" (91) is easily recognizable as the spokesman of Vonnegut, the anthropology graduate without a master's degree, since it is through his socio-critical diagnoses as resulting from the mixture of his deep insights into human desires and his resigned awareness of human limitations that Vonnegut 'lashes' out against the follies and aberrations of his fictional world. Paul first meets the "short, heavy, seemingly soft [. . .] middle-aged" man with "extremely thick glasses" (34f.) when he goes to the dingy Homestead saloon to get whisky for Finnerty and when Lasher confronts him with the plight of his eighteen-year-old son who, although "he just about killed himself studying up" (36) for his National General Classification Tests, did not do well enough to make it to college and will now have to face a senseless future in the Reeks and Wrecks. Then Paul meets Lasher again when he and Finnerty drive over to the saloon for some undisturbed hard drinking and when Lasher tells them that his desperate son has just hanged himself, only to confess a little later to the embarrassed Paul that he does not have a son and has made the story up to see "how one of those superbrains worked" (90). They enter into a long conversation with this eloquent "up-state Socrates" (91), and he aptly defines the people's predicament by explaining that

"For generations they've been built up to worship competition and the market, productivity and economic usefulness, and the envy of their fellow men—and boom! It's all yanked out from under them.

They can't participate, can't be useful any more. Their whole culture's been shot to hell."

[...]

"Things are certainly set up for a class war based on conveniently established lines of demarcation. And I must say that the basic assumption of the present setup is a grade-A incitement to violence: the smarter you are, the better you are. Used to be that the richer you were, the better you were. Either one is, you'll admit, pretty tough for the have-nots to take. The criterion of brains is better than the one of money, but"—he held his thumb and forefinger about a sixteenth of an inch apart—"about *that* much better." (92 and 94)

With this appropriate diagnosis established, Lasher then speculates upon a therapy and comes up with the following conjecture:

"Things, gentlemen, are ripe for a phony Messiah, and when he comes, it's sure to be a bloody business." [...]

"Sooner or later someone's going to catch the imagination of these people with some new magic. At the bottom of it will be a promise of regaining the feeling of participation, the feeling of being needed on earth—hell, *dignity*. The police are bright enough to look for people like that, and lock them up under the antisabotage laws. But sooner or later someone's going to keep out of their sight long enough to organize a following." (93f.)

And before he leaves, he looks at Finnerty and says: "You know, wash your face, and you might do real well as a Messiah." (97)

It is on this eventful evening that Finnerty decides to join the people on the other side of the river, whereas an increasingly drunk Paul, who feels himself teetering "on the verge of a splendid discovery" (101) and then even develops "a feeling of newness—the feeling of fresh, strong identity growing within him." (102), cannot yet make up his mind. Finally he gets so drunk that he feels he must deliver a speech in which "to make himself the new Messiah and Ilium the new Eden," but all he can announce before he collapses is "We must meet in the middle of the bridge!" (105). The metaphorical interplay between *Paul Proteus* dreaming of "some sort of rebirth" (87), Ed Finnerty improvising on the *p*layer *p*iano and thereby reclaiming the mechanical instrument as a means of human expression, and Lasher announcing the imminent appearance of a new Messiah who will deliver men from the machines is subtly enriched when, before leaving, Lasher "pick[s] up a hard-boiled egg at the bar [and] crackle[s] its shell by rolling it along the keyboard of the player piano" (97). That he uses the potent symbol of rebirth to elicit some unprogrammed sounds from the mechanical player might

signal the hope for a new beginning, but that this egg is hard-boiled and its shell
crackled could imply that the new beginning will be abortive and that in the
coming revolt *Paul Proteus*, instead of being liberated, will be instrumentalized
into just another *player piano*, whose utterances are programmed by others.

With his drinking binge in Homestead, with Shepherd's report about
Paul's unlawful admission of an unescorted Finnerty to the Ilium Works,
and with the police having found Paul's illegal pistol, the erstwhile spot-
less manager "pile[s] up a fairly impressive police dossier" (129) in only a
few days, but his chances for being promoted are still excellent. In a heart-
to-heart talk with Kroner, the powerful manager of the Eastern division
and "the archprophet of efficiency" (122), whose German name is certainly
no accident, Paul openly voices his still unspecific doubts about the system,
but the fatherly Kroner tries to reassure him and offers him the prestigious
Pittsburgh job on condition that he testify against Lasher and Finnerty "that
they tried to get [him] into a plot to sabotage the Ilium Works" (130). It is
the outrageous suggestion that he "turn informer on his friend, Ed Finnerty"
(132) which makes Paul finally ready to quit. But the fact that he will not
have to announce his decision before the board meeting at The Meadows,
grants him several weeks to make up his mind. He knows that giving up his
job and all his privileges will certainly make him lose his wife, and since she
is "all he ha[s]" (134) and he shockingly recognizes "that he, like Anita, [is]
little more than his station in life" (134), he decides to pretend that nothing
has happened and keep his decision to quit a secret until he has prepared
Anita and himself for their new life.

The new existence which Paul envisions and clandestinely tries to prepare for is a life out in the open and close to nature, and, avidly reading books
about "woodsmen, sailors, cattlemen" (135), he begins to devise a future in
which he will be able to forget about society and deal "only with Earth as
God had given it to man" (135). These immature dreams coalesce into his
decision to become a farmer: "Somewhere, outside of society, there was a
place for a man—a man and wife—to live heartily and blamelessly, *naturally*,
by hands and wits." (143) Paul dimly remembers that on the margins of his
mechanized world there exists, due to some freakish hereditary twist, an old
farmhouse, "the Gottwald place" (144), and he buys this farm for a small sum.
He is enthused about the ancient farmhouse, the very name of which conjures
up pastoral delights and which is situated "close to the edge of town" (144)
"in a completely isolated backwater, cut off from the rapid boilings of history,
society, and the economy. Timeless" (147). In this house Paul plans to begin
a new existence, and he naïvely hopes that Anita will join him: "Here was a
place where he could work with his hands, getting life from nature without
being disturbed by any human beings other than his wife. Not only that, but

Anita, with her love for things colonial, would be enchanted, stunned, even, by this completely authentic microcosm of the past." (149)

Paul's attempt to escape from his technocratic reality into a pastoral dream and from the artificial complexity of his present into the natural simplicity of a nostalgically transfigured past is easily recognizable as a variation of a constitutive notion of American literature,[24] and it is also easily predictable that such a flight from technological progress to agrarian idealism will not work. Thus it comes as no surprise that Anita, when Paul takes her to the old house and tells her "I've made up my mind to quit my job and live here" (176), enragedly rejects the notion of turning into a farmer's wife as untenable, thereby anticipating an insight which Paul, after his return from The Meadows, will gain himself when he realizes that his training and conditioning as an engineer have irrevocably estranged him from Nature:

> Paul had gone to his farm once, and, in the manner of a man dedicating his life to God, he'd asked Mr. Haycox [the custodian] to put him to work, guiding the hand of Nature. The hand he grasped so fervently, he soon discovered, was coarse and sluggish, hot and wet and smelly. And the charming little cottage he'd taken as a symbol of the good life of a farmer was as irrelevant as a statue of Venus at the gate of a sewage-disposal plant. He hadn't gone back. (246)

With the dream of a pastoral retreat into Jeffersonian agrarianism exploded, the only reaction that is left to Paul is that of open rebellion, and the seeds for that are laid during his days at The Meadows, which mark the climax of his spiritual development. Having been awarded the prestigious function of Captain of the Blue Team, Paul travels to the island not only to take part unwillingly in the annual "orgy of morale building—through team athletics, group sings, bonfires and skyrockets, bawdy entertainment, free whisky and cigars" (44), but also to face the decisive "crisis [that is] coming" and, in meeting the main board, finally to decide whether "to quit or turn informer" (179) and thus to be either expelled from the system or rewarded with the job at Pittsburgh.

In the four chapters which deal with the bizarre events at The Meadows and which are, as unbelievable as it might seem, partly modelled on what really happened on General Electric's Association Island, Vonnegut pulls all the stops in satirically unmasking the organization's ludicrous attempts at creating a corporate identity. Since, in doing so, he enriches the usually serious genre of dystopia with hilarious touches, Hicks was right when he observed in one of the earliest reviews that "nothing could be more amusing than [Vonnegut's] account of the antics of the aspiring engineers when they gather on an island in the St. Lawrence for pep talks, competitive sports, formalized informality, and the careful cultivation of the big shots."[25] On the 'sacred' island, the managers are made to live two in a tent in order to "develop a sort of common-law brotherhood" (182), to call each other only by their first names in order to develop togetherness, to join in constantly singing inane songs from *The Meadows Songbook,* which "look[s] like a hymnal" (136), in order to get into the desired pious mood, to talk only to people they do not know in order to make new buddies, to exert themselves in all sorts of sports in order to "stir up team rivalry" (182), and to drink hard in order to lose their inhibitions. A blaring loudspeaker voice ruthlessly chases them from one activity to the other, and in their carefully orchestrated "orgy of morale building" (44) they behave like frenzied children. The three highlights of the ceaseless island activities are a tearful "memorial service" (190) for the deceased members of the organization, a crudely didactic allegorical play, and a communal swearing of "the Oath of the Spirit of the Meadows" (213). The memorial service, which takes place around an ancient oak, "the official symbol for the entire national organization" (190), is meant to create emotional unity and turn the stirred participants into "a homogenized pudding" (191). The propagandistic drama is a kind of medieval morality play, in which a Radical and a Young Engineer plead their cases before a God-like Sky Manager, and it is meant to convey the organization's central message, which is annually repeated with slight variations and signifies "that the common man wasn't nearly as grateful as he should be for what the engineers and managers had given him, and that the radicals were the cause of the ingratitude" (221). And the oath, which is significantly administered by an aging "professional actor" (212) dressed up as an Indian chieftain and thus relates the required affiliation to the organization to the inseparable bonds of Indian tribal togetherness, makes the impressed "neophytes" (213) swear "by the voice in the pines [. . .] by the lapping of the great blue water, by the whir of the eagle wing [. . .] by the growl of the summer thunder" (213f.) that "I will uphold the Spirit of the Meadows. I will obey the wise commands of my chiefs, for the good of the people. I will work and fight fearlessly, tirelessly for a better world. I will never say the job is done. I will uphold the honor of my profession and what I represent at all times. I will seek out enemies of the people, enemies of a better world for all children, relentlessly." (214)

Paul, however, who has meanwhile made up his mind to opt for 'a separate peace,' is hardly touched by the hubbub around him, because by now "he [is] his own man" (201). But when he is called to the secret meeting of the directors, he knows that the moment of truth has come, and realizes that his previous "easy, comfortable life, with simple answers for every doubt" (216) is drawing to a close. He learns from his superiors that there is an underground movement known as "the Ghost Shirt Society" (217), with its headquarters in Ilium and with the traitorous Finnerty belonging to it, and that they want to infiltrate this society of saboteurs by pretending to fire Paul and thus making him an irresistible bait for the revolutionaries. His reward for acting as a double agent will be the prestigious Pittsburgh job, but he will not even be allowed to tell his wife about the secret operation. When asked whether he will comply with this plan, Paul defiantly announces "I quit" (221), but his bosses laughingly mistake that as his adoption of the intended role. Publicly disgraced as a vile saboteur, Paul is dishonorably discharged from the organization and shipped back to the mainland, where he discovers that Anita is having an affair with the hateful Shepherd and, after an emotional confrontation, loses her as well. Reduced to being what is ironically termed "merely a man" (235) and shamefully demoted from influential manager to "unclassified human being" (239), painfully separated from his wife, and "with his old life gone, and his new one, whatever it was to be, not yet begun" (236), Paul finds himself in an existential limbo and is thus ready for a new beginning.

Having traveled back to Ilium not by managerial plane but on an automatic train filled with swearing soldiers and complaining Reeks and Wrecks, thus getting his first glimpse of life from the point of view of 'the people,' Paul is summoned to the police to have all his privileges revoked. At the precinct he meets an acquaintance from the Homestead bar, with whom he goes for a beer to be filled in on what happened at The Meadows after his departure and, drinking to "the new life he'd chosen," falls "senseless from the barstool" (259). It turns out that the Ghost Shirt Society have knocked him out and abducted him, and when the ex-manager comes to, Finnerty and Lasher are interrogating him under "sodium pentathol" (280), a truth serum, about his beliefs. Admitting that his being fired was a pretense, but insisting that he has also quit, Paul learns from Lasher and Finnerty that the insurgents plan "that the world should be restored to the people" (272) and that they have taken their name from an Indian movement, thus taking recourse to the very Indian lore which also the organization relies upon for its ceremonial oath. The historically knowledgeable Lasher explains:

> With the game and land and ability to defend themselves gone, the Indians found out that all the things they used to take pride in doing, all the things that had made them feel important, all the things that used to gain them prestige, all the ways in which they used to justify their existence—they found that all those things were going or gone. [. . .] The world had changed radically for the Indians. It had become a white man's world, and Indian ways in a white man's world were irrelevant. It was impossible to hold the old Indian values in the changed world. The only thing they could do in the changed world was to become second-rate white men or wards of the white men. [. . .] And the Ghost Dance religion was

the last, desperate defense of the old values. Messiahs appeared, the way they're always ready to appear, to preach magic that would restore the game, the old values, the old reasons for being. There were new rituals and new songs that were supposed to get rid of the white men by magic. And some of the more warlike tribes that still had a little physical fight left in them added a flourish of their own—the Ghost Shirt. [. . .] They were going to ride into battle one last time in magic shirts that white men's bullets couldn't go through. (273)

When Paul finds the freshly manufactured Ghost Shirts presented to him rather silly, Finnerty admits that "we've got to be a little childish, anyway, to get the big following we need" (274), and tells him "It's the symbolism of the thing!" (274). And Lasher explains the parallels: "Don't you see, Doctor? The machines are to practically everybody what the white men were for the Indians. People are finding that, because of the way the machines are changing the world, more and more of their old values don't apply any more." (274)

Paul is cursorily co-opted as a new member of the revolution, and Lasher's aside to Finnerty that "he'll do nicely" (272) makes attentive readers suspect that the still drugged ex-manager does not really proceed from being a cog in the machinery of the ruling powers to being a liberated individual, but that he only shuttles from being the pawn of one to becoming the plaything of another organization. Such suspicions are confirmed when Paul is told that he "[w]on't have to do anything" (275) except put his famous family's name under a letter that has already been drafted by Professor Ludwig von Neumann.[26] In this letter, whose ringing phrases imitate the Declaration of Independence, it is solemnly stated in Paul's name that he and his fellow Luddites "have changed [their] minds about the divine right of machines" (284) and want "to give the world back to the people" (285). And the letter ends by declaring:

Men, by their nature, seemingly, cannot be happy unless engaged in enterprises that make them feel useful. They must, therefore, be returned to participation in such enterprises.

I hold, and the members of the Ghost Shirt Society hold:

That there must be virtue in imperfection, for Man is imperfect, and Man is a creation of God.

That there must be virtue in frailty, for Man is frail, and Man is a creation of God.

That there must be virtue in inefficiency, for Man is inefficient, and Man is a creation of God.

That there must be virtue in brilliance followed by stupidity, for

Man is alternately brilliant and stupid, and Man is a creation of God.

You perhaps disagree with the antique and vain notion of Man's being a creation of God.

But I find it a far more defensible belief than the one implicit in intemperate faith in lawless technological progress—namely, that man is on earth to create more durable and efficient images of himself, and, hence, to eliminate any justification at all for his own continued existence.

Faithfully yours,
Doctor Paul Proteus (285f.)

Paul has hardly digested the meaning of the letter distributed in his name, when the hiding place of the insurgents is raided by the police and Paul, as the only one who does not yet know the escape routes, is arrested and put into prison. There he is visited by Kroner, who still believes that Paul has only fulfilled his duty as informer and will now reveal the plans of the revolutionaries, and by Anita who, having belatedly learnt about Paul's double role, now wants him, and his status, back. But when an expectant Kroner asks who is the leader of the Ghost Shirt Society, Paul says: "I am. And I wish to God I were a better one." (293) Thus, the die has been cast, and Paul, now a confirmed traitor and saboteur, is next seen in the Ilium Federal Courtroom as defendant in a nationwide televised trial. Accused of "conspiracy to advocate the commission of sabotage" (294), he is initially "at ease, filled with the euphoria of well-publicized martyrdom for a cause in which he believe[s]" (295). But he gradually loses his composure, because, revealingly enough, even in the courtroom he finds himself at the mercy of a machine, a sophisticated lie detector which monitors his reactions and reveals that the real reason for his joining the insurgents is not his professed hatred of the machines but his subconscious revolt against the oppressive image of his all-powerful father. Right in the middle of the trial, however, the uprising begins, the courtroom is invaded by hordes of Ghost Shirters, and Paul is carried out, "marionette-like" (304), on the shoulders of triumphant rebels.

The revolution, which is fairly successful in Ilium and a few other cities, nationwide turns out to be a failure, and, what is worse, degenerates into a free-for-all riot in which the frenzied Ghost Shirters indiscriminately destroy everything and engage in senseless "vandalism and looting" (307), giving their chaotic enterprise "all the characteristics of a lynching" (311). Lasher, Finnerty, von Neumann and Paul are unable to prevent their motley troops from burning the museum, blowing up the sewage disposal plant, and playing havoc with everything somehow connected with machinery. Surrounded by massive government forces and faced with an ultimatum that the smoldering ruins of Ilium will be besieged for six months unless the leaders are surrendered, the four disillusioned "brains of the Ghost Shirt Society" warily tour "the strongpoints on the frontiers of their Utopia" (316) and discover to their disgust that their Luddite forces have not only smashed everything, but that a representative group of them are happily repairing the most senseless machine of all, "an Orange-O machine," which dispenses a drink "no one in the whole country" (317) ever drank. And to his deep disillusionment Paul has to recognize that the very men who have just risked their lives in their revolt against the machines are now lovingly creating new ones—a man from the Reeks and Wrecks whom Paul has met earlier as a "desperately unhappy" person is "proud and smiling because his hands were busy doing what they liked to do best, [. . .] —replacing men like himself with machines" (318). Thus it is not so much the hopelessness of their situation, but their shocking insight that they have achieved no real change but only inaugurated another turn of the wheel, another cycle of destruction and reconstruction, which convinces the four leaders that they cannot do anything but surrender.

It is here that a central motif of *Player Piano* achieves its final, and frightening, impact. At the beginning of the novel, Paul wonders about the soft-spoken Bud Calhoun from Georgia, a gifted engineer bearing the name of South Carolina's champion of slavery and nullification. And he muses about Bud, who will later invent a machine which makes himself superfluous and who, as a consequence, also becomes a member of the Ghost Shirt Society: "Bud's mentality was one that had been remarked upon as being peculiarly American since the nation had been born—the restless, erratic insight and imagination of a gadgeteer. This was the climax, or close to it, of generations of Bud Calhouns, with almost all of American industry integrated into one stupendous Rube Goldberg machine." (12) When one of the Reeks and Wrecks cleverly repairs the fuel pump in Paul's car with a piece of leather cut from the sweatband of his cap, he offers another instance of this very mentality (73f.), of which Kroner piously insists that it is not "just gadgeteering, blind tinkering," but "more than that" (126) and of which the founder of the Ilium Works, Thomas Alva Edison, is of course the most outstanding example. When Paul travels back from the Meadows and talks to the old train conductor who has lost his job to a machine, he wonders "at what thorough believers in mechanization most Americans were, even when their lives had been badly damaged by mechanization. The conductor's plaint, like the lament of so many, wasn't that it was unjust to take jobs from men and give them to machines, but that the machines didn't do nearly as many human things as good designers could have made them do." (241)

And when he thinks about the fully mechanized arms which have allowed America to win the final war, he realizes that the men who died in that war "were heirs to another American tradition, as old as that of the rifleman, but once a peaceful tradition—that of the American tinker" (243). Obviously, then, in *Player Piano* it is not the anonymous power of totalitarian systems which enslaves people, but a built-in human flaw, a faulty genetic design, as it were, which time and again makes human beings devise the very instruments of their suffering and lets them become the creators of their own unhappiness. This variation upon the *Zauberlehrling* motif, which shifts the standard dystopian complaint from the level of institutional repression to that of individual failure, is most cynically expressed by Finnerty, when he says: "If only it weren't for the people, the goddamned people, always getting tangled up in the machinery. If it weren't for them, earth would be an engineer's paradise." (313) And it is with this message that Vonnegut significantly deviates from such alleged predecessors of his as Huxley and Orwell. By insisting that it is not the machines which constitute the real enemy, but the built-in flaws of their human inventors, he turns the conventional anti-utopian complaint into a skeptical exploration of the human psyche.[27] And he will explore the limitations of fallen man in his further novels with growing insistence and give this concern its most concise expression in *The Sirens of Titan* (1959) in the parable of the Tralfamadorians' eventual self-annihilation through machines of their own invention (*SoT* 274f.).

When the four leaders of the uprising hold their final conversation, Paul must admit to himself that once more he has not really understood what was going on. Asking Lasher belatedly what happened to "the original Ghost Shirt Society," he not only learns that they all died, since their shirts were of course not bullet-proof, but that Lasher and Finnerty have known from the very beginning that they, too, "were sure to lose" (314) and have intentionally chosen a model for defeat and not for victory. And he realizes that each of the other three leaders has pursued his own individual goal. Finnerty, the cynical iconoclast, has got what he wanted, namely "a chance to give a savage blow to a close little society that made no comfortable place for him" (320). Von Neumann, the former political scientist, has seen the revolution as "a fascinating experiment," since he "ha[s] been less interested in achieving a premeditated end than in seeing what would happen with given beginnings" (320). And Lasher, the "enemy of the Devil" and "man of God" (315) and the "lifelong trafficker in symbols," "ha[s] created the revolution as a symbol, and [is] now welcoming the opportunity to die as one" (320). This is why when the four insurgents have a final drink before surrendering, Lasher's toast is "to the record" (320). Finnerty and von Neumann repeat this toast, joining the calm preacher in his insight that all they have achieved is a footnote in the history books. And when it is Paul's turn to present a toast, the ex-manager of whom Lasher had condescendingly said earlier that "he'll do nicely" (272) as the other-directed figure-head of the revolt and who was revealingly carried "marionette-like" (304) out of the courtroom, has to recognize that he is the only one of the leaders who had no real plan and no precise aim:

> "To a better world," he started to say, but he cut the toast short, thinking of the people of Ilium, already eager to recreate the same old nightmare. He shrugged. "To the record," he said, and smashed the empty bottle on a rock.
>   Von Neumann considered Paul and then the broken glass. "This isn't the end, you know," he said. "Nothing ever is, nothing ever will be—not even Judgment Day."
>   "Hands up," said Lasher almost gaily. "Forward March." (320)

Thus, the novel ends with Paul's insight into the futility of his endeavors, and consequently some critics have found its message to be thoroughly pessimistic. Vanderbilt, for example, sees Paul faced with "not linear progress but hopeless cyclic regression,"[28] and McGrath finds that according to Vonnegut "the postindustrial individual will not likely reach out to embrace the humanistic postbourgeois side of modern liberalism; he will be too preoccupied with a self-defeating struggle against the mechanical world of his industrial predecessor. This is, indeed, the tragic theme that permeates *Player Piano*."[29] But although it is clear that, like the freedom-loving cat which paid with its life for trying to scale the fence, Paul and the others will be severely punished and in all probability even be executed, Hoffman is more convincing when he asserts that "the ending is affirmative because it reassures us that humans will continue to rebel against this prisonhouse of their own creation despite the failure of *this* rebellion, *this* man, or *this* period of history."[30] There is indeed some faint note of optimism in both von Neumann's conviction that "nothing ever is the end" and Lasher's concluding words "Forward March." Human beings are not like the Biblical "lilies of the field," to which the epigraph of the novel refers and which are gloriously beautiful although they neither toil nor spin, but they will always strive for improvement, history will go on, the abortive revolution will not be the last one, and men will not cease in their fight against hateful conditions, even if these conditions are of their own making.

***

The protagonist of *Player Piano* is certainly not a fully rounded character, and Segal rightly observes that none of the novel's actors, "including Paul, is as fully developed as one might wish, and most are two-dimensional characters if not outright stereotypes."[31] Vonnegut would be the first to admit such limitations, since he repeatedly stated that he is not primarily interested in psychological details, and as late as in *Timequake* (1997) made his fictional *alter ego* Kilgore Trout observe that "if I'd wasted my time creating characters, I would never have gotten around to calling attention to things that really matter." And when he added: "Trout might have said, and it can be said of me as well, that he created *caricatures* rather than characters" (*T* 63), he confirmed that his novels are more concerned with the exploration of general ideas than with the development of individual characters. Nevertheless, Paul Proteus is not only a spokesman for humanity's search for freedom and self-fulfillment in a world of oppressive machinery, but also a unique human being with his particular needs and desires. This is why *Player Piano* is not only a socio-critical extrapolation of threatening developments concerning a whole society, but why, on a different and perhaps less obvious level, it is also a psychological exploration of the painful inner development of an individual man.[32]

From the very beginning, Paul Proteus, who "love[s] the machines [as] entertaining and delightful" (16) but also cares for "the people [. . .] replaced by machines" (22), tries in vain to reconcile his conflicting impulses, and he time and again postpones his decision because he is being torn between his interests as a dedicated engineer and his loyalties as a concerned human being. That such a conflict results in some sort of incipient schizophrenia becomes obvious when, after his dishonorable banishment from The Meadows, Paul gives the following piece of advice to young Edmund Harrison, who is the only one to help him and later makes a brief return as an enraged critic of the system: "Don't put one foot in your job and the other in your dreams, Ed. Go ahead and quit, or resign yourself to this life. It's just too much of a temptation for fate to *split you right up the middle* [my italics] before you've made up your mind which way to go." (226) And when Harrison asks whether that has happened to Paul, he answers in the affirmative. On the novel's psychological level, then, Paul's drunken cry in the Homestead bar—"We must meet in the middle of the bridge!" (105)—not only applies to his desire for a reconciliation between the managers and the Homesteaders, but also expresses his need to find some bridge between his divided loyalties.

Another important reason for Paul's mix-up is the fact that he cannot establish true human relationships, since most of the people he has to deal with behave like machines. A typical example is his colleague Baer, who is "just, reasonable, and candid," but also "remarkably *machine-like* [my italics] in that the only problems he interested himself in were those brought to him, and in that he went to work on all problems with equal energy and interest, insensitive to quality and scale" (187). The same is true of Paul's wife Anita, who "has the *mechanics* [my italics] of marriage down pat" (25), and whose machine-like behavior Finnerty comments on when he threatens to "design a machine that's everything you are" (46). However, not only are human relationships reduced to mechanical exchanges, but the conversion also works the other way round, and the engineers' relationships with their machines and the managers' attitudes towards their organization assume sensual aspects and turn into a sort of love affair. The best example of this is Paul's competitor for the Pittsburgh job, Doctor Fred Garth, of whom it is said:

> Garth was [a fine man], desperate to please, and he seemed to have an anthropomorphic image of the corporate personality. Garth stood in relation to that image as a lover, and Paul wondered if this prevalent type of relationship had ever been given the consideration it deserved by sexologists, [. . .] At any rate, Paul had seen Garth at various stages of his love affair, unable to eat for anxiety, on a manic crest, moved to maudlin near-crying at recollections of the affair's tender beginnings. In short, Garth suffered all the emotional hazards of a perennial game of she-loves-me, she-loves-me-not. To carry out directions from above—an irritating business for Paul—was, for Garth, a favor to please a lady. (127f.)

And that Anita has a similar attitude becomes clear, when after the party at Kroner's, where Paul and his wife learn about his forthcoming promotion, "Anita slept—utterly satisfied, not so much by Paul as by the *social orgasm* of, after years of *the system's love play*, being offered Pittsburgh" (133) [my italics]. Thus, even in his marriage Paul does not find the true love which might help him to make the right decision, but all he gets from his socially ambitious wife is the short-lived pleasure of sexual fulfillment. Anita possesses "a sexual genius that gave Paul his one unqualified enthusiasm in life" (134) and regularly uses this talent for making him comply with her plans, as when after the failure of his farmer's dream she calls him her "little boy" and causes him to give "himself over to the one sequence of events that had never failed to provide a beginning, a middle, and a satisfactory end" and of which he thinks as Poe's "Descent into the Maelstrom" (178).

The decisive reason for Paul's depressions and his moral paralysis, however, is his deeply disturbed relationship with his dead father, references to whom punctuate the novel. Not only is Paul regularly confronted with the omnipresent image of his father, who is nationally worshipped as the great hero who made it possible for America to win the war, but whenever he "fancie[s] himself in the image of his father" (38), he must realize to his chagrin that he cannot fill the old man's shoes. As a child and young man Paul hardly saw his busy father, and when Finnerty asks him about details, he angrily states: "How do I know what my father was? The editor of *Who's Who* knows about as much as I do. The guy was hardly ever home." (85) But he cannot rid himself of the overbearing shadow, and whenever he meets Kroner, that paternalistic archpriest of the organization either admonishes him "to follow in his father's footsteps" (66) or praises him for progressing "in the footsteps of your father" (49), and when he promotes Paul he does so "always in the name of his father" (127). Paul's psychological arrest becomes obvious when, in the presence of Kroner, he cannot help but feel "docile" and "childlike," as though he "stood in the enervating, emasculating presence of his father again" (48). Although Paul is angrily aware that he is not up to his father's expectations—"He could handle his assignments all right, but he didn't have what his father had, [...] the ability to be moved emotionally, almost like a lover, by the great omnipresent and omniscient spook, the corporate personality." (66f.)—he is never allowed to forget the great man, since Anita has put up a picture of Paul's father on his bureau so that "he could see it the first thing in the morning and the last thing at night" (66). And it is of course the crowning irony that she will later deceive Paul with Shepherd, a man about whom she tells her cuckolded husband that "he's the spitting image of your father" (67). Even in his dreams Paul is haunted by the old man's shadow, and when after his dishonorable dismissal from The Meadows he sleeps with a prostitute, he awakes "From a dream in which he saw his father glowering at him from the foot of the bed" (246).

The long chain of these references climaxes at Paul's trial, which Seed rightly calls "a cross between legal interrogation and psychoanalysis."[33] There the prosecutor accuses Paul that he did not fight against the organization because of his professed humanitarian motives, but for another, and much baser, reason:

> [...] your red-white-and-blue patriotism is really an expression of hate and resentment—hate and resentment for one of the greatest true patriots in American history, your father! [...] I submit that this man before you is little more than a spiteful boy, to whom this great land of ours, this great economy of ours, this civilization of ours, has become a symbol of his father! A father whom, subconsciously, he would have liked to destroy! (298)

And when the unerring lie detector confirms this diagnosis as correct, a chastised Paul confesses that he "can't deny" (299) the prosecutor's argument that his "treason" originates from an "Oedipus complex" (298). Thus, there is sufficient textual evidence that Paul Proteus serves not only as the spokesman of Vonnegut's social criticism but also as the individual object of his psychological exploration. On this level, by the way, certain aspects of Paul's rejection of his father can be read as referring back to Vonnegut's disturbed relationship with his own father,[34] and this is one of the reasons why Broer, who finds "Paul's psychodrama" more central to the book than its socio-political message, reads Vonnegut's apprentice novel as the first in a series of narrative attempts at exorcizing the growing threats to his own mental sanity in "a career-long process of cleansing and renewal."[35]

***

The main plot of *Player Piano* is restricted to the interaction of a relatively small cast of characters from either the management of the Ilium Works or the people of Homestead, and therefore it offers no possibilities for a scenic presentation of such other important facets of the fictional post-World-War-III America as the military complex, the educational system or the realm of organized sports, which readers need to learn about in order to make up their minds about the new society. Fortunately, Vonnegut refrains from integrating these necessary aspects into his tale by having an omniscient narrator present the long descriptive passages which make many well-known dystopias come across as almost plotless treatises, but he resorts instead to a clever combination of two venerable fictional strategies. He gives eight of his thirty-five chapters to a wholly independent subplot centering around the Shah of Bratpuhr, the "wizened and wise [. . .] spiritual leader of 6,000,000 members of the Kolhouri sect" (26), who is on a state visit to the U.S. "to see what he could learn in the most powerful nation on earth for the good of his people" (26). Since he and his hilariously named translator Khashdrahr Miasma are shown around as guests of the government with Doctor Ewing J. Halyard from the State Department as their concerned guide, the Shah's travels through the country allow Vonnegut to combine the survey functions of the picaresque mode with the defamiliarizing effects of the Martian perspective.

The Shah, who is first introduced as driving through Ilium, is then taken to an army camp to speak to some soldiers, to the Carlsbad Caverns to see EPICAC XIV and be introduced to the President, to "Proteus Park, Chicago" to see how an "average man" (156) lives, and to Miami Beach to have his hair cut. On his way to Ithaca he has a revealing encounter with a failed writer's wife, and then he is shown Cornell University, where Vonnegut studied chemistry and biology from 1940–1943. While passing through Ilium on his way to New York, he and his entourage are accidentally caught in the riots, and he and his interpreter are last seen, "huddled together, asleep in a slip trench" (319) on the deserted battlefield of downtown Ilium. The Shah's itinerary allows Vonnegut to use him as a kind of picaresque guide for presenting his readers with diverse segments of society, and the fact that he comes from a different cultural and linguistic universe and looks at America with the astonished eyes of a stranger who is both naïve and wise makes him serve the same purpose which foreign visitors served from Montesquieu's *Lettres Persanes* (1721) through Goldsmith's *The Citizen of the World* (1762) to Howells' *Traveller from Altruria* (1894).

Critics have complained that the Shah-subplot is unrelated to the main action, but this is simply not true. It is right that Paul and the Shah never meet, but Vonnegut links the different strands of his narrative in an indirect way, which is both ingeniously realized and highly meaningful. When the Shah is first introduced as driving through Ilium, it is said about his car: "The limousine came to a halt by the end of the bridge, where a large work crew was filling a small chuckhole. The crew had opened a lane for an old Plymouth with a broken headlight, which was coming through from the north side of the river. The limousine waited for the Plymouth to get through, and then proceeded." (27) And when Paul drives over to Homestead in "his cheap and old Plymouth" (29) to buy whiskey for Finnerty, he is stopped at the bridge by a group of Reeks and Wrecks, but then can "ease through the work crew, past a black government limousine, and into Homestead" (31). Unbeknownst to each other, then, the Shah in his state limousine and Paul in his old car pass each other by, and it is certainly no accident that they meet on the bridge, which connects the worlds of the haves with that of the have-nots, which is introduced with the narrator's comment that "not many people on either side ha[d] reasons other than curiosity for crossing" (9), and to which Paul refers when in his drunken appeal in the Homestead bar he demands that "we must meet in the middle of the bridge!" (105). At the end of the novel, the State Department limousine "crosse[s] the Iroquois River at Ilium once more" (300), and this repetition is driven home to the readers when Halyard answers the Shah's question about where they are by saying "Ilium. Remember? We crossed here before, going the other way" (301). And once more the car is stopped, "blocked this time, not by a Reconstruction and Reclamation Corps crew, but by a phalanx of Arabs" (302), who are, of course, Reeks and Wrecks disguised for the imminent riots, the first stage of which is then narrated from the perspective of the puzzled Shah.

This connecting 'frame' provides by no means the only way in which the Shah-episodes are connected to the main plot. When the Shah visits the army, this episode is presented mostly through the enraged mind of Private First Class Elmo C. Hacketts, Jr., who has "only twenty-three more years to go on his hitch" (68) and dreams about going overseas to escape what will be one of Vonnegut's favorite targets in his later novels as well, namely the dehumanizing effect of senseless military drill. Nineteen chapters later this subsidiary character briefly reappears when Paul overhears a group of soldiers on the train and learns that "Pfc Elmo Hacketts is shipping out" to Tamanrasset in "the Sahara Desert" (244). Later the Shah visits the house of Edgar R. B. Hagstrohm and his family from Chicago, whom, in what is perhaps the most scathingly satirical episode of the novel, the computer has selected as a representative "average man" (156):

Edgar R. B. Hagstrohm [. . .] was statistically average in every
respect save for the number of his initials: his age (36), his height
(5'7"), his weight (148 lbs.), his years of marriage (11), his I.Q.
(83), the number of his children (2: 1 m., 9; 1 f., 6), the number of
his bedrooms (2), his car (3 yr. old Chev. 2 dr. sad.), his education
(h.s grad, 117th in class of 233; maj. in business practice; 2nd string
f'ball, b'k'th'l; soc. comm., sen'r play; no coll.), his vocation (R&R),
his avocations (spec'r sports, TV, softb'l, f'sh'g), and his war record
(5 yrs. 3 ov'sea; T-4 radioman; 157th Inf. Div.; battle stars: Hjoring,
Elbesan, Kabul, Kaifen, Ust Kyakhta; wounded 4 times; P'ple H't,
3 cl.; Star Br'ze Star, 2 cl.; G'd Cond. Med.)
    And the machine could have made an educated guess that, since
Hagstrohm had gone that far in being average, he had probably
been arrested once, had had sexual experience with five girls before
marrying Wanda (only moderately satisfying), and had had two
extramarital adventures since (one fleeting and foolish, the other
rather long and disturbing), and that he would die at the age of
76.2 of a heart attack. (156f.)

Ten chapters after this 'transparent' man is presented to the Shah as *the*
average American, Paul is waiting at the police station to have his privileges
revoked, and he accidentally observes a 'Wanted' report coming out of the
"radiophoto machine," which calls for the arrest of Edgar Rice Burroughs
Hagstrohm, R&R 131313, and reads:

Hagstrohm cut up his M-17 home in Chicago with a blowtorch,
went naked to the home of Mrs. Marlon Frascati, the widow of an
old friend, and demanded that she come to the woods with him.
Mrs. Frascati refused, and he disappeared into the bird sanctuary
bordering the housing development. There he eluded police, and
is believed to have made his escape dropping from a tree onto a
passing freight—(250)

This narrative bracket not only contrasts the orderly appearance proudly
presented to the visiting Shah with the chaotic reality smoldering under-
neath it, but it also demonstrates through the pathetic escape of a desperate
man, who bears the programmatic name of Edgar Rice Burroughs, the creator of Tarzan, that in the mechanized world of *Player Piano* the only jungle
left to which a Tarzan can try to take his Jane is a "bird sanctuary bordering
the housing development."
    When the Shah meets a desperate woman, whose husband has just lost
all his privileges because, as a writer, he has refused to lower the "readability

quotient" (233) of his manuscript, Halyard cannot understand such obstinacy and asks "Why doesn't he write about clipper ships, or something like that? This book about the old days on the Erie Canal—the man who wrote that is cleaning up. Big demand for that bare-chested stuff" (233). This passing remark establishes yet another ingenious cross-reference to what happens much earlier in the main plot. There a disgruntled Paul Proteus begins to develop "an appetite for novels wherein the hero lived vigorously and out-of-doors, dealing directly with nature, dependent upon basic cunning and physical strength for survival—woodsmen, sailors, cattlemen" (135), and he shows his secretary the book he is reading and which is "all about bargemen on the old Erie Ship Canal" and sports "the broad, naked chest of the hero on the book jacket" (135). For readers who catch this hidden link it becomes obvious that Paul's desire to escape into a world of romantic nostalgia is being anticipated by the ruling powers and that the books which Paul now reads are published for the very purpose of stabilizing the existing order by diverting discontent through the provision of vicarious wish-fulfillment in the imaginative adventures of literature. The main plot and the subplot, then, not only meet when the Shah's government car is accidentally caught up in the Ilium riots, but are skillfully intertwined throughout the novel in an oblique and rather unusual way. Thus Mallard, who is a little rash in arguing that Vonnegut has discarded "all the mechanical aspects of pictorialism associated with Henry James and the mimetic novel" in favor of what Marshall McLuhan defined as a new medium and described as "'non-literate,' 'implicit, simultaneous, and discontinuous,'"[36] is right in so far as *Player Piano* really shows some first, albeit still tentative, indications of what will then become one of the hallmarks of Vonnegut's mature novels, namely the spatialization of narration through the presentation of seemingly disparate episodes that form a polyphonic structure which it is the readers' task to rearrange into a meaningful whole.

The Shah functions not only as a kind of picaresque travel guide through diverse segments of America's 'brave new world,' but he also provides a "wise" (26) spiritual counterpart to a soulless technological society. And since he cannot speak English and his interpreter has to translate whatever is being said, his journey becomes a sequence of eye-opening cultural clashes as well as hilarious linguistic misunderstandings, which have a defamiliarizing effect and subversively unmask as questionable achievements what the U.S. technocrats consider impressive proofs of their cultural progress. The most obvious example is the recurring problem with the translation of "average man" and "citizen" (28), the terms with which Halyard refers to the people who are neither managers nor engineers but members of the army or the R&R. When this problem occurs for the first time, Khashdrahr Miasma is lost, as ironically befits his name, in the 'heavy vapors' of linguistic uncertainties and doubtingly says "Please, this *average man,* there is no equivalent in our language, I'm afraid." When Halyard answers "You know, the ordinary man, like, well, anybody" (28), and Khashdrahr dutifully translates, the following dialogue ensues:

> "Aha," said the Shah, nodding, "*Takaru.*"
> "What did he say?"
> "*Takaru,*" said Khashdrahr, "*Slave.*"
> "No *Takaru,*" said Halyard, speaking directly to the Shah. "*Ci-ti-zen.*"
>   "Ahhhhh," said the Shah. "*Ci-ti-zen.*" He grinned happily. "*Takaru—citizen. Citizen—Takaru.*"
> "No *Takaru!*" said Halyard.
>   Khashdrahr shrugged. "In the Shah's land are only the Elite and the *Takaru.*"
>   Halyard's ulcer gave him a twinge, the ulcer that had grown in size and authority over the years of his career as an interpreter of America to provincial and ignorant notables from the backwaters of civilization. (28f.)

Here, in a very funny and most effective way, the alien's unprejudiced view unmasks the fact that the social structure of a "divided" (9) America, with the managers and the engineers on the one hand and 'the people' on the other, hardly differs from that of the Shah's allegedly backward country with its dichotomy between the elite and the slaves.

When the Shah is shown an impressive army drill, he praises the parading soldiers as "a fine bunch of slaves" and, when Halyard rejects his renewed use of the *Takaru* concept as inappropriate, he quite innocently asks "if these not slaves, how you get them to do what they do," making an enraged General produce the rather helpless answer "Patriotism" (69). Since this dialogue is framed by the desperate ruminations of Private Hacketts as one of the performing marionettes, once again the situational context proves the Shah right. And when later an exasperated Halyard complains to the General that the Shah "thinks of everything he sees in terms of his own country, and his own country must be a Goddamn mess" (71), the fact that he is sublimely unaware of his own ethnocentrism and the ironic implication that he might as well be speaking about his own country makes this comment all the more revealing. A similar disclosure takes place when the Shah's request that "he might see the home of a typical *Takaru*, freely translated from one culture to another, as 'average man'" (156), is granted and he is taken to the Hagstrohms' house. There the guide proudly points out how fast the diverse labor-saving machines complete Mrs. Hagstrohm's household chores, and when the Shah wants to know why she "has to do everything so quickly [...] What is it she has to do, that she mustn't waste any time on these things?" all the exasperated guide can come up with is "Live! Live! Get a little fun out of life" (159). But it turns out that Mrs. Hagstrohm is glad that the breakdown of her ultrasonic clotheswasher forces her to do the washing in a tub, because it "gives [her] something to do" (160). Thus, once again, the visiting stranger sees through the surface and reveals that the life of the 'average' citizen is a *Takaru*, a slave-existence, since it is devoid of meaning and purpose and filled with nothing but unending boredom.

But it is in the key scene of the subplot, namely, the Shah's visit to the Carlsberg Caverns there to see EPICAC XIV and be introduced to the President, that the clash between the two cultures becomes most obvious and that the shortcomings of the American technocracy are most drastically revealed. When the President, a "gorgeous dummy" (119) who turns out to be a prophetic anticipation of real American presidents to come, has read out a ghostwritten text improperly praising the supercomputer as "the greatest individual in history" (119), the Shah begs permission to ask EPICAC a question. When his request is granted, the following scene ensues:

The Shah dropped to his knees on the platform and raised his hands over his head. The small, brown man suddenly seemed to fill the entire cavern with his mysterious, radiant dignity, alone there on the platform, communing with a presence no one else could sense.

"We seem to be witnessing some sort of religious rite," said the announcer.

"Can't you keep your big mouth shut for five seconds?" said Halyard.

"Quiet!" said Khashdrahr.

The Shah turned to a glowing bank of EPICAC's tubes and cried in a piping singsong voice:

> "Allakahi baku billa,
> Moumi a fella nam;
> Serani assu tilla,
> Touri serin a sam."

"The crazy bastard's talking to the machine," whispered Lynn [the President].

"Sssh!" said Halyard, strangely moved by the scene.

"*Siki?*" cried the Shah. He cocked his head, listening. "*Siki?*" The word echoed and died—lonely, lost.

"*Mmmmmm,*" said EPICAC softly. "*Dit, dit. Mmmmm. Dit.*"

The Shah sighed and stood, and shook his head sadly, terribly
let down. "*Nibo,*" he murmured. "*Nibo.*"
"What's he say?" said the President.
"*Nibo*'—'nothing.' He asked the machine a question, and the
machine didn't answer," said Halyard. "*Nibo.*"
"Nuttiest thing I ever heard of," said the President. (120)

In this brilliantly executed scene, in which the shamanistic chant of the
Shah is contrasted with the theatrical nonsense of the President, in which
the archetypal test of solving a riddle is used for ascertaining the transcendental, that is, the sense-making powers of the testee, and in which even
the skeptical Halyard is unwillingly impressed by the "mysterious, radiant
dignity" of the oriental sovereign, EPICAC is unmasked as nothing but a
soullessly humming machine. Khashdrahr explains that his people believe
"that a great, all-wise god will come among us one day, and we shall know
him, for he shall be able to answer the riddle, which EPICAC could not
answer. When he comes, there will be no more suffering on earth" (121).
In the Shah's eyes, therefore, the computer has miserably failed, and thus
for him the mechanical wonder, of which the technocrats believe that it has
already ended all earthly suffering by creating a utopian society, is revealed
as what it really is, namely *baku,* a "false god" (122).

In the final talk which the Shah has with Halyard before he is accidentally drawn into the Ilium riots, Halyard offers him the generous devel-
opmental aid of America: "At no expense whatsoever to you, America will
send engineers and managers, skilled in all fields, to study your resources,
blueprint your modernization, get it started, test and classify your people,
arrange credit, set up the machinery." (302) But the Shah wants one question answered before embarking on the 'modernization' of his country, and
when he has his interpreter request from Halyard: "would you ask EPICAC
what people are for?" (302), he sums up the very problem which stands at the
center of *Player Piano* and which will be varied time and again in Vonnegut's
further novels.[37]

When, in 1981, Vonnegut "graded [his] separate works from A to D,"
he gave a straight B to *Player Piano* (*PS* 311) and thus indicated that he still
thought well of it. But the critical evaluation of his apprentice novel ranges
from its condescending dismissal as yet another variation of an exhausted formulaic genre on the one hand to its enthusiastic praise as an outstanding and
original masterpiece on the other. Thus, Giannone sees the book as a mere
rehashing of Huxley and Orwell and as "markedly conventional,"[38] Ketterer
takes it to be just one more dystopia "in somewhat conventional fashion,"[39]
Tanner sees it as "a fairly orthodox futuristic satire,"[40] Samuels dismisses it
as "a sort of *Man in the Gray Flannel Suit* as it might have been revised by

George Orwell,"[41] and Karl dubs it a "gentle allegory" with "minimal life"[42] because of its dealing with a tired theme. At the other end of the critical spectrum, however, Hillegas praises *Player Piano* as "the best of the science-fiction anti-utopias—and indeed the best of all the recent anti-utopias,"[43] Vanderbilt enthusiastically calls Vonnegut "the writer who would soon own the best utopian imagination in American literature since World War Two,"[44] Mustazza grants the book "brilliant originality,"[45] and the Woods even call it "one of the best science-fiction novels ever written."[46]

Of course, in the final analysis all these judgments reveal as much about the standpoint and taste of each critic as about the literary achievement of Vonnegut's first novel. But even the detractors of *Player Piano* must admit that this is an admirable accomplishment for an apprentice novel, since with regard to its central topic it not only turns out to be eerily prophetic, but with regard to its narrative properties it manages to add new and thought-provoking aspects to the exhausted genre of dystopia, to enliven the usually deadly serious form with strategically functional humor, to change the actors from mere carriers of ideas into at least partially individualized and psychologically believable characters, to make ingenious usage of both the picaresque mode and the Martian perspective, and to connect the main plot and the subplot into a polyphonic structure that unfolds a broad panorama of the world depicted. Moreover, if read in the context of Vonnegut's later novels, it reveals the roots of many of the idiosyncratic techniques which would then develop into the hallmarks of his oeuvre.

NOTES

1. Page numbers in brackets refer to *Player Piano* (New York: Avon Books, 1967); other Vonnegut texts are quoted from the following editions: *BSB* = *Bagombo Snuff Box; Uncollected Short Fiction* (New York: Putnam's, 1999); *BC* = *Breakfast of Champions; or, Goodbye Blue Monday!* (New York: Dell Books, 1974); *CwKV* = *Conversations with Kurt Vonnegut,* ed. by William Rodney Allen (Jackson: University Press of Mississippi, 5th ed., 1999); *GBY*= *God Bless You, Mr. Rosewater; or, Pearls Before Swine* (London: Panther Books, 1972); *PS* = *Palm Sunday; An Autobiographical Collage* (London: Jonathan Cape, 1981); *SoT* = *Sirens of Titan* (New York; Dell Books, 1972); *T* = *Timequake* (New York: Putnam's, 1997); *WFG* = *Wampeters, Foma, and Granfalloons (Opinions)* (New York: Delta Books, 1974).

2. Charles Lee, "New Terms and Goons," *Saturday Review,* 30 August 1952, p. 11; quoted from the reprint in *Critical Essays on Kurt Vonnegut,* ed. by Robert Merrill (Boston, 1990), 29f.

3. Robert W, Henderson, untitled review, *Library Journal,* 77 (August 1952), 1303.

4. For these figures see Jerome Klinkowitz, *Kurt Vonnegut* (London, 1982), 40.

5. Theodore Sturgeon, "A Brace, 3 Singles, and a 10-Strike" *National Review,* 18 (17 May 1966), 478.

6. Louise Armstrong, "Ruling Robots and Secret Agents," *Saturday Review,* 49 (14 May 1966), 44.

7. H. Bruce Franklin, "Fictions of Science," *Southern Review,* 3 (n.s.) (Autumn 1967), 1036, 1037, 1038.

8. For details about GE's Association Island see Paul Keating, *Lamps for a Brighter America* (New York, 1954), 83–86.—David Y. Hughes, "The Ghost in the Machine: The Theme of *Player Piano,*" in *America as Utopia,* ed. by Kenneth M. Roemer (New York, 1981), 114, note 14, refers to the former GE President Charles Wilson, whose career shows obvious parallels to that of Gelhorne in *PP,* and the title page of whose collection of speeches as edited by GE shows the Island's Sacred Elm, which obviously provided the model for Vonnegut's Sacred Oak.

9. Carolyn Rhodes, "Tyranny by Computer: Automated Data Processing and Oppressive Government in Science Fiction," in *Many Futures, Many Worlds: Theme and Form in Science Fiction,* ed. by Thomas D. Clareson (Kent, 1977), 67.

10. Norbert Wiener, *The Human Use of Human Beings: Cybernetics and Society,* 2nd enl. ed. (New York, 1967), 185, 216, 220, 220f.

11. Norbert Wiener, *The Human Use of Human Beings,* 251.

12. Stanley Schatt, *Kurt Vonnegut, Jr.* (Boston, 1976), 17, postulates a connection between the name of the central computer, the city of Ilium, and Homer's *Ilias,* when he observes that the name EPICAC "suggests that the only epic to which man can look forward in his post-Christian technological age is one found on computer paper"—Thomas P. Hoffman, "The Theme of Mechanization in *Player Piano,*" in *Clockwork Worlds. Mechanized Environments in SF,* ed. by Richard D. Erlich and Thomas P. Dunn (Westport, 1983), 135, note 6, states: 'There is implicit irony in the 'EPIC' portion of the computer's name, an irony which underscores the machine's lack of response to anything heroic while also suggesting the imposing aspect of EPICAC XIV as the ruler of an automated America." And he suggests yet another implication of the computer's name by observing that "EPICAC is Vonnegut's advertent transposition of Ipecac (an emetic), which humorously emphasizes the computer's ability to vomit back information, but only that information fed into it by its human operators." With this he follows, without mentioning him, Wayne D. McGinnis, who, in "Names in Vonnegut's Fiction," *Notes on Contemporary Literature,* 3, 4 (September 1973), 8, pointed out ten years earlier that EPICAC is "a transmutation of *ipecac,* the name of an emetic that induces vomiting, just as a computer swallows information and regurgitates it."

13. The choice of "Ilium" was probably influenced by the fact that in the vicinity of Schenectady there really is a town named "Troy," which is also mentioned in *PP* when "the clubs in Albany, Troy, or Schenectady" (165; see 180) are referred to.

14. The General Electric Company, which came into being through a consolidation of Thomas Alva Edison's various companies, was founded in 1886 in Schenectady, and this is another confirmation of the fictional Ilium being a barely disguised version of the real Schenectady.

15. Whereas Lawrence Broer, "Pilgrim's Progress: Is Kurt Vonnegut, Jr., Winning His War with Machines?" in *Clockwork Worlds: Mechanized Environments in SF,* ed. by Richard D. Erlich and Thomas P. Dunn (Westport, 1983), 140, unduly exaggerates when he calls this scene "one of the most revealing symbolic episodes in all of Vonnegut's work," the charged constellation of a wild animal caught in a mechanized plant is certainly of crucial significance in *Player Piano,* and Vonnegut

would later expand on it in one of his better-known short stories, which was also successfully filmed. In "Deer In the Works" (*Esquire*, 1955), collected in both *Canary in a Cat House* and *Welcome to the Monkey House,* the young copy writer David Potter squanders his newly acquired job at the "Ilium Works of the Federal Apparatus Corporation" by freeing a deer that has strayed onto the factory grounds

16. Aldous Huxley, *Brave New World* (Harmondsworth, 1955), 85 and 88.

17. George Orwell, *1984* (Harmondsworth, 1954), 102.

18. In a 1969 symposium Vonnegut said: "We are our own old men, our own wrestling opponents. We're all Proteus." (in Roger Henkle, "Wrestling [American Style] with Proteus," *Novel: A Forum on Fiction,* 3 [Spring 1970], 198).—in his interview with Zoltán Abádi-Nagy, "'Serenity,' 'Courage,' 'Wisdom': A Talk with Kurt Vonnegut," *Hungarian Studies in English,* 22 (1991), 33, he observed: "In order to survive we must be Protean. [. . .] To respond to this or that damned fool invention or to the hydrogen bomb or to the destruction of the ozone layer we *must* change, and chances are we *can't.*"

19. Thomas P. Hoffman, "The Theme of Mechanization in *Player Piano,*" 134.

20. Vonnegut uses the same onomatopoeic joke in *Breakfast of Champions,* where a truck bearing the name of the car-rental firm Hertz "seemed to cry out in pain to Wayne, because he read the message on the side of it phonetically" (*BC* 205).

21. Peter J. Reed, *Kurt Vonnegut, Jr.* (New York, 1972), 30.

22. Peter J. Reed, *Kurt Vonnegut, Jr.,* 54.

23. Richard Giannone, *Vonnegut: A Preface to His Novels* (Port Washington, 1977), 19.

24. See Leo Marx, *The Machine in the Garden: Technology and the Pastoral Ideal in America* (New York, 1964); Mary Sue Schriber, "You've Come a Long Way, Babbitt! From Zenith to Ilium," *Twentieth Century Literature,* 17 (April 1971), 105; and John Walter Knorr, "Technology, Angst, and Edenic Happiness in Kurt Vonnegut's *Player Piano* and *Slaughterhouse-Five,*" in *The Image of Technology in Literature, the Media, and Society,* ed. by Will Wright and Steve Kaplan (Pueblo, 1994), 103.

25. In *The New York Times Book Review,* 17 August 1952; quoted from the reprint in Granville Hicks and Jack Alan Robbins, *Literary Horizons: A Quarter Century of American Fiction* (New York, 1970), 176.

26. This name may allude to John von Neumann (1903–1957), the Hungarian-born scientist who was the founder of the mathematical theory of games and whose development of *maniac* (mathematical *a*nalyzer, *n*umerical *i*ntegrator, *a*nd *c*omputer) enabled the U.S. to produce and test the world's first hydrogen bomb. Such a reference is all the more probable because it is later said about the fictional von Neumann that "he had been less interested in achieving a premeditated end than in seeing what would happen with given beginnings" (320), thus experimenting with what Paul calls the "most fascinating *game* [my italics] there is, keeping things from staying the way they are" (313).

27. This reading is shared by most critics. See, e.g., David Hughes, 'The Ghost In the Machine: The Theme of *Player Piano,*" 113; Howard P. Segal, "Vonnegut's *Player Piano:* An Ambiguous Technological Dystopia," in *No Place Else: Explorations In Utopian and Dystopian Fiction,* ed. by Eric S. Rabkin and Martin H. Greenberg (Carbondale, 1983), 174; or Leonard Mustazza, "The Machine Within:

Mechanization, Human Discontent, and the Genre of Vonnegut's *Player Piano*," *Papers on Language and Literature*, 25 (Winter 1989), 113.

28. Kermit Vanderbilt, "Kurt Vonnegut's American Nightmares and Utopias," in *The Utopian Vision: Seven Essays on the Quincentennial of Sir Thomas More*, ed. by E. D. S. Sullivan (San Diego, 1983), 143.

29. Michael J. Gargas McGrath, "Kesey and Vonnegut: The Critique of Liberal Democracy in Contemporary Literature," in *The Artist and Political Vision*, ed. by him (New Brunswick, 1982), 381.

30. Thomas P. Hoffman, "The Theme of Mechanization in *Player Piano*," 130.

31. Howard P. Segal, "Vonnegut's *Player Piano:* An Ambiguous Technological Dystopia," 168.

32. Lawrence R. Broer, *Sanity Plea: Schizophrenia In the Novels of Kurt Vonnegut*, rev. ed. (Tuscaloosa and London, 1994), 5, argues that, "while Vonnegut's role as a social critic is not to be denied, his reputation as America's most popular prose satirist has obscured the more personal and intensely psychological nature of his art," and he investigates "the bizarre phobias, paranoid delusions, masked aggression, and desperate escapist compulsions of Vonnegut's psychically maimed heroes."

33. David Seed, "Mankind vs. Machines: The Technological Dystopia in Kurt Vonnegut's *Player Piano*," in *Impossibility Fiction: Alternativity, Extrapolation, Speculation*, ed. by Derek Littlewood and Peter Stockwell (Amsterdam, 1996), 19.

34. See *PS* 59, and Lynn Buck, "Vonnegut's World of Comic Futility," *Studies in American Fiction*, 3 (Autumn 1975), 185, about the "theme of conflict between father and son." With regard to Kroner's collecting of guns and using them "for props" (124) see Vonnegut's references to his father's gun collection in *WFG* 214 and *CwKV* 275 and his literary exploration of this motif in *Deadeye Dick* (1982).

35. Lawrence R. Broer, *Sanity Plea*, 28 and 152.

36. James M. Mellard, "The Modes of Vonnegut's Fiction: or, *Player Piano* Ousts *Mechanical Bride* and *The Sirens of Titan* invade the *Gutenberg Galaxy*," in *The Vonnegut Statement*, ed. by Jerome Klinkowitz and John Somer (New York, 1973), 180 and 188.

37. In Kilgore Trout's novel *2BRO2B*, for example, which is retold In *God Bless You, Mr. Rosewater; or Pearls Before Swine*, this question is taken up almost verbatim when a character asks "What in hell are people *for*?" (*GBY* 25)

38. Richard Giannone, *Vonnegut: A Preface to His Novels*, 13.

39. David Ketterer, *New Worlds for Old: The Apocalyptic Imagination, Science Fiction, and American Literature* (Garden City, 1974), 296.

40. Tony Tanner, *City of Words: American Fiction 1950–1970* (London, 1971), 181.

41. Charles Thomas Samuels, "Age of Vonnegut," *The New Republic*, 12 June 1971, 30.

42. Frederick Karl, *American Fictions: 1940–1980: A Comprehensive History and Critical Evaluation* (New York, 1983), 246.

43. Mark Hillegas, *The Future as Nightmare: H. G. Wells and the Anti-Utopians* (Carbondale and Edwardsville, 1974), 159.

44. Kermit Vanderbilt, "Kurt Vonnegut's American Nightmares and Utopias," 140.

45. Leonard Mustazza, "The Machine Within: Mechanization, Human Discontent, and the Genre of Vonnegut's *Player Piano*," 113.

46. Karen and Charles Wood, "The Vonnegut Effect: Science Fiction and Beyond," in *The Vonnegut Statement*, 142.

FUMIKA NAGANO

Surviving the Perpetual Winter:
The Role of Little Boy in Vonnegut's Cat's Cradle

Introduction

"Call me Jonah," says the narrator at the beginning of Kurt Vonnegut's *Cat's Cradle* (1963), echoing the famous exordium of Herman Melville's *Moby-Dick* (1851), "Call me Ishmael." Just like Ishmael who witnesses Captain Ahab's desperate quest for the white whale and the ultimate death of all the crew but himself, Jonah is a survivor of a devastating catastrophe which dooms the world to perpetual winter. In Jonah's case, however, he is not the only survivor: among others, the midget Newton and his brother Franklin also find shelter in a cave in Mt. McCabe, the belly of "a fearful hump, a blue whale" (142). Nor is Jonah a victim of uncanny nature: the worldwide freeze is caused by a lethal substance called ice-nine, an invention of modern science.

As the playful naming suggests, the midget Newton is intimately connected with this scientific disaster, for his father, like Stanley Kubrick's Dr. Strangelove, was an influential scientist who worked for the American military machine, inventing both the A-bomb and ice-nine. Newton's deformed body may appear to be the biological result of some nuclear irradiation, of the kind caused by the 1986 explosion of the Chernobyl nuclear power plant, but it is rather the product of his father's preoccupation with inventing atomic weapons and carelessness with regards to his children. Newton's small body, which invites the verbal abuse from his peers, originates from his own family.

Journal of the American Literature Society of Japan, Number 2 (February 2004): pp. 73–90.
Copyright © 2004 The American Literature Society of Japan.

The science fiction of the same period saw the birth of boy-robots depicted as freakish and therefore alienated even from their producers. However, unlike Brian Aldiss's "Supertoys Last All Summer Long" (1969) and Osamu Tezuka's *Tetsuwan Atomu* (*Mighty Atom* 1951–1968),[1] Vonnegut's Newton is a human character who is transformed into the equivalent of a scientific invention through the writer's narratology.

In fact, Vonnegut's allusions to *Moby-Dick* and the biblical *Jonah* only imply his conscious effort to initiate a "fiction" by blurring the narrator's identity: "Call me Jonah. My parents did, or nearly did. They called me John" (7). Therefore, with the profound implication of the world's icy end, Vonnegut's novel examines the political abuse of technology as well as the narrative of the Cold War, introducing a midget man caught up between two women from the US and the USSR. Having lost his childhood faith in science when he realized that "we dropped scientific truth on Hiroshima" (*Wampeters* 161), Vonnegut not only suggests "the truth" is merely the product of power games manipulated by those whose interests they may serve, but he also criticizes the Cold War dynamic by introducing such binary oppositions into his story and negating them using a technique of foregrounding Cold War super-textuality.

1. Genealogy of the Little Boy

Vonnegut is conscious of the nuclear age in his highly stylistic novel published in 1963, one year after the Cuban Missile Crisis, for he symbolically situates the locus of total annihilation in the Republic of San Lorenzo, an imaginative post-colonial nation in the Caribbean Sea.[2] Yet from the epigraph of *Cat's Cradle,* any reader will appreciate how Vonnegut weaves its self-referential textuality: "Nothing in this book is true. 'Live by the foma [harmless untruths] that make you brave and kind and healthy and happy.—The Book of Bokonon, 1.5.'" This enigmatic contrast between the actuality of crisis in this novel and its hyper-fictionality is resolved when the narrator explains how this book came to carry such a disclaimer: Jonah, a freelance writer, starts the story with his historical ("factual") study of the nuclear attack on Hiroshima entitled *The Day the World Ended,* but despite the author's intention, this turns out to be a different book—*Cat's Cradle* based on Bokononist lies—because he himself lives to witness another day the world ends and subsequently converts to Bokononism. The apocalypse he himself experiences marks a strange twist, forcing him to reconsider the way he depicts the world, just like the Biblical Jonah, who repents after being swallowed by the whale. Yet again, as Douglas Robinson points out, Jonah-John is not a prophet like his predecessor (152), for he claims that he was just compelled by "somebody or something" to find himself at "certain places at certain times, without fail" (11). And in this narrative of modern apocalypse, it is the atomic bomb and the Hoenikker family that control this witness-author in the wake of the catastrophe, entangling him with the tendrils of his life (what Bokononists call *sinookas*) into their *karass*, a team of people who "do God's will without ever discovering what they are doing" (11).

Along with this comical Vonnegutian terminology, the relationships between characters are described with familial metaphors. To "emphasize the *human* rather than the *technical* side of the bomb" (14), Jonah's survey focuses on the late Dr. Felix Hoenikker, father of the A-bomb and inventor of the deadly substance ice-nine, which freezes water at 114°F. The first of his heirs that Jonah makes contact with is Newton, the youngest son and member of Jonah's fraternity from Cornell University. Jonah calls this pre-med student *"Brother"* in a letter asking for any recollections of the day of the Hiroshima bombing; he assures Newton that anything seen "through the eyes of a 'baby'" will suit his purpose (15). Newton answers his request by revealing an essential part of Dr. Hoenikker's character, confessing that his childhood was not happy with a father whose specialty was not "people" but science (21).

The playful language also reflects the nature of the Hoenikkers. In the course of his survey, Jonah discovers that despite the extreme danger of his inventions, Dr. Hoenikker was not a mad scientist who intended to destroy the world, but a childish and innocent man who played with the laws of nature: "Apparently, before he sat down in his wicker chair and died, the old man played puddly games in the kitchen with water and pots and pans and *ice-nine*" (166). Dr. Hoenikker invented ice-nine in response to a request by a top army officer who needed a way to advance into swampland. It also answered his own curiosity. All three of his children are also creative in their own ways: Angela, the oldest sibling, is an excellent flute player; Franklin's hobby is to make refined miniatures of the world; and Newton creates abstract paintings. The Hoenikker children inherit their father's playfulness and inquisitiveness together with the threat of danger: following the Doctor's death, ice-nine spreads to other countries through three apparently innocent children. Eventually it falls accidentally into the sea, thus freezing the entire earth.[3]

The problems created by the curious Hoenikkers are introduced through their peculiar sense of ethics. In a letter to Jonah, Newton writes about an anecdote that illustrates the Doctor's ethical failing:

> After the thing [in an experiment] went off, after it was a sure thing that America could wipe out a city with just one bomb, a scientist turned to Father and said, 'Science has now known sin.' And do you know what my Father said? 'What is sin?' (21)

This absent-minded behavior of Dr. Hoenikker was surely inherited by his children. He succeeded in extracting crystals of ice-nine and, after his death, the children divided up the deadly material: "The Hoenikkers [three children] couldn't remember that anyone said anything to justify their taking ice-nine as personal property. They talked about what ice-nine was . . . but no talk of morals" (168). Jonah speculates on the reason why the Hoenikkers did not talk of "morals" in possessing the substance, and writes "Angela, Franklin, and Newton Hoenikker had in their possession seeds of ice-nine, seeds grown from their father's seed—chips, in a manner of speaking, off the old block" (43). Interestingly, the Hoenikkers and the dangerous invention are depicted as if they were brothers: their ownership of ice-nine is vindicated through both the logic of inheritance of parental property and their duty to care for a younger sibling.

Thus, ice-nine, which a naive scientist created without the slightest inkling of impending planetary destruction, is released from the laboratory. Leonard Mustazza observes that the Doctor's invention may be the result of innocent curiosity but his lack of morals leads to the world's end because of his short-sighted children (*Forever Pursuing Genesis* 79). Franklin, for example, gives ice-nine to the despotic ruler of San Lorenzo in exchange for being made a minister. Here, one should note that Vonnegut does not suggest that the Hoenikker children were especially immoral: they are as "short-sighted as almost all men and women are" (164). They are *amoral* rather than immoral because they lack the intention to do others harm. Therefore, Dr. Hoenikker's rhetorical question, "What is sin?" designates not a deplorable lack of strong ethics, but rather the inventor's hopeless inability to see the various consequences any action may entail.

This absent-mindedness of Dr. Hoenikker is most strongly reflected in the youngest son, Newton. When Jonah visits the laboratory where Dr. Hoenikker used to work on the A-bomb, he learns how Newton came into the world. One day the scientist left his car in the middle of a traffic jam and continued on foot to his laboratory. The police called and made his pregnant wife fetch the car, and, as a result, she was involved in a traffic accident, leading to Newton's birth and her death. Hence, Newton is another product of the Doctor's absent-mindedness.

What should be emphasized here is that Newton was stigmatized because of a freakish body. In a letter to Jonah, Newton writes: "P. P. S. You call our family 'illustrious,' and I think you would be making a mistake if you called it that in your book. I am a midget for instance—four feet tall" (21). As a young man at the age of twenty-one, he is extremely short and has been perpetually teased or pitied because of his body. For instance, in the airplane to San Lorenzo, a passenger addresses Newton: "It isn't size that makes a man a pissant. It's the way he thinks" (91). The ironic way of associating a little body with broad-mindedness reminds us of a tradition of the nineteenth-century freak show. When the most famous midget of all time, Tom Thumb, visited the Victorian court, he claimed: "The Prince is taller than I am, but I *feel* as big as anybody" (Drimmer 164). This paradoxical presentation is possible since a little body necessarily evokes the immaturity of children. Newton's freakish body, too, is misconstrued as something infantile.

Newton as an "immature" child of his father's absent-mindedness is also unwittingly entangled in an erotic and proprietary dynamic because of his body. Lori Merish's study of "little people" in freak shows clarifies a conceptual fabric concerned with such "cute" people, through which "the Other" is domesticated and (re)contexualized within the human "family" (188):

> Like the cute child, the little person (like all "freaks") is culturally positioned as an object, not a subject. But unlike other freaks, the little person—by virtue of her identification with the child—could be drawn into the cute's [*sic*] structure of maternal proprietorship and "protection" . . . (190)

In Newton's case, there are two possible "mothers" who try to put this "little boy" under their protection: his older sister and foster mother Angela, and his fiancée Zinka, a Ukrainian ballet dancer. Angela persists "in treating Newt like an infant" (80) even after his coming of age. Newton grasps the opportunity to escape from her containment when he falls in love with Zinka, who is also a midget, and they begin a new life together in a retreat. However, he makes a surprise discovery after she abandons him: "Zinka was not, as she claimed, only twenty-three years old. She was forty-two—old enough to be Newt's mother" (22). He is caught in a cradle of mothering even with another midget.

The midgets' relationship is seen as just a love affair, but the truth becomes clear later:

> I [Jonah] gathered that the Republic of San Lorenzo and the three Hoenikkers weren't the only ones who had ice-nine. Apparently the United States of America and the Union of Soviet Socialist Republics had it, too. The United States had obtained it through Angela's husband. . . . And Soviet Russia had come by it through Newt's little Zinka, that winsome troll of Ukrainian ballet. (164)

Thus the two "mothers" of Newton and the two superpowers are related: while Zinka, a Soviet spy, cheats the innocent Newton out of the deadly weapon,[4] Angela willingly sells the weapon to the United States through her husband in order to please him.[5]

Newton as "an infant"—at the mercy of two women from the U.S. and the Soviet Union—seems to reflect the Cold War structure, the tension between East and West with nuclear power as a node. One is reminded of the code-name for the atomic bomb dropped on Hiroshima: "Little Boy." However, Vonnegut does not imply that Newton himself is a danger; instead, he emphasizes Newton's helplessness and perseverance in the face of abuse. On seeing Newton being embarrassed by the man on the airplane, Jonah writes: "Never had I seen a human being better adjusted to such a humiliating physical handicap" (91). His stigmatized body permits such humiliation because he invites a category mistake between objects and subjects. As Gaby Wood points out, while science has historically pursued the dream of mechanical life, such as Frankenstein's monster and AI, small people were seen "as inanimate things brought magically to life" as dolls or automata (220). In comparison with the human nickname "Little Boy," this little boy is transformed into something like a scientific invention, a disfiguration of the bomb: he certainly serves Jonah's purpose since he embodies the *"human"* side of the superweapon. Though Vonnegut's writing intended to reveal the politics of an objectified body, Newton parallels the production of science, which, in the course of political conflict, may be abused.

2. Textuality of the Cold War

The network surrounding Newton originates in his family history and develops into worldwide political conflict as countries strive to obtain his younger sibling, ice-nine. This is reflected in the title of the book *Cat's Cradle:* the name of a game that inevitably suggests the tension between poles. In this book, it mainly refers to an uneasy equilibrium between the tyrannical government and an underground cult (Bokononism) on the island of San Lorenzo, but it also literally alludes to Newton's memoir of a rare chance to play with his father on August 6, 1945, *the day the world ended.*

On that very day, Dr. Hoenikker unexpectedly started to make a cat's cradle, using a string that had been tied around a package. It was the manuscript for a novel called *2000 A.D.* and written by an insane criminal who asked Dr. Hoenikker for advice on a deadly bomb with which fictional mad scientists were to wipe out the whole world. With no interest in the novel, the scientist tried to play cat's cradle with little Newton whom "he had hardly ever spoken to." He urged the infant to "see the cat" and started to sing, "Rockabye catsy, in the tree top . . . when the wind blows, the cray-dull [cradle] will fall. Down will come cray-dull, catsy and all" (18). Frightened, Newton burst into tears and ran out of the room. Dr. Hoenikker's lullaby back in 1945 was traumatic for little Newton, because "[i]n the conceit of the cat's cradle metamorphosing into the baby cradle, Newt becomes the cat (or baby) falling when the wind blows, but with no one there to catch him" (Simons 38), and because it also refers to the A-bomb dropped on Hiroshima on that very day. Considering his status as the disfigured invention of his father, he effectively becomes an object that can fall at any moment from an ostensibly secure supportive network.[6] The cat's cradle might even prefigure the supposed balance between the two superpowers in the Cold War, in which Newton is to become entangled.

This harrowing experience torments Newton so much that as an adult he composes a picture of a cat's cradle, which, according to Jonah, looks something like "sticky nets of human futility hung up on a moonless night to dry" (113). As if trying to break the spell of this cat's cradle, he tells Jonah, "No wonder kids grow up crazy. A cat's cradle is nothing but a bunch of X's between somebody's hands, and little kids look and look and look at all those X's. . . . *No damn cat, and no damn cradle*" (114). Having gone through the torment of power games in the hands of Angela and Zinka, Newton not only denunciates his father who insisted on him seeing the cat, but also speculates on the fictionalization of truth in the political dynamic. As Jerome Klinkowitz argues, Newton emotionally objects to his father's cat's cradle since it failed to subsume his son's humanity (86). Yet, on a deeper level, he criticizes the political discourse that feigns internal truth: just as he denies seeing any cat or cradle in the conceit of the cat's cradle, the political conflicts around him are perceived merely as crossing relationships without any intrinsic justification. Thus, Newton's art intends to reduce the cat's cradle into no more than "a bunch of X's," resetting his metamorphosis back to reality.

At first sight Newton's denunciation of the cat's cradle in his painting seems to reflect his restrictive artistic imagination, which clearly contrasts with the author's disclaimer of fictionality in epigraph. However, this articulation is directed against his unimaginative father, who, in spite of his usual comment "Why should I bother with made-up games when there are so many real ones going on?" tried to create a cat's cradle with string as he remembered his own childhood with his father, a tailor (17). Therefore, Newton wants to escape from this lineage of failed imagination. His art actually records the deletion of himself in the texture of cat's cradle with a resentful exclamation that he was never there. In other words, while discussing the impossibility of lying about reality, Newton stays within the text/texture, though signifying his own absence: his claim of artistic reality stresses the necessary perception of the absence of the cat/baby or the bomb between the bunch of X's. Thus, his artistic aspiration leads to his deletion, his claim of non-existence, which seems like "the sticky nets of human futility" to Jonah.

With Newton's art, Vonnegut dramatically features the nuclear weaponry surrounded by the framing narrative and the paradoxical nature of the bomb, which remains textual in spite of its real existence. With the growing possibility of nuclear devastation, critics like Alan Nadel and William Chaloupka have studied the discourse surrounding nuclear arms, especially the all-encompassing metanarrative of the Cold War. Concerning the over-whelming inclusiveness of this narrative, Chaloupka observes:

> Like few other issues, nuclearism strains to become more than an instance. It aspires to be context and case, to shape public and private life. It seeks a symbolic position of such force that other concerns would arise within the context of nuclear technology, sometimes even when explicit connections are absent. . . . In short nuclearism organizes public life so thoroughly that, in another era of political theory, we would analyze it as an ideology. (1)

Donald E. Pease argues in the same vein that in totalizing the globe into an opposition between the two superpowers, "the Cold War economizes on any opposition to it by relocating all options within its frame" to such an extreme point that "there appear to be no alternatives to it" (114). In other words, the power of containment is at work even on the narrative/textual level.[7]

Along with the textual power of the Cold War as a framing narrative, the bomb itself is invested with textuality: as Jacques Derrida contends, be-cause a nuclear war has not taken place, "[t]he terrifying reality of the nuclear conflict can only be the signified referent, never the real referent (present or past) of a discourse or text" (23). We can only speak about nuclear war in the future, and this rhetorical context is marked with the ultimate absence. At this point, the nuclear age comes closest to literature, for it is *"fabulously tex-tual"* (24) just like literature, without any necessary referent outside the words by which it is constructed.

In addition, Derrida goes as far as to say that a missile is a missive. In nuclear deterrence diplomacy, the missile of one side is aimed at the enemy, but its real purpose is not to reach the target: whereas each side accuses the other of destroying the equilibrium of deterrence, there is a "tacit recognition on both sides that only by such destabilization can deterrence be maintained" (McCanles 18). In other words, despite terminology that dismisses the en-emy as an "evil" empire, each superpower retains belief in the other's common sense, believing it will not allow worldwide catastrophe. Indeed, if a missile is a missive, it carries a message that paradoxically annihilates itself the moment it reaches its destination: it can never deliver the message because it explodes and annihilates itself along with the addressee, and quite possibly, the sender. Following Derrida's theory, Peter Schwenger concludes: "Thus the tenets of deconstruction are validated: a literal and all-encompassing disaster enacts the 'disaster' that is a figurative way of speaking about the annihilation coeval with every act of creation" (10).

Vonnegut's creation of Newton easily accepts this style of writing, or what Chaloupka calls "speaking unspeakables." In his attempt to deal with the contradiction between his father's fable and his own reality, Newton deconstructs the conceit of the cat's cradle. By doing so, he thus discovers a most profound absence of the bomb framed in the web of the Cold War, providing an intersection with the author's emphasis on textuality.

3. The Crystallization of History

The midget's body as a locus of binary oppositions is further examined in its relationship to two of the writer's own invention, San Lorenzo and Bokononism, for both give witness-narrator Jonah a chance to reconsider his own writing. Jonah flies to San Lorenzo with his manuscript of *The Day the World Ended* left unfinished: he has been assigned by a magazine to write about an American millionaire who founded a hospital for the poor on the island. To his great surprise, he soon learns that the middle sibling of the Hoenikkers, who went missing after his father's funeral and was suspected of running stolen cars to Cuba, is now the Minister of Science and Progress in San Lorenzo: in fact, Franklin bought himself this job by giving his share of ice-nine to the despotic president, "Papa" Monzano. It is on the plane that Jonah meets Newton and Angela, who are on the way to attend the celebration of Franklin's engagement to Monzano's adopted daughter and his nomination as the next president.

Surrounded by the Caribbean, this third-world nation was founded as part of a utopian experiment. Jonah learns from a history book that in 1922 Lionel Boyd Johnson, a black born in Tobago, was shipwrecked on the way to Miami; he reached the post-colonial island in the company of a "brilliant, self-educated, idealistic Marine deserter" named Earl McCabe (77). They tried to play "Prospero on the disease-ridden island that had been dominated by Castle Sugar and the Catholic Church" by converting it into a utopia (Vanderbilt 148). McCabe reformed the island's economic and legal systems, while Johnson, whose name was pronounced "Bokonon" by the natives, designed the new religion. McCabe's first attempt at socialism turned out to be completely wrong for San Lorenzo: the overpopulated nation's income was "between six and seven dollars" per person (94). As a result, they eventually became dependent on a theatrical device called "Dynamic Tension": "a living legend of the cruel tyrant in the city and the gentle holy man in the jungle" (119). All the island's inhabitants believe in Bokononism, while the tyrant, himself a Bokononist, perpetually threatens to execute Bokonon. After McCabe's death, "Papa" Monzano took his place and ruled San Lorenzo with an adopted daughter of mixed blood, Mona Aamons, serving as the national muse. Monzano, now on his deathbed, chooses Franklin, "the *blood son* of Dr. Felix Hoenikker" as the next president (61).

Utopian as it is, San Lorenzo is not autonomous: it is in fact dominated by America. As a poor country with limited resources, it has depended on speculation by American investors and visits by tourists. The utopian experiment is based on the supposed equality of people, mirroring the American founding myth. It might even be assumed that this fantasy island is part of the United States in the Cold War era with its policy of "pitting good against evil" (74) and deferring the final resolution by a narratological device. In addition, one of the national holidays, the "Day of the Hundred Martyrs to Democracy," celebrates the time when San Lorenzo declared war on Germany and Japan an hour after the attack on Pearl Harbor. In the air show staged as part of the celebrations, the San Lorenzan Air Force attacks cardboard dolls of the enemies of freedom: Stalin, Castro, Tojo and Hitler among others (154). Jonah falls instantly in love with Mona and accepts Franklin's offer to make him the next president and husband of Mona. From his deathbed, Papa persuades Jonah and Franklin to teach the people science: "Science is magic that *works*" (147). At this point, Jonah dreams of bringing "a sort of millennium" to the island with the help of Bokonon (152). Ironically, his utopian—that is, American—dream is never to be: Papa commits suicide by swallowing a piece of ice-nine with the profoundly disfigurative effect of his last speech, "Now I will destroy the whole world" (160). In the subsequent air show accident, the palace with Papa's frozen body collapses into the sea, literally bringing about the world's end.[8]

This anecdote is intriguing because American employment of the bomb resulted from the American pursuit of democracy and expansion. In his study of the atomic bomb, Ronald Takaki traces the reason for this "racist" atrocity back to the heritage of American democracy. As Frederick Jackson Turner noted in 1891, American democracy was born on the frontier: "the frontier is productive of individualism. . . . The tendency is anti-social. It produces antipathy to control, and particularly to any direct control" (53). Moreover, so long as "vacant lands" existed, economic power supported political power with the opportunity for a competency. Thus, democracy was secured by expansion westward, including the "opening" of Japan in 1853. When the frontier vanished and a flood of immigrants arrived on American shores, however, the intrinsic contradiction of democracy emerged. Takaki proposes that, because democracy requires that society be composed of "a same people," a person had to be "white" to be eligible for naturalized citizenship. To people who believed in American democracy, the expansion of the ethnical other into their own country signaled a threat to America as a white society (77).

Similarly in the name of democracy, Harry Truman practiced "the diplomacy of masculinity" and encouraged racism toward Japanese "beasts" and vigilance toward the threat of Russian expansionism. Tellingly, the success of the explosion in New Mexico was conveyed to Truman "in terms of a father receiving news about the birth of his son" (115):

To Secretary of War from Harrison [Interim Committee member]. Doctor has just returned most enthusiastic and confident that the little boy is as husky as his big brother [the bomb exploded in New Mexico]. The light in his eyes discernible from here to Highhold [Secretary of War Henry Stimson's estate] and I could have heard his screams here to my farm. (qtd. in Takaki 115)

As Takaki contends, "the atomic bomb symbolized [the] virility" of American expansionism (115) and Truman used it to American advantage to negotiate at the Potsdam conference (thereby setting the scene for the Cold War) and to force Japan's unconditional surrender.

It is significant, therefore, that on the plane to San Lorenzo Jonah hears a conscientious woman say, "Americans . . . are forever searching for love in forms it never takes, in places it can never be. It must have something to do with the vanished frontier" (71). In journeying from New York to the utopian island of San Lorenzo, Jonah symbolizes American expansion: he unexpectedly finds the tombstone for his lost ancestors—German immigrants—near the graveyard where Newton's mother Emily lies under "an alabaster phallus twenty feet high and three feet thick" (48); tempted by a Creole beauty, he accepts the presidency and dreams of his own utopia.

After the world actually *ends*, however, Jonah converts to Bokononism and abandons his utopianism; instead, he begins to dream of "climbing Mount McCabe with some magnificent symbol and planting it there" (190). Yet he hesitates to accept a plan proposed by another survivor, who calls herself "Mom"—that is, for Jonah to plant the American flag. When he drives with Newton to the city center to forage for paints, he accidentally encounters Bokonon and hears of an alternative plan. In the chapter entitled "The End" literally located at the end of the book, Bokonon tells Jonah that he was thinking about the final sentence of his *Books of Bokonon:* "If I were a younger man, I would write a history of human stupidity; and I would climb to the top of Mount McCabe . . . and I would take from the ground some of the blue-white poison that makes statues of men" (191). In contrast to the "alabaster phallus" erected as a memorial for Newton's ill-fated mother, Bokonon transforms himself into a metonymy of human stupidity, lying horizontally on the ground. Jonah, seeing his plan performed by Bokonon, decides to write "a history of human stupidity" following the last lesson of Bokonon. This book of history is delivered to us with the title *Cat's Cradle*, virtually crystallizing history in the statue of Bokonon. Thus, Jonah's writing is not only a denial of his earlier life, but a critique of American history itself.

Newton is also reborn as a result of the cataclysm: as a Bokononist, he finds consolation in *The Books of Bokonon:* "Midget, midget, midget, how he struts and winks, / [f]or he knows a man's as big as what he hopes and

thinks!" As Jonah notes, this is a crucial sentence referring to "the cruel paradox of Bokononist thought, the heartbreaking necessity of lying about reality,
and the heartbreaking impossibility of lying about it" (189); this paradox, as
expressed in the body of a midget, is found to be quite similar to that of the
bomb. Therefore, the ultimate solution in this story is the liberation of the
"little boy" via the death of the two women in the literal nuclear winter. Earlier, Newton was obsessed with virility as symbolized by his mother's eccentric tombstone: he devoured the pornographic scenes in *2000 A.D.* delivered
on the day of the Hiroshima bombing and admits "I used to dream of women
twenty, thirty, forty feet tall. . . . " But, like Jonah, he has lost his sexual urge:
"God, I can't even remember what my Ukrainian midget looked like" (188).
Now, he is free of oversized political abusers or hands that hold the cat's
cradle, including Bokonon, and begins to paint the devastated landscape. He
is a midget and therefore embraces his dual nature, but he has understood
his paradox with the help of Bokononism—that is, he is conscious of its own
textuality, composed of lies.

Conclusion

Since the earliest reviews of *Cat's Cradle,* critics have focused on its metafictional structure and Vonnegut's ethical caution: Tony Tanner, discussing
the potential danger in the artists' playfulness, observes that "the artist
cannot rest in confidence as to the harmlessness of his inventions" (188);
Klinkowitz argues the only possible way to elude such dangers is to compose
fiction "which will handle the finite on its own terms, without recourse to
'lies'" and stresses the importance of the tragicomical design of Bokononism (86). Yet, by focusing attention on a midget and his nuclear family, and
by reading his body as a disfigured metaphor of the atomic bomb itself, we
can say that Vonnegut's design is deeply concerned with the issue of Cold
War politics, which has transformed scientific inventions into monstrous
weapons with its textual power. Vonnegut calls attention to those "morally
innocent scientists" like Dr. Hoenikker who unwittingly allow their work
to be abused.[9] However, the style of his depiction of Newton's body is not
so simple. Vonnegut first reveals the lineage of the Hoenikker family and
how the history of Hiroshima has led the family members into political
conflict, and then he introduces the textuality typical of the nuclear age,
combating it with his own highly self-reflexive textual devices. Newton's
stigmatized body, a disfiguration of scientific artifice, permits the two
superpowers' interventions reflecting the Cold War opposition. This network, along with his father's game of the balance and imbalance, not only
threatens Newton but also arouses his artistic sense to a new recognition of
his profound absence in the textuality of the atomic bomb.

Here the self-referential textuality of this novel itself mirrors the fiction of nuclear deterrence. The only difference between nuclear politics and Vonnegut's fiction is that Vonnegut actually introduces the world's end, thereby disrupting the network that disguises the truth in itself, and pursues the fiction in the nuclear age with the help of the Bokononist system to presuppose fictionality per se. In this sense, as a novelist of what Steve Erickson calls "nuclear imagination," Vonnegut not only recognizes the impending danger and examines it, but his imagination is liberated by it (42). What Vonnegut tries to annihilate "[a]t a certain amount of expense to the world" (187) is the worldwide political *cat's cradle* that entangles the little boy. Of course, this is Vonnegutian black humor, but it is in this particular way that he has fought the metanarrative of the Cold War.

NOTES

1. *Atomu* in Japan conveys the sense of *Mighty Atom*, a literal translation, whereas recent American editions (2002–) have been published under the title *Astro Boy*, which has been used by American TV producers and unlicensed rewriters since 1965.

2. In studies of *Cat's Cradle*, Albert E. Stone regards this geographical similarity as especially important. Focusing on Franklin's portion of ice-nine which freezes the ocean first in San Lorenzo, Stone argues, "the Third World Caribbean country accomplishes what the Cuban Missile Crisis barely failed to do" (63).

3. On this complex nature of playfulness (i.e. that of pure curiosity and the potential danger it poses), Tony Tanner has pointed out, "the whole novel is an exploration of the ambiguities of man's disposition to play and invent, and the various forms it may take" (189).

4. In defense of Newton's failure to prevent Zinka from stealing the lethal substance, Angela insists, "Newt didn't give it to her. She *stole* it" (164). His innocence, though "uninteresting" to Jonah, is emphasized through her patronizing rhetoric.

5. Angela was also the one who urged her father to develop the atomic bomb, removing the turtles in which Dr. Hoenikker had become so engrossed that he stopped going to the laboratory. In both cases, her intention was not political but selfish: with the A-bomb, she wanted a brilliant father, and with ice-nine, she hoped to gain her husband's love. As is the case with Newton, her quest for familial and erotic love leads to the emergence of highly political problems.

6. The episode of the cat's cradle gives us a good chance to reconsider the notion of security. According to the *OED*, the Latin origin of the word "secure" conveys the meaning "without care" (*se-* without, *cura* care). In other words, it means the state of being "carefree" without the need to feel special anxiety or pain. A cradle that primarily signifies a secure place for a baby (Newton) is in fact *insecure* for him since his father is carefree and absent-minded. As is discussed later, Cold War politics also relies on the bomb for security, for each superpower can trust that the enemy will never use the weapon since it will lead to mutually assured destruction (MAD). Yet, in maintaining security, both countries had to prepare for the ultimate *insecurity*, avoiding the imbalance that might lead to the bomb being dropped.

7. According to Tobin Siebers, whereas the Cold War metanarrative resulted from modernist world wars, postmodernists see it as a wrong-minded attempt to convert all contradictory relations into a super opposition, and as a failure "to include a great deal that could not be defined in terms of the superpower duality of the postwar world" (7).

8. Papa Monzano's last speech is a Bokononist way of speaking about committing suicide, but it clearly prefigures the literal world's end which results from Papa's poisoning.

9. Vonnegut, *Wampeters, Foma & Granfalloons* 97. In an address given to the American Physical Society (1969) Vonnegut expresses his sympathy for young scientists who cannot do without a question as to whether the atomic bomb is "a sin or not" (98). In contrast, Daniel L. Zins records a "chilling testimony" by J. Robert Oppenheimer, the leader of the Manhattan Project and one of those scientists Vonnegut calls "old-fashioned": " . . . it is my judgment in these things that when you see something sweet you go ahead and do it and you argue about what to do about it only after you have had your technical success. That is the way it was with the atomic bomb" (71). Zins's argument stresses the exploitation of scientists by technocracy, and reads this novel as a didactical lesson on the danger of nihilism.

Works Cited

Aldiss, Brian. *A. I. Supertoys Last All Summer Long: And Other Stories of Future Time.* London: Orbit, 2001.

Chaloupka, William. *Knowing Nukes: The Politics and Culture of the Atom.* Minneapolis: University of Minnesota Press, 1993.

Derrida, Jacques. "No Apocalypse, Not Now (full speed ahead, seven missiles, seven missives)." Trans. Catherine Porter and Philip Lewis. *Diacritics* 14.2 (1984): 20–31.

Drimmer, Frederick. *Very Special People.* 1973. New York: Citadel, 1991.

Dr. Strangelove or: How I Learned to Stop Worrying and Love the Bomb. Dir. Stanley Kubrick. Perf. Peter Sellers and George C. Scott. Columbia, 1963.

Erickson, Steve, *Leap Year.* 1989. New York: Avon, 1991.

George, Peter. *Dr. Strangelove or: How I Learned to Stop Worrying and Love the Bomb.* 1963. London: Prion, 2001.

Klinkowitz, Jerome. "*Mother Night, Cat's Cradle,* and the Crimes of Our Time." Mustazza, *Critical Response* 79–89.

McCanles, Michael. "Machiavelli and the Paradoxes of Deterrence." *Diacritics* 14.2 (1984): 12–19.

Melville, Herman. *Moby-Dick.* 1851. Ed. Hershel Parker and Harrison Hayford. New York: Norton, 2002.

Merish, Lori. "Cuteness and Commodity Aesthetics: Tom Thumb and Shirley Temple." *Freakery: Cultural Spectacle of the Extraordinary Body.* Ed. Rosemarie Garland Thomson. New York: New York University Press, 1996. 185–203.

Mustazza, Leonard, ed. *Critical Response to Kurt Vonnegut.* Westport, CT: Greenwood, 1994.

———. *Forever Pursuing Genesis. The Myth of Eden in the Novels of Kurt Vonnegut.* Lewisburg: Bucknell University Press, 1990.

Nadel, Alan. *Containment Culture. American Narratives, Postmodernism, and the Atomic Age.* Durham: Duke University Press, 1995.

Pease, Donald E. "*Moby Dick* and the Cold War." *The American Renaissance Reconsidered*. Ed. Walter Benn Michaels and Donald E. Pease. Baltimore: Johns Hopkins University Press, 1985. 113–155.

Robinson, Douglas. *American Apocalypses: The Image of the End of the World in American Literature*. Baltimore: Johns Hopkins University Press, 1985.

Schwenger, Peter. *Letter Bomb: Nuclear Holocaust and the Exploding Word*. Baltimore: Johns Hopkins University Press, 1992.

Simons, John L. "Tangled Up in You: A Playful Reading of *Cat's Cradle*." *Kurt Vonnegut's Cat's Cradle*. Ed. Harold Bloom. New York: Chelsea, 2002. 33–48.

Siebers, Tobin. "Introduction: What Does Postmodernist Want? Utopia." *Heterotopia: Postmodern Utopia and the Body Politic*. Ed. Tobin Siebers. Ann Arbor: University of Michigan Press, 1994. 1–38.

Stone, Albert E. *Literary Aftershocks: American Writers, Readers, and the Bomb*. New York: Twayne, 1994.

Takaki, Ronald. *Hiroshima: Why America Dropped the Atomic Bomb*. Boston: Little, 1995.

Tezuka, Osamu. *Astro Boy*. Vol. 1–13+. Trans. Fredrick L. Schodt. Milwaukie: Darkhorse, 2003.

Tanner, Tony. *City of Words: American Fiction, 1950–1970*. New York: Harper, 1971.

Turner, Frederick Jackson. "The Significance of the Frontier in American History." 1893. *Rereading Frederick Jackson Turner*. Ed. John Mack Faragher. New York: Holt, 1994. 31–60.

Vanderbilt, Kermit. "Kurt Vonnegut's American Nightmares and Utopias." *The Utopian Vision: Seven Essays on the Quincentennial of Sir Thomas More*. Ed. E. D. S. Sullivan. San Diego: San Diego University Press, 1983. 138–173.

Vonnegut, Kurt. *Cat's Cradle*. 1963. New York: Dell, 1988.

———. *Wampeters, Foma & Granfalloons: Opinions*. 1974. New York: Dell, 1989.

Wood, Gaby. *Edison's Eve: A Magical History of the Quest for Mechanical Life*. New York: Knopf, 2002.

Zins, Daniel L. "Rescuing Science from Technocracy: *Cat's Cradle* and the Play of Apocalypse." Mustazza, *Critical Response* 67–77.

JOSH SIMPSON

"This Promising of Great Secrets": Literature, Ideas, and the (Re)Invention of Reality in Kurt Vonnegut's God Bless You, Mr. Rosewater, Slaughterhouse-Five, and Breakfast of Champions

Or "Fantasies of an Impossibly Hospitable World": Science Fiction and Madness in Vonnegut's Troutean Trilogy

> I resent a lot of science fiction. This promising of great secrets just beyond our *grasp*—I don't think they exist.
> —Kurt Vonnegut, interview with Frank McLaughlin, 1973

> [Mushari] didn't understand that what Trout had in common with pornography wasn't sex but fantasies of an impossibly hospitable world.
> —*God Bless You, Mr. Rosewater,* 20

The novels, short stories, and plays that collectively form Kurt Vonnegut's literary canon are unique in that they can be read two ways—as autonomous texts that in and of themselves contain meaning and as parts of a larger whole. Thus the question emerges: What, to borrow Henry James' phrase, is "the string" on which Vonnegut's "pearls are strung?" The answer can be found in a fan letter printed in the prologue to Vonnegut's 1979 novel *Jailbird:*

Critique: Studies in Contemporary Fiction, Volume 45, Number 3 (Spring 2004): pp. 261–271.
Copyright © 2004 Heldref Publications.

John Figler is a law-abiding high-school student. He says in his letter that he has read almost everything of mine and is now prepared to state the single idea that lies at the core of my life work so far. The words are his: "Love may fail, but courtesy will prevail." This seems true to me—and complete. So now I am in the abashed condition [...] of realizing that I needn't have bothered to write several books. A seven-word telegram would have done the job. Seriously. (x)

Courtesy will prevail. Kurt Vonnegut is a writer setting out to discover the mysteries of the human condition. Using irony, satire, and black humor as his helmet, breastplate, and flaming sword for battling the existential malaise of the twentieth century, Vonnegut forces his readers to consider what it means to be human in a chaotic, often absurd, and irrational universe.

Because at various points in his career Vonnegut has employed aspects of science fiction such as time travel, spaceships, machinery, and distant galaxies in his novels, many critics, scholars, and readers in general have, over the years, written him off as a hack writer, existing in the subculture of pulp fiction. In his scathing 1965 essay "Science Fiction," he states: "I learned," in 1952 from the reviewers of *Player Piano,* "that I was a science fiction writer [...]. I have been a soreheaded occupant of the file drawer labeled science fiction ever since, and I would like out, particularly since so many serious critics regularly mistake the drawer for a urinal" ("Science Fiction" 1). A decade after Vonnegut's essay first appeared in the *New York Times,* Stanley Schatt, in the preface to his now-classic *Kurt Vonnegut Jr.,* wrote that "Kurt Vonnegut Jr., has been labeled at various times as a mediocre science fiction writer, a social satirist, a Black Humorist, and a major novelist" (9).

I claim that far from being a science fiction writer, Kurt Vonnegut is a writer whose works, when read closely, ultimately warn against the dangerous ideas that exist within science fiction. At the center of his canon resides the notion that science fiction is capable of filling humanity with false realities and empty promises for utopian societies that do not and, perhaps most important, cannot exist. I have labeled *God Bless You, Mr. Rosewater* (1965), *Slaughterhouse-Five* (1969), and *Breakfast of Champions* (1973) as Vonnegut's Troutean trilogy. In each of these novels, the ideas found in the science fiction novels of Kilgore Trout succeed in distorting the realities of Vonnegut's protagonists. A close examination of each novel reveals that through Trout, Vonnegut realizes the dangers that lie at the heart of science fiction if it is read and interpreted as reality.

God Bless You, Mr. Rosewater:
Humanity, Compassion, and the Birth of Kilgore Trout
God Bless You, Mr. Rosewater, like virtually all of Vonnegut's novels, has been read and misread on a number of different levels. Leonard J. Leff argues that

"[. . .] despite its title, [*God Bless You, Mr. Rosewater*] is concerned less with Eliot Rosewater than with the dehumanizing power of money upon man" (30). Leff's article reveals an important question that Vonnegut scholars have wrestled with for almost fifty years: On what level does Vonnegut write? Does he pose parabolic questions and deliver metaphorical answers about the human condition in particular and the world in general—as do self-confirmed science fiction writers such as Theodore Sturgeon, Ray Bradbury, and Harlan Ellison? Or, in any given novel, does he present his audience of readers, scholars, critics, and, most important, thinkers with characters and individuals that are to be admired and pitied? I argue that Vonnegut works on both levels. The situations with which his characters find themselves struggling—and what these situations represent in reality—are always more important than the characters themselves. However, to read Vonnegut as strict allegory is to lose sight of the human condition as it occurs, through characterization, inside his novels. The problem that many readers have with Vonnegut is that they are unable to see the humans because of the parable—an occurrence on the level of missing the proverbial forest because of the trees. Vonnegut's fictional world has many forests but also many trees.

Critics and readers who focus on the allegorical aspects of Vonnegut's novels have many textual moments to which to turn for support. In the opening line of *God Bless You, Mr. Rosewater,* Vonnegut states, "A sum of money is a leading character in this tale about people, just as a sum of honey might properly be a leading character in a tale about bees" (7). Although money is *a* leading character in *God Bless You, Mr. Rosewater,* it is not *the* leading character—the novel is, after all, a "tale about people." The reader should remember that whatever the theme—money, war, politics, class, or race—Vonnegut is always concerned with how the theme influences, shapes, molds, and, as is often the case, distorts the individual, on a human level.

The plot of *God Bless You, Mr. Rosewater,* on the surface, is simple. On returning home from World War II, Eliot Rosewater, the son of a famous senator, receives a large sum of money—$87,472,033.61 to be exact—when he becomes president of The Rosewater Foundation. Rosewater, knowing that he has done nothing to earn such wealth and comfort, is filled with grief and compassion when he recognizes how impoverished virtually everyone else in America is. Overcome with guilt, he develops a severe drinking problem and turns to the arts—science fiction in particular—in an attempt to understand better himself and the world in which he lives. Into this situation, Vonnegut introduces Kilgore Trout, the obscure writer of science fiction whose ideas, he later learns in *Breakfast of Champions,* can be nothing less than "mind poison." Indeed, they *are* poison to Eliot Rosewater. Early in the novel, Rosewater crashes a science fiction convention in Milford, Pennsylvania, where he delivers the following speech:

> I love you sons of bitches. You're all I read any more. You're the only ones who'll talk about the really terrific changes going on, the only ones crazy enough to know that life is a space voyage [...]. You're the only ones with guts enough to *really* care about the future, who *really* notice what machines do to us, what wars do to us, what cities do to us, what big, simple ideas do to us, what tremendous misunderstandings, mistakes, accidents, and catastrophes do to us. (18)

Rosewater turns to science fiction as a form of ideological salvation because they are "the only ones" who realize the catastrophes that plague the human condition. Of these writers who, according to Rosewater, have their fingers on the pulse of humanity, Kilgore Trout is king: "I only wish that Kilgore Trout was here, so I could shake his hand and tell him that he is the greatest writer alive today [... he is society's] greatest prophet" (19). Rosewater feels that Trout, like the biblical prophets of the Old Testament, offers truth, wisdom, comfort, and, perhaps above all, warnings of what is to come.

Vonnegut's portrayal of Trout as a postmodern prophet is not so farfetched. The prophets of the Bible warned Israel of what would happen if they did not change their ways. They wrote in metaphors to convey their messages to the people. Kilgore Trout's novels are structured similarly. Describing Trout's style, Vonnegut writes: "Trout's favorite formula was to describe a perfectly hideous society, not unlike his own, and then, toward the end, to suggest ways in which it could be improved" (20). Trout's warnings, viewed and understood as such, are published in cheap paperbacks that can only be found and purchased in smut shops, "amidst the rawest pornography" (19). When Norman Mushari, the eager young lawyer who is hell-bent on proving Rosewater insane and thus depriving him of his fortune, learns of Rosewater's love for Trout's works, he attempts to find samples of his writing to use as testaments to Rosewater's insanity. The only place that he can locate the novels is in a pornography shop.

The link between science fiction, Trout, and pornography is a central aspect in Vonnegut's novels. Vonnegut is not saying that science fiction is pornography; on the contrary, he is arguing quite the opposite. "[...] what Trout had in common with pornography wasn't sex but fantasies of an impossibly hospitable world" (20). Pornography, understood as images representing the complete carnal gratification of the flesh, presents the reader with a distorted view of reality, as do science fiction novels. Both science fiction and pornography, Vonnegut suggests, present the reader with blissful images of a world that cannot be reached or achieved in reality.

Rosewater is psychologically unhinged by Trout's ideas in much the same way that sex addicts are unhinged by pornography. He seeks to turn the ideas found in Trout's novels into realities in his own world. Rosewater's self-professed "work of art," loving Americans "even though they're useless and unattractive" and distributing his wealth to the needy—the very act that causes his father, Mushari, and the world at large to consider him crazy and legally insane—is inspired by Trout's short story "2BRO2B" (36). In this story, Trout asks the following question: "What in hell are people for?" (21). From the moment he first encounters the question, Rosewater devotes his life to discovering an answer. According to Vonnegut scholar Jerome Klinkowitz, Rosewater takes Trout's ideas and uses them to "reinvent reality," a theme that Vonnegut develops more fully in *Slaughterhouse-Five* (60).

At the end of the novel, Rosewater is clearly mad. Readers will realize, however, that Trout is not responsible for Rosewater's mental condition. As a result of his horrid experiences in the war—in which he accidentally killed a group of volunteer firemen, one of them a fourteen-year-old boy—Rosewater is emotionally and mentally unbalanced before he encounters Trout's fiction. He believes that the promises for a brave, new love-centric utopian society that he encountered in Trout's fiction could be realized. Those ideas send Rosewater over the edge.

In the last section of the novel, before Rosewater is to take the stand and prove his sanity before a judge, his father tells him that he has contacted Trout. "You said Trout could explain the meaning of everything you'd done [. . .] even if you couldn't," Rosewater's father states (182). This is the central passage in the novel, revealing Rosewater's dependence on Trout. Far from being able to defend himself before a judge, Rosewater is unable to defend his actions even to himself. He requires Trout to explain to him the reality that he constructed when he set out to answer the question posed in "2BRO2B." Trout, the writer who asks "What in hell are people for?" never provides an answer to his own question.

Kilgore Trout, an elderly man "who looked like a frightened, aging Jesus whose sentence to crucifixion had been commuted to imprisonment for life, supplements his income by working as a clerk in a trading-stamp redemption center. Behind his small desk, surrounded by stamps, he is safe—far removed from the ideas presented in his own books, which apparently few people but Rosewater read. He knows, in the end, that his ideas are nothing more than "the fantasies of an impossibly hospitable world" (115). He does not attempt

to make them realities—he would rather hide behind his desk and write
about what *could be* rather than what *is.*

Slaughterhouse-Five:
Billy Pilgrim, Science Fiction, and the Reinvention of the Universe

Stanley Schatt once remarked that "[j]ust as money is a central character in
God Bless You, Mr. Rosewater, death serves that role in *Slaughterhouse-Five*,"
Vonnegut's much-anticipated and long-awaited Dresden book (Schatt 1976,
81). A prisoner of war behind German lines at the end of World War II,
Vonnegut was present when the city was firebombed in February 1945.
Although few would deny that *Slaughterhouse-Five* is Vonnegut's undisputed
masterpiece, they seem to agree on little else. William Rodney Allen argues
that the novel is Vonnegut's "story" of Dresden (*Understanding* 77–79). William E. Meyer Jr. claims: "[. . .] [w]e need to concede that *Slaughterhouse-
Five* is not, finally, about the fire-bombing of Dresden [. . .]. Rather, the
work stands, albeit stumblingly, in that long line of New-World 'fiery hunts'
for self-discovery—for the excitement and horror of 'the great principle of
light'" (96). Perhaps the truth lies somewhere between Allen's and Meyer's
equally astute observations. I argue that although *Slaughterhouse-Five* on the
surface is Vonnegut's Dresden novel, on a much deeper level it is also the
story of Billy Pilgrim, a man so tormented and haunted by the burden of the
past that he finds it necessary to "reinvent" his own reality. As is the case
with Eliot Rosewater, Kilgore Trout's science fiction novels are responsible
for Billy's reinvention.

As a result of the unspeakable atrocities and mounds of human wreck-
age and carnage that he saw in Dresden, Billy, on returning home, checks
himself into a "ward for nonviolent mental patients in a veterans' hospital" in
the spring of 1948 (127).[1] Pilgrim finds himself sharing a room with Eliot
Rosewater, who had voluntarily committed himself to cure his all-consuming
drinking habit. In this crucial scene, Vonnegut skillfully links the themes of
God Bless You, Mr. Rosewater and *Slaughterhouse-Five.* He states: "[Rosewater
and Billy] had both found life meaningless, partly because of what they had
seen in war. Rosewater, for instance, had shot a fourteen-year-old fireman,
mistaking him for a German soldier. So it goes. And Billy had seen the greatest massacre in European history, which was the fire-bombing of Dresden.
So it goes" (128). Vonnegut continues: "So they were both trying to reinvent
themselves and their universe. Science fiction was a big help" (128). At this
point, readers remember that the action of *God Bless You, Mr. Rosewater* took
place in 1965, the year that Eliot Rosewater establishes The Rosewater Foundation. *Slaughterhouse-Five*, however, written four years later than *God Bless
You, Mr. Rosewater*, takes readers back in time to 1948 and introduces them to
a younger, healthier Eliot Rosewater. Vonnegut's novels build on each other

and yield interesting—and sometimes surprising—results when each work is read as a part of a larger whole and not just for itself. In this case, the reader learns that Rosewater's insanity, like Billy's, is brought about by his reinvention of himself and his universe in 1948, three years after the end of World War II.

Kilgore Trout's novels, of which Rosewater has an extensive collection, are the tools with which Billy constructs his new, postwar reality. According to Vonnegut: "Kilgore Trout became Billy's favorite living author, and science fiction became the only sort of tales he could read" (128). This passage echoes Rosewater's comments at the Milford science fiction convention, in which he blurted out to the assembled body of writers, "I love you sons of bitches. You're all I read anymore" (18).[2] Using the novels of Kilgore Trout as their guides, Rosewater and Billy set out on journeys of reinvention. Readers of *God Bless You, Mr. Rosewater* know that Rosewater's journey fills him with dreams of a classless, Marxesque utopia; Billy, on the other hand, journeys to Tralfamadore, a planet in a distant galaxy where free will does not exist.

For years, scholars, critics, and readers of *Slaughterhouse-Five* have been asking whether Tralfamadore exists or whether it is a figment of Billy's warped imagination. One writer suggests, "Billy [...] increasingly withdraws from reality and ultimately loses his sanity" (Broer 88), whereas another argues that "[...] from the moment he comes 'unstuck in time,' Billy continually tries to construct for himself an Edenic experience out of the materials that he garners over the course of some twenty years" (Mustazza 299). Yet another admits that "[t]he novel is so constructed that one cannot determine whether or not what Billy sees is real" (Schatt 65). Vonnegut leaves the question of Tralfamadore's existence open to debate; however, a close reading of the novel strongly suggests that it exists only in Billy's mind, having been placed there by Kilgore Trout's particular brand of literary "poison."

According to Billy, he has been to Tralfamadore many times. He claims that he was first kidnapped by a flying saucer on a clear night in 1967—nineteen years after he first encountered Trout's fiction in the psychiatric ward: "The saucer was from the planet Tralfamadore, [Billy] said. He was taken to Tralfamadore where he was displayed naked in a zoo, he said. He was mated there with a former Earthling movie star named Montana Wildhack" (32). Throughout the novel, it is unclear whether Billy was abducted by a flying saucer or whether he has lost his mind. In 1969, near the end of the novel, a Kilgore Trout novel catches Billy's eye in the window of a New York adult bookshop. He quickly enters the shop and begins inspecting the novel. At this point, Vonnegut breaks into the narration: "He got a few paragraphs into it, and then he realized that he *had* read it before—years ago, in the veterans' hospital. It was about an Earthling man and an Earthling woman who were kidnapped by extraterrestrials. They were put on display in a zoo on a planet called Zircon-212" (257). Comparing the description of Billy's abduction with the plot of Trout's *The Big Board* makes it clear that Tralfamadore is nothing more than a product of Billy's mind. He first read the novel in the veterans' hospital in 1948—during the spring of his reinvention. As a result, he created Tralfamadore as a way of escaping his troubled past. In that light, his Tralfamadorian existence must be approached as an escape mechanism grounded in mental instability but—and this is key—fueled by Troutean science fiction.

Slaughterhouse-Five shows two things simultaneously and with equally chilling clarity: what war and bad ideas can do to humanity. War psychologically wounds Billy Pilgrim; however, the ideas contained in Kilgore Trout's science fiction novels are, ultimately, responsible for his complete divorce from reality. Vonnegut, in his next novel, *Breakfast of Champions*, forces Trout to confront the dangers that exist at the heart of his own printed words.

Breakfast of Champions:
Free Will, Bad Chemicals, and the Creation of Conscience

In a widely cited interview, Vonnegut remarked: "Well, *Slaughterhouse-Five* and *Breakfast of Champions* used to be one book. But they just separated completely. It was like a pousse-café, like oil and water—they simply were not mixable. So I was able to decant *Slaughterhouse-Five* and what was left was *Breakfast of Champions*" (Standish 108). To discuss *Slaughterhouse-Five* at length without considering *Breakfast of Champions* is impossible. Considering their origins, it is surprising that the two novels have received such drastically different critical receptions. Many critics who sing the praises of *Slaughterhouse-Five*, claiming it to be one of the most innovative, rich novels of the twentieth century, often dismiss *Breakfast of Champions* as a vastly inferior novel. Others see it as a thematic return to earlier work. Peter Messent argues, "[I]n *Breakfast of Champions* [. . .] Vonnegut moves back to the *God Bless You, Mr. Rosewater* approach, as he draws up a wide scale indictment of the numerous flaws of American life" (103). Messent goes on to note that "[f]or most of the time *Breakfast of Champions* expresses Vonnegut's personal despair and his despair at his society" (104). *Breakfast of Champions* thematically relates to *God Bless You, Mr. Rosewater*, just as it relates to *Slaughterhouse-Five*. However, far from being a novel with "considerable flaws" as Allen suggests (*Understanding* 103), or a novel that borrows perhaps a little too heavily from the past, *Breakfast of Champions* is one of Vonnegut's most important books, for in it, the third and final installment of what I term the Troutean trilogy, Vonnegut forces Kilgore Trout to examine his work's influence on humanity.

In *Breakfast of Champions*, Kilgore Trout receives more attention than in either *God Bless You, Mr. Rosewater* or *Slaughterhouse-Five*. Along with

Dwayne Hoover, he is the central character in the novel. In the opening lines of the first chapter, Vonnegut states:

> This is a tale of a meeting of two lonesome, skinny, fairly old white men on a planet that was dying fast. One of them was a science-fiction writer named Kilgore Trout. He was a nobody at the time, and he supposed his life was over. He was mistaken. As a consequence of the meeting, he became one of the most beloved and respected beings in history. (7)

Dwayne's descent into madness causes Trout, for the first time in his career, to gain a conscience and an understanding of the power that is both possible and available in and with the written word.

Dwayne's mental breakdown, unlike that of Eliot Rosewater or Billy Pilgrim, is caused by "bad chemicals" rather than war. "Dwayne's incipient insanity was mainly a matter of chemicals. [...] Dwayne Hoover's body was manufacturing certain chemicals which unbalanced his mind. But Dwayne, like all novice lunatics, needed some bad ideas too, so that his craziness could have shape and direction" (13–14). The "bad ideas" that Dwayne requires are provided by the writings of Kilgore Trout. As Vonnegut writes:

> The bad ideas were delivered to Dwayne by Kilgore Trout. Trout considered himself not only harmless but invisible. The world had paid so little attention to him that he wished he was dead. He hoped he was dead. But he learned from his encounter with Dwayne that he was alive enough to give a fellow human being ideas which would turn him into a monster. (14)

In this passage, Vonnegut suggests that, throughout the course of the novel, Trout will realize that his ideas matter and that they can have a profound impact on the world. Because he thinks of himself as being "invisible," his works, from his perspective, can be understood only as the writings of an "invisible" man. Much like Rosewater, Billy, and Dwayne, Trout reinvents the reality of his own universe. For him, invisibleness allows him to think that who he is and what he does will not and cannot have an influence on humanity. In much the same way that Billy creates Tralfamadore to rid himself of the responsibility for his actions, Trout clings to invisibleness. However, in the end, unlike Billy, he is forced to re-enter reality. He learns that he is *not* invisible and that his ideas *do* matter.

Although Eliot Rosewater and Billy Pilgrim find themselves psychologically damaged by Trout's ideas in earlier novels, the damage they receive is self-satisfying. Both men get what they want: Rosewater becomes a hero, if not quite a god, to the people of Rosewater, Indiana, whereas Billy escapes his haunted past by inventing Tralfamadore. Dwayne Hoover, on the other hand, is transformed into a ravenous monster, hell-bent on destruction and thirsty for blood. In the cocktail lounge of the Holiday Inn, he goes on a destructive rampage, setting out to destroy everything and everyone in his way. Dwayne's violent outbreak occurs because Trout's science fiction destroys his understanding of the human "other." In Trout's *Now It Can Be Told*, Dwayne reads: "You are the only creature in the entire universe who has free will [...]. Everybody else is a robot, a machine" (259). After reading that passage, he sees humanity as nothing more than a series of robots and machines; at least in his own sick mind, he is "the only creature in the universe with free will." When he goes on his bloody rampage, he feels he is attacking machines and robots rather than human beings.

Dwayne's mental breakdown forces Trout to examine his role as a science fiction writer. Vonnegut writes: "It shook Trout up to realize that even *he* could bring evil into the world—in the form of bad ideas. And, after Dwayne was carted off to a lunatic asylum in a canvas camisole, Trout became a fanatic on the importance of ideas as causes and cures for diseases" (15). The reader learns that by the time of his death in 1981, Trout had become a respected and decorated scientist. These words are written on his tombstone: "We are healthy only to the extent that our ideas are humane" (16). In the end, Trout realizes that as a writer he has a responsibility to the human community.

With *Breakfast of Champions*, Vonnegut ends his Troutean trilogy. Kilgore Trout, however, is not fully "set free" at the novel's end; the sci-fi writer appears in such later works such as *Jailbird* (1979) and *Timequake* (1997). With *God Bless You, Mr. Rosewater, Slaughterhouse-Five*, and *Breakfast of Champions*, however, Vonnegut uses Trout as a comical character who, through his interactions with Eliot Rosewater, Billy Pilgrim, and Dwayne Hoover, learns a profound lesson: Literature matters, and the writer-artist has an obligation to the world. In an age when random acts of violence and horror are blamed on literature, music, film, and the arts in general, Trout is an important literary figure with much to offer the masses.

When asked his feelings about science fiction during a 1973 interview with Frank McLaughlin, Vonnegut responded: "I think it is dangerous to believe that there are enormous new truths, dangerous to imagine that we can stand outside the universe. So I argue for the ordinariness of love, the familiarity of love" (74). Vonnegut is, above all, a literary messenger of love. Eliot Rosewater, Billy Pilgrim, and Dwayne Hoover are all examples of literary characters who attempted to stand outside the universe. The science fiction novels of Kilgore Trout were the stepping stones that allowed them to seek "enormous new truths" that exist exclusively "outside the universe." Vonnegut would argue that the fatal, damning flaw that resides at the heart of science fiction in general, and Kilgore Trout's novels in particular, is that, as a genre, it all too often seeks to find answers outside the universe, outside the human condition, and outside the realms of human kindness. The answers to the mysteries of the human condition, he would argue, can be found not in space or in theory, but rather, in humanity itself. As Trout ultimately learns, "We are only healthy to the extent that out ideas are humane."

Love may fail, but courtesy will prevail.

Notes

1. I intend to use dates whenever possible in order to locate Billy Pilgrim in his own narrative. Because, as the opening line of the novel suggests, he has become "unstuck in time," it is often difficult to tell where he is at any given moment in the novel. Time, not sequence, I argue, is crucial to understanding Pilgrim's progression.

2. It is difficult to keep track of time in Kurt Vonnegut's novels. For example, Vonnegut's comment on Billy (referring to a time in the late 1940s) directly relates to remarks that Rosewater made almost twenty years later (mid- to late 1960s). For the purposes of this essay—and my own sanity—I approach Vonnegut's works in chronological order. Because *Slaughterhouse Five* was written later than *God Bless You, Mr. Rosewater,* I include in this section any light that the former can shed on the latter.

Works Cited

Allen, William Rodney, ed. *Conversations with Kurt Vonnegut.* Jackson: University Press of Mississippi, 1999.

———. *Understanding Kurt Vonnegut.* Columbia: University of South Carolina Press, 1991.

Broer, Lawrence R. *Sanity Plea: Schizophrenia in the Novels of Kurt Vonnegut.* Rev. ed. Ann Arbor: UMI Research Press, 1989.

Klinkowitz, Jerome. *Kurt Vonnegut.* London: Methuen, 1982.

Leff, Leonard J. "Utopia Reconstructed: Alienation in Vonnegut's *God Bless You, Mr. Rosewater.*" *Critique* 12.3 (1971): 29–37.

McLaughlin, Frank. "An Interview With Kurt Vonnegut Jr." Allen 66–75.

Messent, Peter B. "*Breakfast of Champions:* The Direction of Kurt Vonnegut's Fiction." *Journal of American Studies* 8 (1974): 101–114.

Meyer, William H. E. Jr. "Kurt Vonnegut: The Man With Nothing to Say" *Critique* 29.2 (1988): 95–109.

Mustazza, Leonard. "Vonnegut's Tralfamadore and Milton's Eden." *Essays in Literature* 13.2 (1986): 299–312.

Schatt, Stanley. *Kurt Vonnegut Jr.* Boston: Twayne, 1976.

———. "The World of Kurt Vonnegut Jr." *Critique* 12.3 (1971): 54–69.

Standish, David. "Playboy Interview." Allen 76–110.

Vonnegut, Kurt. *Breakfast of Champions.* 1973. New York: Delta, 1999.

———. *God Bless You, Mr. Rosewater.* 1965. New York: Dell, 1980.

———. *Jailbird*. New York: Delacourte, 1999.

———. "Science Fiction." *Wampeters, Foma, & Granfalloons: Opinions*. 1974. New York: Delta, 1999.

———. *Slaughterhouse-Five*. 1969. New York: Delta, 1999.

GILBERT MCINNIS

Evolutionary Mythology
in the Writings of Kurt Vonnegut, Jr.

The first [function of mythology] is what I have called the mystical function:
to waken and maintain in the individual a sense of awe and gratitude in
relation to the mystery dimension of the universe, not so that he lives in fear
of it, but so that he recognizes that he participates in it, since the mystery of
being is the mystery of his own deep being as well. [...] The second function
of a living mythology is to offer an image of the universe that will be in
accord with the knowledge of the time, the sciences and the fields of action
of the folk to whom the mythology is addressed. [...] The third function of
a living mythology is to validate, support, and imprint the norms of a given,
specific moral order, that, namely, of the society in which the individual is to
live. [...] And the fourth is to guide him, stage by stage, in health, strength,
and harmony of spirit, through the whole foreseeable course of a useful life.
—Joseph Campbell, *Myths To Live By* (221–222)

Campbell's description of the four functions of a mythology reflects
the extent to which the theory of evolution functions as a mythology in
the lives of Kurt Vonnegut's characters—Mary Hepburn *(Galápagos)*, Unk
(The Sirens of Titan), Billy Pilgrim *(Slaughterhouse-Five)*, Howard Campbell
(Mother Night), and Dwayne Hoover *(Breakfast of Champions)*—and in the
American culture depicted by Vonnegut's novels.

Critique: Studies in Contemporary Fiction, Volume 46, Number 4 (Summer 2005): pp. 383–396. Copyright 2005 Heldref Publications.

In *Galápagos*, the notion of natural selection discloses a world of mystery and awe, and we observe this wonder when we examine the chance element in natural selection. According to what we learn from *Galápagos*, the chance element in natural selection shares characteristics with the mystery element of God and is, therefore, also a possible surrogate for that mystery. However, the characters are not active participants in "the mystery dimension of the universe," but rather are victims of the deterministic force underlying the chance mechanism of natural selection. When we further examine that malicious force, we conclude that it, too, resembles the mechanistic view of the universe propounded by evolutionary science. Therefore, the cosmological function of evolutionary mythology offers "an image of the universe" that is in accord with evolutionary science.

Vonnegut's readers experience the power or awe in Darwin's notion of natural selection in *Galápagos*. Leon accents this omnipotent power when he says, "I am prepared to swear under oath that the Law of Natural Selection did the repair job without outside assistance of any kind" (291). That "repair job" is natural selection's "job" of correcting human evil: At the outset of *Galápagos*, Vonnegut portrays the "big brains" destroying the earth and humanity; yet later, through the material workings of natural selection, these big brains evolve to "smaller skulls," and consequently the planet and humanity are saved from destruction. Some may argue that Mary Hepburn plays an important role in this new creation because her genetic engineering creates a new family that survives the apocalypse. However, Mary does so by the prodding of her big brain, which natural selection also repairs. Therefore, we are led to believe that natural selection alone is an almighty power that governs humanity and the universe.

Furthermore, according to the image that the novel impresses on us, the universe is determined by chance, and evolutionary science is employed to validate this image so that the mythology will be in accord with the prevalent ideas of our time. Leon tells us that natural selection played a mysterious role in correcting human evil, but we conclude that natural selection operates according to the force of chance. Moreover, chance is portrayed as a materialistic alternative to the mysterious role of God. Philip Johnson asserts that "[a] materialistic theory of evolution [...] must be based on chance, because that is what is left when we have ruled out everything involving intelligence or purpose" (22). According to Leon and Philip Johnson, either the universe is governed by chance or God, but not both, because, as R. C. Sproul states, "If chance existed, it would destroy God's sovereignty. If God is not sovereign, he is not God. If he is not God, he simply *is* not. If chance is, God is not. If God is, chance is not. The two cannot coexist by reason of the impossibility of the contrary" (3; emphasis in original). Moreover, Mary Midgley, discussing the popular evolutionist Jacques Monod and his book *Chance and Necessity*, helps us to understand how his philosophy of chance is also evident in the gambling-casino-luck view of the universe depicted in *Galápagos*. Midgley also asserts that "Monod's interest in contingency, however, does not center on this causal disconnection between elements of matter, but on the removal of God" (41). Thus, according to Midgley and Monod, accepting the sovereignty of chance undermines the belief in God's existence. In fact, Boodin advocates that when this happens, chance becomes our new god. He states:

> By some magic the antecedent factors [of evolution] are supposed to yield new forms and characters. By chance variation the structure of protoplasm is supposed to build up from inorganic matter, and by further chance variation the various life characters and forms appear. Intelligence is but a favourable chance variation of material antecedents. Chance is God. (82)

Evolutionary science is employed to validate such an image of the universe so that the mythology will accord with the prevalent ideas of our time because, as Monod argues, "Chance *alone* is at the source of every innovation, of all creation in the biosphere. Pure chance, absolutely free but blind, at the very root of the stupendous edifice of evolution [. . .] is today the *sole* conceivable hypothesis, the only one that squares with observed and tested fact" (112, emphasis in original). Therefore, according to Leon, our observations of Mary, and Monod's image of the universe, "chance alone" is at the source of every innovation, of all creation; and evolutionary science is employed to validate such a mythology so it will be accepted by our current culture as tested fact.

However credible Darwin's notion of natural selection is, whether in the sciences or in culture, it fails to serve a fundamental role pertinent to a mythology, especially when the characters cannot participate in its "mystery of being." Hence, this mystery of being is not connected to the character's deep sense of being but is a disconnected and fatalistic force that determines the course of evolution without any consideration of horizontal or vertical relationship. Consequently, when the characters believe in the evolutionary mythology, they live according to its materialistic principles, or the chance mechanism of natural selection. In comparison to a Greek-Calvinistic view of characters as mere actors on a stage, the evolutionary mythology would have us believe now that we are nothing more than mere cogs in a machine.

Both Unk *(The Sirens of Titan)* and Billy Pilgrim *(Slaughterhouse-Five)* experience the awe of their chance-driven universe, yet like Leon and Mary, they do not participate in that "mystery dimension" because a mechanistic and deterministic philosophy characterizes the "mystery" depicted in both *The Sirens of Titan* and *Slaughterhouse-Five*. Unk has a revelation that provides a description of that awe governing his life when he claims, "I was a victim of a series of accidents [. . . a]s are we all." His final revelation exemplifies how the random impersonal force, or chance, not only governs his universe but also the human biological dimension. About the accidents that Unk had while in the chrono-synclastic infundibula, Rumfoord asks, "Of all the accidents which would you consider the most significant?" Unk "cocked his head and said, 'I'd have to think—.'" However, Rumfoord answers the question himself with, "I'll spare you the trouble [. . .]. The most significant accident that happened to you was your being born" (258–259). Unk's initiation into the chrono-synclastic infundibula brings together a cosmogonic experience (typified by his statement: "I was a victim of a series of accidents") and an origins experience (Rumfoord's explains that Unk's biological birth was also an accident). Unk does not experience these two revelations until he has been "baptized" into the chrono-synclastic infundibula, which functions as a syncretic element of myth because the cosmic and biological elements of the evolutionary mythology merge here. Moreover, Vonnegut's invention of the chrono-synclastic infundibula shares traits with the "unstuck in time" in his later novel, *Slaughterhouse-Five*.

Like Unk, Billy has an epiphany when he becomes "unstuck" in time. Billy's subsequent quest helps us come to terms with the antagonism between chaos and order, but Vonnegut synthesizes the theories of Einstein and Darwin in the fictional invention of unstuck in time. After Billy's initiation of becoming unstuck in time, the Tralfamadorians teach him that there is no beginning, middle, or end to life. "There isn't any particular relationship between all the messages [. . .]. There is no beginning, no middle, no end, no suspense, no moral" (88). Moreover, Boodin argues that this "modern point of view which finds its typical expression in Darwinism [. . .] runs on like an old man's tale without beginning, middle, or end, without any guiding plot. It is infinite and formless. Chance rules supreme. It despises final causes" (77). Hence, Billy believes in no initial or final cause or a God; instead, his realization leads him to concur that "chance rules supreme" in the universe.

Moreover, Billy does not participate in that mystery dimension of chance because as the opening page of *The Sirens of Titan* declares, "Everyone now knows how to find the meaning of life within himself." Unk's epiphany is a summation of his lifelong journey, climaxing with his understanding that he cannot relate to that impersonal force or awe because it is beyond his control. Like Unk, Billy can only conclude that "everything is all right, and everybody has to do exactly what he does" (198). Or, as he learns from the Tralfamadorians, "'Well, here we are, Mr. Pilgrim, trapped in the amber of this moment. There is no why'" (76). In fact, when "chance rules supreme [. . .] there is no why" (Boodin 77) because as Sproul argues, "To say that something happens or is caused by chance is to suggest attributing instrumental power to nothing" (13). If the myth of chance is allowed to govern our beliefs, then there is no meaning to life because we are "attributing instrumental power to nothing." Peter Freese argues a similar point: "Billy attempts to teach his fellow humans that their repeated question 'Why?' is useless and inappropriate" (155). Moreover, the question "Why?" is useless and inappropriate for both Billy and Unk because there is no "mystery dimension of the universe" other than the awe of nothingness or chaos, and this conclusion is justified in terms of evolutionary science. Therefore, both novels investigate how evolutionary science provides a cosmological function that is in accordance with the prevalent ideas of our time, but the two novels also reveal how myth is sanctioned by the principles of evolutionary science.

Through Howard Campbell's description of the force underlying the totalitarian mind (wartime Nazi Germany in *Mother Night*), the mystical function of the evolutionary mythology depicts how chance rules supreme. As in other novels, Vonnegut here portrays a chance element as a substitute for God. Moreover, Campbell, like previous characters, does not participate in the mystery dimension of that chance-driven universe because the mystery of being that governs his universe operates according to the terms of contemporary evolutionary science. Like the big brains in *Galápagos*, the human mind in *Mother Night* operates as a simulacrum of the mechanical and random universe, and Campbell describes this mechanical, random thought machine as a totalitarian mind. Moreover, as with the big brains in *Galápagos*, each totalitarian mind that is transformed by the random thought machine in *Mother Night* is the result of the awful force that we have observed operating in *The Sirens of Titan* and *Slaughterhouse-Five*. According to Campbell, the totalitarian mind "might be likened unto a system of gears whose teeth have been filed off at random. Such a snaggle-toothed thought machine, driven by a standard or even substandard libido, whirls with the jerky, noisy, gaudy pointlessness of a cuckoo clock in Hell" (162). Therefore, the human mind is likened to a universe or thought machine that operates randomly, a view of the universe also espoused by evolutionary science. The totalitarian mind, or that force guiding the universe, is responsible for much of the chaos in the novel; and Campbell is in awe of its power to transform the human mind. He informs us:

> That was how my father-in-law could contain in one mind an indifference toward slave women and love for a blue vase—
> That was how Rudolf Hoess, Commandant of Auschwitz, could alternate over the loudspeakers of Auschwitz great music and calls for corpse-carriers—
> That was how Nazi Germany could sense no important difference between civilization and hydrophobia—

That is the closest I can come to explaining the legions, the nations of lunatics I've seen in my time. (162–163)

Therefore, that random thought machine not only governs the universe but also conditions the totalitarian minds of Campbell, Campbell's father-in-law, Rudolf Hoess, and "nations of lunatics."

However meaningless the "God of Chance" appears in *Mother Night,* the characters nevertheless attempt to participate in relation to its "mystery dimension." They do so by adapting, but as they adapt, their transformation signals the power they relinquish to this random thought machine to alter their minds into totalitarian minds. For example, once war begins, Campbell, a successful playwright, makes a double adaptation: he becomes a radio propagandist for Hitler and—to secure his future after the war—an American agent. However, his adaptations, or series of accidents, make him schizophrenic. Schizophrenia, the "first fruit" of his new totalitarian mind, eventually leads to his destruction. Campbell's sister-in-law Resi concludes: "He is so used up that he can't love any more. There is nothing left of him but curiosity and a pair of eyes" (166). Like Campbell, "nations of lunatics" in *Mother Night* fail to participate in the mystery dimension of the universe, precluded by their successful adaptation to the ruling mythology of social Darwinism. Therefore, according to *Galápagos, The Sirens of Titan, Slaughterhouse-Five,* and *Mother Night,* the universe operates according to the material principles of a chance mechanism or Darwin's notion of natural selection.

In addition, the cosmological function of the evolutionary mythology, or the random thought machine, is justified by evolutionary science's explanation of the constitution of the universe, and is, therefore, relevant to our time. First, the totalitarian mind, or that random thought machine of the universe, not only governs the universe but also conditions Campbell, his father-in-law, Rudolf Hoess, and "nations of lunatics." Moreover, the science of social Darwinism also makes the evolutionary mythology relevant to our time. Campbell's radio broadcasts propagate a mythology that permitted Nazi Germany to "sense no important difference between civilization and hydrophobia" or between civilization and an environment that would sanction the killing of millions of so-called inferior human beings. The Nazi mythology justified, or made relevant, his message, or truth. According to the social Darwinist Dr. Jones, Campbell was brave enough to "tell the truth about the conspiracy of international Jewish banking and international Jewish Communists who will not rest until the bloodstream of every American is hopelessly polluted with Negro and/or Oriental blood" (56). Moreover, Campbell informs us that the articles in Jones's fascist newspaper were "coming straight from Nazi propaganda mill," and it "is quite possible, incidentally, that much of his more scurrilous material was written by me" (60). Finally, the biological racism or

Nazi mythology "was developed from the theory of eugenics developed by Charles Darwin's cousin, Francis Galton" (Bergman 109). Therefore, it is possible for anyone, including scientists, to develop mythology from evolutionary science.

In *Breakfast of Champions*, we observe that the principal character, Dwayne Hoover, is controlled by the "awe-full" power of materialism, which transforms his mind. Hoover, like the other characters I have discussed, does not participate in "relation to the mystery dimension" of this materialistic universe but is a victim of its deterministic force. Kilgore Trout exemplifies the "awe-full" power of this materialistic dimension of the universe when he claims, "There were two monsters sharing the planet with us when I was a boy [. . .]. They were determined to kill us, or at least to make our lives meaningless [. . .]. *They inhabited our heads.* They were the *arbitrary* lusts for gold, and God help us, for a glimpse of a little girl's pants" (25; emphasis added). According to Trout, "arbitrary" nature characterizes this mysterious power. And as with other Vonnegut characters, this arbitrary mystery inhabits Dwayne's head. His "incipient insanity was mainly a matter of chemicals, of course. Dwayne Hoover's body was manufacturing certain chemicals which unbalanced his mind" (14). However, if, according to evolutionary science, natural selection determines the course of all material things in the natural world, then Dwayne's "unbalanced mind" is determined by it, too. His mind is controlled arbitrarily, like the "big brains" in *Galápagos* or the totalitarian minds in *Mother Night*.

These arbitrary bad chemicals that determine Dwayne's mind to do bad things cause many other minds to do evil as well.

> Dwayne certainly wasn't alone, as far as having bad chemicals inside of him was concerned. He had plenty of company throughout history. In his lifetime, for instance, the people in a country called Germany were so full of bad chemicals for a while that they actually built factories whose purpose was to kill people by the millions. The people were delivered by trains. (133)

Moreover, Vonnegut's narrator makes it clear that these bad chemicals are not drug-induced but are created by the natural functions of the body. "A lot of people were like Dwayne: they created chemicals in their own bodies which were bad for their heads" (70).

Dwayne behaves according to the materialistic principles of evolutionary science, but he does not participate in the mysterious dimension of the universe. In his relationship with Francine Pefko, we see that they cannot exercise free will but behave according to the principles of materialism. Shortly after Dwayne and Francine have sexual intercourse, Vonnegut's narrator gives one material yet metaphysical reason for Dwayne's suffering. "Here was the problem: Dwayne wanted Francine to love him for his body and soul, not for what his money could buy. He thought Francine was hinting that he should buy her a Colonel Sanders Kentucky Fried Chicken franchise" (157). Hence, Dwayne fails to meet his "invisible need" because the malicious force of materialism prevents him and Francine from participating in a meaningful relationship. The evolutionist Richard Lewontin claims this is because Dwayne exists as one of many material beings "in a material world, all of whose phenomena are the consequences of material relations among material entities" (Johnson 70). In brief, Dwayne must come to terms with Lewontin's materialistic cosmogony by the end of *Breakfast*. He cannot meet his immaterial needs by attempting to solve his problems according to the rules of an arbitrary materialistic worldview.

Moreover, this arbitrary and materialistic understanding of the universe by which Dwayne and others in *Breakfast of Champions* live derives its credibility from the scientific materialism of evolutionary science, which is in accord with the prevalent ideas of our time. The two monsters that Trout says are determined to kill the human race—the desire for gold and "a glimpse of a little girl's pants"—are materialistic pleasures derived from materialistic values, or a logical manifestation of scientific materialism. According to Runes, materialism is "a proposition about values: that wealth, bodily satisfactions, sensuous pleasures, or the like are either the only or the greatest values man can see or attain." Furthermore, scientific materialism is the belief that "the universe is not governed by intelligence, purpose, or final causes" but "that matter [money or sex] is the primordial or fundamental constituent of the [human] universe" (Runes 189). Money and sex seem to be the fundamental constituents of the universe of *Breakfast*. Hence, scientific materialism, or evolutionary science, serves the cosmological function in the novel because it explains the constitution of the universe in a way that makes the mythology practical for the characters.

Joseph Campbell's third and fourth functions of mythology are "to validate, support, and imprint the norms of a given, specific moral order [. . .] of the society in which the individual is to live," and "to guide [the individual] stage by stage in health, strength, and harmony of spirit throughout the [. . .] course of a useful life." If Campbell is correct, the sociological function of the myth should "validate, support, and imprint" a certain social order and the pedagogical function should instruct individuals how to live "in health, strength, and harmony of spirit." However, we have concluded that the social organization that is informed by the evolutionary mythology is justified by the ideology of Darwin's notion of natural selection, or the notion of survival of the fittest. For some individuals, an equal treatment of Darwin's notion of natural selection and the notion of survival of the fittest may seem far-fetched, but Darwin in *The Origin of Species* often used the two terms interchangeably. He states that the "preservation of favourable individual differences and variations, and the destruction of those which are injurious, I have called Natural Selection, or the Survival of the Fittest" (89). Therefore, the social or moral implications of the notion of survival of the fittest would be the same for the notion of natural selection.

One essential human value that is supported and validated by Darwin's notion of the survival of the fittest is also depicted in the Vonnegut novels under discussion, most directly in the opening page of *The Sirens of Titan*. This value asserts that human beings will not find meaning "out there" but instead must look within themselves and that to become the fittest, individual interest must be their supreme goal. Moreover, through the survival-of-the-fittest mythology, each individual's reliance on a meaningful relationship with a human community is transformed into an overburdened self-reliance on individualism. If there is to be a relationship with someone "out there," it is either to procreate individual genes or to consume pleasure. Vonnegut's characters are ill-served by allowing themselves to let Darwin's evolutionary mythology or the survival of the fittest validate their moral order and guide them stage by stage throughout the course of their lives. The resulting moral order, making individual interest the supreme goal, negates human connectedness to a larger pattern or the human community.

In *Galápagos*, Mary's decision to create a new race is supported and validated by a Darwinian social order or the materialistic morality of survival of the fittest, and that order or morality guides her stage by stage in strength throughout life. According to the sociological function of the evolutionary mythology, Mary, following Darwin, must preserve the "favourable individual differences and variations" and allow for the "destruction of those which are injurious." She accomplishes this by creating a new race out of the genetics of the innocent simple folk Akiko and Kamikaze. However, as Leon informs us, Darwin's notion of natural selection or the survival of the fittest guides Mary's "big brain," and by this guidance, she accomplishes the repair job for all of humanity. Also, when Mary learns that there is a classification between favorable individuals and injurious ones, we learn "how to live a human lifetime under these circumstances." We learn that to evolve in a world dominated by these values, we must, like Mary, accept that classification.

Although Vonnegut exploits Darwin's notion of a superior race for his fictive purpose, this idea or ideology has mythic implications, according to Northrop Frye. He states: "The coming of mythical analogies to evolution in the nineteenth century [. . . or] what is called social Darwinism, for instance, tried to rationalize the authority of European societies over 'inferior' ones" (174). According to Frye, the belief that Europeans are superior to savages is mythic in itself. He also points out how this ideology becomes a "popular mythology" that can he used to "rationalize the authority of European societies over 'inferior' ones" like that of Akiko and Kamikaze. Therefore, according to Vonnegut's *Galápagos* and the evolutionary mythology, a specific moral order can be derived from the science of Darwin's notion of the survival of the fittest, and it can guide individuals "stage by stage" in "strength" through the whole foreseeable course of a useful life. However true this moral order is, it nevertheless reduces society to tribalism or harsh individualism, because, as Darwin argues, natural selection, or the central mechanism of the evolutionary mythology, must preserve "favourable individual differences and variations" and destroy "those which are injurious."

However, Vonnegut rejects this harsh individualism or tribalism when, by inversion, he parodies in *Galápagos* the European element in Darwin's myth. Moreover, Vonnegut's inversion or perversion of Darwin's narrative adds an ironic element to his novel. Mary Hepburn is of European descent, and the common progenitor of Akiko's descendants. Instead of beginning the story of evolution with the savage Akiko and ending it with the superior European Mary Hepburn (as Darwin's myth does), Vonnegut reverses Darwin's line of descent by beginning it with Mary and continuing it with Akiko and her descendants. In doing so, Vonnegut rejects the myth, or morality, that Europeans are superior to savages. Moreover, he constructs his narrative so that the European white savagery is repaired instead (ironically, by Darwin's notion of natural selection) by evolving to innocent fisherfolk. Hence, Vonnegut feels that those who have invented a myth to dominate other races in the name of evolutionary science are injurious to the whole of humanity.

In *The Sirens of Titan* and *Slaughterhouse-Five*, the same evolutionary science sanctions a Darwinian morality in the societies portrayed, and this evolutionary morality instructs both Unk and Billy Pilgrim about how to live. As in *Galápagos*, the specific moral order in *Sirens* derives its justification from Darwin's notion of natural selection. Unk, the principle character in *Sirens*, no longer believes in an absolute moral authority "out there" and therefore in no absolute universal meaning. Yet, the opening page of *Sirens* declares, "Everyone now knows how to find the meaning of life within himself." The key word to understanding the sociological change that Unk's society is undergoing is "now." It implies that society has changed since World War II, and the cause of that change is probably the impact of evolutionary science on the human condition. As Vonnegut's narrator in *Galápagos* declares of Darwin (and I agree), "He thereupon penned the most broadly influential scientific volume produced during the entire era of great big brains. It did more to stabilize people's volatile opinions of how to identify success or failure than any other tome" (13). Consequently, the meaning of life in *The Sirens of Titan* is "now" sought within oneself and not "out there" in the community, or even in a realm beyond the natural confines of the human brain.

Moreover, Unk principally learns this evolutionary morality from an experience he has in the chrono-synclastic infundibula, which is also a popular form of moral relativism. According to the chrono-synclastic infundibula, "there are so many different ways of being right" (9). Therefore, according to the morality Unk experiences there and to the declaration in the opening page of *Sirens*, "Everyone now knows how to find the meaning of life within himself." This belief engenders a social order in the novel that is sanctioned by Darwin's notion of natural selection. First, we read on the opening page of the novel that "[w]hat mankind hoped to learn in its outward push was who was actually in charge of all creation, and what all creation was all about." Unk learns that the meaning of life is within himself, but he is instructed "what all creation was about" after experiencing the chrono-synclastic infundibula. That experience teaches him that "I was a victim of a series of accidents [...] As are we all." Hence, Unk learns the cosmic explanation sanctioned by Darwin's ideology of natural selection. Also, the pedagogical function of the mythology, or the ideology of the phrase "I was a victim of a series of accidents [...] As are we all," informs him how to live stage by stage under his evolutionary circumstances. For example, if his life is determined by accidents, then he has no free will and is not responsible for his actions. That is why the meaning of life is reduced to his own individual interpretation, which is nothing other than moral relativism. Consequently, moral relativism, or "the different ways of being right," or that meaning within himself guides him in life, sanctioned by the science of evolution—or that "series of accidents."

Similarly, in *Slaughterhouse-Five*, Billy understands the sociological implications of the evolution mythology. For him, too, there is no God and, therefore, no universal morality governing his life and his universe. In Billy's universe, Darwinian ideology replaces God or any absolute universal meaning. The Tralfamadorians instruct him first about this when they tell him about their system of beliefs: "There is no beginning, no middle, no end, no suspense, no moral, no causes, no effects" (88). However, the Tralfamadorian mythology can be explained in terms of Darwin's ideology. Boodin states that according to Darwinism, "History runs on like an old man's tale without beginning, middle, or end, without any guiding plot. It is infinite and formless" (77). According to Boodin's view of Darwinism and the Tralfamadorian mythology, history is infinite and has no "beginning, middle, or end." Because there is no first or final cause, "Chance is God." Moreover, if chance is God, then, as Vonnegut's narrator concurs, there is no moral to be learned in this "certain social order" other than that our lives, fundamentally, are explained in terms of a series of accidents or Darwin's notion of the survival of the fittest. In this way, Darwin's notion of survival of the fittest becomes the existing morality.

Like Unk's experience in the chrono-synclastic infundibula, Billy's becoming unstuck in time (a "time" that has no beginning, middle, or end) symbolizes his entry into the Darwinian order, and like Unk, Billy also experiences
a "baptism" into moral relativism. Moreover, once Billy becomes unstuck in
time, the Tralfamadorians instruct him on how to live according to these circumstances. They teach him that in life, "[t]here is no beginning, no middle,
no end, no suspense, no moral, no causes, no effects" (88); that "[a]ll moments,
past, present, and future always have existed, always will exist" (26). However,
Boodin, discussing S. Alexander's *Space, Time and Deity,* states that

> [t]he abstractions of space and time are invested with metaphysical
> properties which have nothing to do with the mathematical origin
> of these concepts. Space becomes a metaphysical continuum and
> not just a mathematical continuum, and thus space furnishes
> continuity to the instants of time. Space also has the property of
> conserving the instants of time. Space furnishes the continuity and
> time the content. (87)

According to Alexander, time and content are inseparable, so becoming
unstuck in time would also mean becoming unstuck in content. Thus, Billy's
"unstuck" experience has loosened him from any absolute meaning. In fact,
that is the philosophy that the Tralfs teach Billy: "There isn't any particular
relationship between all the messages. [. . .] There is [. . .] no [absolute]
moral." Moreover, once Billy "converts" to the Tralf mythology, he becomes
unstuck from any content or meaning; therefore, the moral relativism of the
evolutionary mythology replaces his earlier absolute morality.

In *Mother Night,* the moral implications of evolution mythology im-
press on its central character, Howard Campbell, the specific social order of
Darwin's ideology of survival of the fittest and instruct him "stage by stage"
throughout the course of his life to adapt to his environment at all cost.
Moreover, like Vonnegut's other characters, Howard Campbell suffers the
gravest consequences when he lives according to the ideology of this mythology. For example, by the end of the novel, "He is so used up that he can't love
any more. There is nothing left of him but curiosity and a pair of eyes" (166).
His demise is the result of many precarious adaptations to the war-time environment of the novel. Before the war, he is a successful American-born
playwright in Germany. Once the war begins, Campbell adapts to the role
of radio propagandist for Hitler; once the United States enters the war (and,
consequently, threatens Hitler's success) Campbell adapts to the role of an
American double agent. The evolutionary mythology or morality impressed
on him that it is more important to adapt to his environment and survive
than to be loyal to one absolute position.

After there "is nothing left of him but curiosity and a pair of eyes," Campbell blames these precarious adaptations on the Nazi totalitarian mind. However, on examining this totalitarian mind, we conclude that it is the ideology of social Darwinism that conditioned him. Campbell describes the totalitarian mind as follows: "I have never seen a more sublime demonstration of the totalitarian mind, a mind which might be likened unto a system of gears whose teeth have been filed off at random. [. . .] The missing teeth, of course, are simple, obvious truths, truths available and comprehensible even to ten-year-olds, in most cases" (162). He admits that those teeth, or absolute truths, have been removed by a "random-thought" machine, or Darwin's mechanism of natural selection, and this "random-thought" machine conditions the whole culture described in the novel. Hence, as Campbell says, "That was how Nazi Germany could sense no important difference between civilization and hydrophobia" (163).

Moreover, Campbell tells us the extent to which social Darwinism has transformed Adolf Eichmann's mind into a totalitarian, "relativistic" mind: "I offer my opinion that Eichmann cannot distinguish right and wrong—that not only right and wrong, but truth and falsehood, hope and despair, beauty and ugliness, kindness and cruelty, comedy and tragedy, are all processed by Eichmann's mind indiscriminately" (123–124). Tragically, in embracing the Nazi mythology derived from social Darwinism, Eichmann, Hoess, Campbell's father-in-law, Nazi Germany, and Campbell have all explained any absolute morality indiscriminately, and now they must find their own relative meaning within themselves to survive, stage by stage, through the course of their lives.

In *Breakfast of Champions*, the evolutionary mythology sanctions a materialistic moral order in the American society portrayed by Vonnegut, and these materialistic values inform Dwayne Hoover "stage by stage" through the course of his life. Accordingly, in *Breakfast*, the evolutionary mythology imposes on the characters the belief that human value and self-worth increase proportionately with the accumulation of valuable possessions or measurable things; consequently, measurement and the accumulation of "things" toward an absolute amount of possessions will supposedly provide meaningful value. Dwayne's materialistic morality is evident when he reduces the meaning of happiness and fulfillment to bodily pleasures or the acquisition of material things. Dwayne owned

not only the Pontiac agency and a piece of the new Holiday Inn. He owned three Burger Chefs, too, and five coin-operated car washes, and pieces of the Sugar Creek Drive-In Theatre, Radio Station WMCY, the Three Maples Par-Three Golf Course, and seventeen hundred shares of common stock in Barrytron, Limited,

a local electronics firm. He owned dozens of vacant lots. He was
on the Board of Directors of the Midland County National Bank.
(64–65)

Dwayne's wealth is large; he has consumed the whole city, and the value of
his measure provokes awe in others. An employee who overhears Dwayne
singing at the Holiday Inn comments, "If I owned what he owns, I'd sing,
too" (41). Vonnegut portrays a materialistic moral order in *Breakfast* that
captivates and controls many characters in the society. These materialistic
values are sanctioned by the ideology of scientific materialism or a Darwinian "*a priori* commitment to materialism" (Johnson 76).

Moreover, Vonnegut would have us believe that scientific materialism
provides the basis for his characters' values. Sallye Sheppeard states:

> That the values fostered by science and technology prove more
> detrimental than beneficial to mankind also finds expression in
> Vonnegut's other early novels, but of these, *Breakfast of Champions*
> (1973) contains their grimmest exposé. Its setting and narrative
> clearly reflect the debilitating effects of contemporary American
> society, via science and technology, upon the human spirit. (17)

According to Sheppeard, contemporary American society lives by the values fostered by science and technology, leading us to conclude that when
science sanctions these values, science functions like myth. Moreover, the
Americans in *Breakfast* derive their values according to certain rules of
science, and more specifically an evolutionary science. The "debilitating
effects" of those rules on American society manifest themselves in the form
of popular materialism.

The implications of these materialistic values raise new questions. First,
for how long will Darwinist theory have an affect on our human geography?
George Streeter provides at least one answer when he stated: "Our great [sci-
entific] heroes are those who succeed in cleverly expressing the complex phenomena of nature in the form of precisely stated laws, or archetypal patterns,
and we grade our heroes according to the length of time their laws or patterns
endure" (405). Darwin's theory was published almost one hundred and fifty
years ago (1859); earlier in this essay I quoted praise for Darwin by the narrator of *Galápagos*. To that statement, I would add that Darwin's *Origin of
Species* is also the most broadly influential scientific volume of the twentieth
century and perhaps of decades to come.

A second question raised by this study is, will the evolution mythology
replace the traditional Judeo-Christian mythology and become the dominant
mythology in Western society? From what we have learned from Vonnegut's

writings, the answer is "No"—unless those who espouse it can overcome three barriers mentioned by Suzi Gablik in *Has Modernism Failed?*

Although we may value technological power more than sacred wisdom, scientific rationalism has so far failed to prove itself as a successful integrating mythology for industrial society; *it offers no inner archetypal mediators of divine power, no cosmic connectedness, no sense of belonging to a larger pattern.* (94; emphasis added)

The relevance of Gablik's three barriers (taken in reverse order) can be verified with examples from any Vonnegut novel discussed in this essay. Unk's conversion to the evolutionary mythology provides *"no sense of belonging to a larger pattern"* because he now "knows how to find the meaning of life within himself" (1). In fact, examples from the other characters examined here— Mary Hepburn, Billy Pilgrim, Howard Campbell, and Dwayne Hoover— could also support this point. In the novels discussed, a *"cosmic connectedness,"* appears to be operating within the evolutionary mythology, especially when we consider that Darwin's theory serves many mythological functions, but once these pertinent properties are raised from the deepest unconsciousness, the sole cosmic connectedness we find in the mythology is characterized by the material and ruthless workings of natural selection, hardly enough to keep a community together.[1] The strongest example of *"inner archetypal mediators of divine power"* in the novels is, again, natural selection. Although natural selection plays a pseudo-divine role in evolutionary mythology in its apparent ability to select life or death, I conclude that Darwin's notion is no more than a materialistic replacement for the Judeo-Christian notion of the Holy Spirit. Natural selection impels us to reduce all the workings of the universe to materialistic ends, so there can be no mention of "spirit" or any teleological element in science per se.

NOTE

1. A recent computer-animated film, *Dinosaur,* written by John Harrison (1999), is a clever expression of the newer neo-Darwinian notion of evolution through cooperation rather than the old Darwinian competition (Godawa 122).

WORKS CITED

Bergman, Jerry. "The History of Evolution's Teaching of Women's Inferiority." *Perspectives on Science and Christian Faith* 48.3 (June 1992): 109–123.
Boodin, John E. *Cosmic Evolution.* New York: Kraus, 1972.
Campbell, Joseph. *Myths to Live By.* New York: Bantam, 1972.
Darwin, Charles. *The Origin of Species.* New York: Mentor, 1859.

Freese, Peter. "Vonnegut's Invented Religions as Sense-Making System." *The Vonnegut Chronicles: Interviews and Essays.* Ed. Peter J. Reed. Westport, CT: Greenwood, 1996. 145–164.

Frye, Northrop. *Words with Power.* Markham, Ontario: Viking, 1990.

Gablik, Suzi. *Has Modernism Failed?* New York: Thames, 1984.

Godawa, Brian. *Hollywood Worldviews.* Downers Grove, IL: InterVarsity, 2002.

Johnson, Phillip E. *Objections Sustained.* Downers Grove, IL: InterVarsity, 1998.

Midgley, Mary. *Science as Salvation: A Modern Myth and Its Meaning.* New York: Routledge, 1992.

Monod, Jacques. *Chance and Necessity.* New York: Knopf, 1971.

Runes, Dagobert D. *Dictionary of Philosophy.* 15th ed. New York: Philosophical, 1960.

Sheppeard, Sallye. "Kurt Vonnegut and the Myth of Scientific Progress." *Journal of the American Studies Association of Texas* 16.1 (1985): 14–19.

Sproul, R. C. *Not a Chance: The Myth of Chance in Modern Science and Cosmology.* Grand Rapids, MI: Baker, 1994.

Streeter, George L. "Archetype and Symbolism." *Science* 65.1687 (Apr. 29, 1927): 405–412.

Vonnegut, Kurt, Jr. *Breakfast of Champions.* New York: Dell, 1973.

———. *Galápagos.* New York: Dell, 1985.

———. *Mother Night.* New York: Dell, 1962.

———. *The Sirens of Titan.* New York: Dell, 1959.

———. *Slaughterhouse-Five.* New York: Dell, 1969.

KEVIN BROWN

"A Launching Pad of Belief":
Kurt Vonnegut and Postmodern Humor

Humor critics have argued that satire is not possible any longer, largely due to the horrors of the twentieth century and the postmodern belief in the lack of objective truth, especially in relation to morality. Because of these developments, they argue that no moral stance can be taken through satire; instead, satirists now write merely for pleasure, not to instigate any change in morality. Several postmodern authors, including Kurt Vonnegut, however, still attempt to provide moral messages through their writing. John Gardner, for example, attacked existentialism in *Grendel*. Several critics, though, misread the novel and viewed the narrator and the author as having the same worldview. Because he did not establish a moral norm from which to work, he was misunderstood. Vonnegut, however, did not assume that there is a common set of values held by their readers. Instead, he laid out a moral base from which to work from within the work itself.

Postmodern humor is often characterized as rebelling against the norms of literature and trying to subvert them with no motivation other than pleasure. In *Circus of the Mind in Motion*, Lance Olsen shows the purpose of postmodern humor to be revolutionary in its motivation. Using Duchamp as an illustration of the motivation behind postmodern art (writing included), Olsen writes that "Duchamp had no intention of improving or even changing the critics' minds. Rather, his impulse was to subvert a power structure for

Studies in American Humor, Volume 3, Number 14 (2006): pp. 47–54. Copyright © 2006 Kevin Brown.

171

no other reason than the pleasure of subverting a power structure" (18). Olsen takes this idea farther to do away with any authority and any final interpretation the reader may hope to gather; instead, "the impetus of postmodern humor is to disarm pomposity and power. The postmodern creator becomes aesthetic and metaphysical terrorist, a freeplayer in a universe of intertextuality where no one text has any more or less authority than any other" (18). This lack of authority causes the idea of a final authorial position to be radically thrown into question: "The audience often senses a complexity and subtlety of tone, but because the postmodern creator manipulates a system of private instead of public norms, his or her final position remains uncertain . . . Because of this, his or her text exists to be interpreted in radically different, even contradictory, ways" (18).

While Olsen's theory destroys all sense of a final meaning, Harry Levin proposes a different view of how one interprets humor. In *Playboys and Kill-joys*, Levin proposes that there is a basis that the author draws upon in humor, especially in satire: "Every satirist, negative though he may sound, must project his guided missiles from a launching-pad of belief" (196). What Levin attempts to do here is to illustrate how the satirist creates a set of public norms, as Olsen describes them, by taking his or her private norms and declaring them openly. This approach would be akin to Swift's beginning "A Modest Proposal" with some sort of introduction letting the reader know that eating children is, for one reason or another, morally wrong. He would not even have to do this didactically, but he would have to convey it clearly in order to create a public norm the reader would react to.

Olsen, however, argues that there is no "launching-pad of belief" anymore; he argues that college freshmen misread "A Modest Proposal" because we live in a world where "in fact a portion of the global population *did* believe it right to kill children and turn them into lampshades and gloves" (86–87). However, this approach presupposes that the students in these classes believe that eating children is a moral norm somewhere in the world. Instead, all of my students argue that Swift needs some sort of counseling or punishment, showing that they still do rely on moral norms in their reading. In fact, they believe in these norms so strongly that they cannot imagine anyone suggesting we break them, even satirically, which is why they actually misread Swift.

However, Leonard Feinberg shows other difficulties that arise when one argues that satire relies on moral norms for its effectiveness: "The assumption that satire relies on moral norms is so widely accepted that one hesitates to challenge it. But moral norms are not easy to define. Many satirists consider their work moral even when it contradicts the satire of other writers who also call themselves moralists" (9). Feinberg, however, does admit that satire relies on some type of norm when he writes, "Of course satire relies on norms. The moment one criticizes and says that something has been done in the wrong way, he is implying that there is a right way to do it" (11). Levin argues that the satirist can persuade his or her reader that something is wrong with an idea and then satirize that idea, thus creating his or her own moral norm:

> Yet the satirist must convince his audience that, when something is rotten or someone goes astray, there has been a departure from a certain ethos. It is simpler for him when the norms of that ethos have already been accepted by convention. Otherwise, it becomes a part of his job to inculcate those norms—in other words, to preach to the unconverted. He must be hortatory before he can wax sardonic, like Bernard Shaw in the prefaces to his plays. (197)

In *Slaughterhouse-Five*, Kurt Vonnegut establishes his moral norm by showing the outcome of Billy Pilgrim's philosophy in relation to the bombing of Dresden and the Germans' massacre of the Jews.

Billy Pilgrim learns his philosophy of passive acceptance from the Tralfamadorians, aliens who capture him. They teach him that one should not look for reasons why things happen; he or she should simply allow them to happen. When Billy asks, "How—how did I get here?" they respond, "It would take another Earthling to explain it to you. Earthlings are the great explainers, explaining why this event is structured as it is, telling how other events may be achieved or avoided. I am a Tralfamadorian, seeing all time as you might see a stretch of the Rocky Mountains. All time is all time. It does not change. It does not lend itself to warnings or explanations. It simply *is*" (85–86). Since everything simply is, one does not question what happens or believe that one could change the course of events. When Billy asks how the universe ends, the Tralfamadorians say, "We blow it up, experimenting with new fuels for our flying saucers. A Tralfamadorian test pilot presses a starter button, and the whole Universe disappears." Billy responds, "If you know this . . . isn't there some way you can prevent it? Can't you keep the pilot from *pressing* the button?" The Tralfamadorian guide answers, "He has *always* pressed it, and he always *will*. We *always* let him and we always *will* let him. The moment is *structured* that way" (116–117). This philosophy denies the human capability to prevent any event. Wayne McGinnis comments concerning the Tralfamadorian philosophy, "Their little formula 'so it goes' said ritualistically throughout the novel whenever death, no matter how trivial, is mentioned, is from the human point of view, the height of fatalism" (116). By merely accepting the end of the universe and any other catastrophe, they deny the human potential for change.

Vonnegut ridicules this idea by connecting the Tralfamadorian view to the views of those who defend the bombing of Dresden. When Billy is in the hospital after a plane crash, he shares a room with Professor Rumfoord, who is writing a book on the bombing of Dresden. Rumfoord tells Billy, "It *had* to be done," which echoes the Tralfamadorian view of the end of the universe. Billy accepts this justification because of the philosophy he learned from the Tralfamadorians: "It was all right . . . *Everything* is all right, and everybody has to do exactly what he does. I learned that on Tralfamadore" (18). Critics' neglect of this connection leads to misinterpretation, as Merrill points out when he writes, "The interpretive problem with *Slaughterhouse-Five* is roughly the same as with the books already discussed. The objective evidence of the text is supposed to persuade us that the Tralfamadorian philosophy, as reflected in such characters as General Rumfoord, is *humanly* unacceptable" (178). Vonnegut's paralleling of Rumfoord's defense of the bombing of Dresden with the quietism practiced by Billy shows the outcome of the Tralfamadorian philosophy.

Vonnegut further mocks the idea of unquestioning acceptance by connecting the Tralfamadorian philosophy with the philosophy of the Germans. When Billy is taken aboard the Tralfamadorian spaceship, he asks, "Why me?" The Tralfamadorians respond, "That is a very *Earthling* question to ask, Mr. Pilgrim. Why *you?* Why *us* for that matter? Why *anything?* Because this moment simply *is.* Have you ever seen bugs trapped in amber? . . . Well, here we are Mr. Pilgrim, trapped in the amber of this moment. There is no *why*" (76–77). This exchange parallels a scene that takes place in a German prison camp. One of the American soldiers makes a comment that a guard does not like; the guard then knocks out two of the American's teeth. The American asks the guard, "Why me?" The guard responds, "Vy you? Vy anybody?" (91). This type of unquestioning acceptance of the status quo leads to a bombing of Dresden or to a slaughter of the Jews, and it is this type of philosophy to which Vonnegut is opposed.

Vonnegut further criticizes Billy's philosophy by presenting him as self-deluded and possibly insane. When Billy commits himself to a mental institution, he meets Eliot Rosewater, who is trying to deal with the same problem Billy has:

> They had both found life meaningless, partly because of what they had seen in the war. Rosewater, for instance, had shot a fourteen-year-old fireman, mistaking him for a German soldier. So it goes. And Billy had seen the greatest massacre in European history, which was the fire-bombing of Dresden . . . So they were trying to re-invent themselves and their universe. (101)

Rosewater tells Billy at one point that everything there was to know about life was in *The Brothers Karamazov,* adding "But that isn't *enough* any more" (101). Later, Billy hears Rosewater tell the psychiatrist, "I think you guys are going to have to come up with a lot of wonderful new lies, or people aren't going to want to go on living" (101). As Merrill points out, "Like [John] Gardner, Vonnegut creates a sympathetic protagonist who adopts a deterministic philosophy in order to make sense out of life's apparent randomness" (177). Billy, therefore, tries to develop new lies to live his life; but in his attempt, he creates the Tralfamadorians and their philosophy.

Billy develops the Tralfamadorians through Kilgore Trout, a science fiction author whose books Rosewater collects and allows Billy to read while in the hospital. One of these books was *Maniacs in the Fourth Dimension*, which was about "people whose mental diseases couldn't be treated because the causes of the diseases were all in the fourth dimension, and three-dimensional Earthling doctors couldn't see those causes at all, or even imagine them" (104). One of the Tralfamadorians' teachings was that many things, such as other genders, exist in the fourth dimension. Another Kilgore Trout book that influenced his Tralfamadorian experience was *The Big Board*, which was "about an Earthling man and woman who were kidnapped by extra-terrestrials. They were put on display in a zoo on a planet called Zircon-212" (201). Billy is supposedly captured by the Tralfamadorians and put on display in a zoo with a woman named Montana Wildhack. His development of the Tralfamadorians is a self-defense mechanism to deal with the horrors he saw at the bombing of Dresden.

Slaughterhouse-Five has been misinterpreted by critics who argue that Vonnegut is advocating a passive stance in view of the horrors of the world. For example, Robert W. Uphaus writes, "To put it another way: people, including Kurt Vonnegut, Jr., are free to self-actualize but they must never expect such self-actualization to alter, fundamentally, the course of human history" (167). Robert Merrill points out this misinterpretation when he comments, "Even such excellent critics as Alfred Kazin and Tony Tanner have agreed that 'The main idea emerging from *Slaughterhouse-Five* seems to be that the proper response to life is one of the rejected acceptance'" (178). Merrill goes on to add,

> As it happens, however, our problems in reading *Grendel* [by John Gardner] are very similar to our difficulties in reading such recent fabulations as John Barth's *The Floating Opera* (1956), Joseph Heller's *Catch-22* (1961), Kurt Vonnegut's *Slaughterhouse-Five* (1969), and many other well-known books in this mode. For reasons I will discuss later, modern fabulators have tended to produce works in which it is essential that we perceive the errors of their basically sympathetic protagonists. If we fail to note these errors, or if we interpret them inappropriately, we are in danger not only of misconstruing the author's meaning but of actually reversing it. (162)

The reason for this misinterpretation is that critics believe that Billy Pilgrim's attitudes are synonymous with Vonnegut's; however, Vonnegut distances himself from Pilgrim by showing the hazards of Pilgrim's philosophy and by presenting Pilgrim as a questionable, if not unreliable, narrator.

Another reason that *Slaughterhouse-Five* has been misinterpreted results from a comment that Vonnegut makes in the opening chapter. He relates a conversation he had about *Slaughterhouse-Five:*

> Over the years, people I've met have often asked me what I'm working on, and I've usually replied that the main thing was a book about Dresden. I said that to Harrison Staff, the movie-maker, one time, and he raised his eyebrows and inquired, "Is it an anti-war book?" "Yes," I said, "I guess." "You know what I say to people when I hear they're writing anti-war books?" "No. What do you say, Harrison Star?" "I say, 'Why don't you write an anti-*glacier* book instead?'" What he meant, of course, was that there would always be wars, that they were as easy to stop as glaciers. I believe that, too. And even if wars didn't keep coming like glaciers, there would still be plain old death. (3–4)

This interchange has been seen as a confirmation of the passive acceptance of wars and other such atrocities; however, Vonnegut is merely viewing the situation realistically. Vonnegut has certainly done this in many of his other works and speeches. In an address to the graduating class of Bennington College in 1970, he said, "I know that millions of dollars have been spent to produce this splendid graduating class, and that the main hope of your teachers was, once they got through with you, that you would no longer be superstitious. I'm sorry—I have to undo that now. I beg you to believe in the most ridiculous superstition of all: that humanity is at the center of the universe, the fulfiller or the frustrator of the grandest dreams of God almighty" (163). As John May writes, "There is, it seems to me, considerable evidence that Vonnegut would steer us from one course of action because he has something better in mind, although there is a marked inclination to dwell on the limitations of the possibilities before us. His tendency to limit the humanly possible so severely is, in fact, an almost desperate plea to the reader to avoid the destructively quixotic" (123). Vonnegut knows that one book is not going to end wars, and even if it did, there would still be death.

This recognition of the effects of satire is reminiscent of Jonathan Swift's comment in the letter from Captain Gulliver to his cousin Sympson at the beginning of *Gulliver's Travels:* "And so it hath proved; for instead of seeing a full Stop put to all Abuses and Corruptions, at least in this little Island, as I had Reason to expect: Behold, after six Months Warning, I cannot learn that my

Book hath produced one single Effect according to mine Intentions . . ." (viii). Vonnegut, like Swift, realizes that change will not come in six months, or even more, based on one book. Instead, change happens in individuals long before it happens in societies. John May supports this view: "We may not be able, Vonnegut is saying, to undo the harm that has been done, but we can certainly love, simply because they are people, those who have been made useless by our past stupidity and greed, our previous crimes against our brothers. And if that seems insane, then the better the world for such folly" (125). Vonnegut encourages local action, rather than hoping that society will change in a short period of time.

Not only does he encourage pacifism, he practices it in relation to his own family. In the opening chapter he writes, "I have told my sons that they are not under any circumstances to take part in massacres, and that the news of massacres of enemies is not to fill them with satisfaction or glee. I have also told them not to work for companies which make massacre machinery, and to express contempt for people who think we need machinery like that" (19). Even if no one is changed by this book, Vonnegut promises to try to pass his peaceful philosophy on to his children. He seems to have succeeded at least at this: His son, Mark, is a doctor; his oldest daughter, Edith, is an artist, as is his second daughter, Nanette.

Vonnegut's message in *Slaughterhouse-Five* is not ambivalent, as Olsen argues concerning postmodern humor; instead, the reader must read carefully to separate Billy Pilgrim from Kurt Vonnegut. Vonnegut even clearly states his viewpoint in opposition to Pilgrim in the last chapter of the book when he says, "If what Billy Pilgrim learned from the Tralfamadorians is true, that we will all live forever, no matter how dead we may sometimes seem to be, I am not overjoyed" (211). If it is taken out of context, Billy Pilgrim's viewpoint could be seen as that of Vonnegut; however, when one examines the connections between Pilgrim's views and those of the Germans and the supporters of the bombing of Dresden, Vonnegut's message of working toward peace becomes evident.

The problem Vonnegut faced in 1969 with *Slaughterhouse-Five* is one that continues to plague both writers and readers. Readers are hesitant to accept any writer's view of the world as true; thus, the writers must establish the view of the world they are taking. In so doing, the reader knows what to expect, preparing the way for norms that can be used to satirize differing opinions. Otherwise, misreading, such as what happened with many critics who commented on *Slaughterhouse-Five* and *Grendel*, will continue to happen.

WORKS CITED

Feinberg, Leonard. *Introduction to Satire*. Iowa: Iowa State University Press, 1967.
Levin, Harry. *Playboys and Killjoys*. New York: Oxford University Press, 1987.

May, John R. "Vonnegut's Humor and the Limits of Hope." *The Critical Response to Kurt Vonnegut.* Ed. Leonard Mustazza. Westport, Ct.: Greenwood Press, 1994. 123–133.

McGinnis, Wayne D. "The Arbitrary Cycle of *Slaughterhouse-Five.*" *The Critical Response to Kurt Vonnegut.* Ed. Leonard Mustazza. Westport, Ct.: Greenwood Press, 1994. 113–122.

Merrill, Robert. "John Gardner's *Grendel* and the Interpretation of Modern Fables." *American Literature* 56:2 (May 1984): 162–180.

Olsen, Lance. *Circus of the Mind in Motion.* Detroit: Wayne State University Press, 1990.

Swift, Jonathan. *Gulliver s Travels.* 1727. New York: Modern Library, 1985.

Uphaus, Robert W. "Expected Meaning in Vonnegut's Dead-End Fiction." *The Critical Response to Kurt Vonnegut.* Ed. Leonard Mustazza. Westport, Ct.: Greenwood Press, 1994. 165–174.

Vonnegut, Kurt. "Address to Graduating Class at Bennington College, 1970." *Wampeters, Foma, and Granfaloons.* New York: Dell Publishing Group, 1974. 159–168.

———. *Slaughterhouse-Five.* 1969. New York: Dell Publishing Group, 1988.

Chronology

1922   Kurt Vonnegut born on Armistice Day, November 11, in Indianapolis, Indiana. His grandfather was the first licensed architect in Indiana; his father, Kurt Vonnegut Sr., is a wealthy architect; his mother, Edith Lieber Vonnegut, is the daughter of a socially prominent family. He has an older brother, Bernard, and a sister, Alice.

1929   With the Great Depression, the family fortune disappears.

1936–1940   Attends Shortridge High School, where he becomes editor of the *Shortridge Daily Echo*, the first high-school daily newspaper in the country.

1940   Enters Cornell University as a chemistry and biology major. Becomes columnist and managing editor of the *Cornell Daily Sun*.

1943   Hospitalized for pneumonia and loses draft deferment; enlists in the United States Army.

1943–1944   Studies mechanical engineering at Carnegie Mellon University as part of military training.

1944   Returns home before shipping out; mother commits suicide by overdosing on sleeping pills, Mother's Day, May 14. Joins 106th Infantry Division; on December 19, Vonnegut becomes German prisoner of war after being captured at Battle of the Bulge. Sent to Dresden, an "open city" presumably not threatened with Allied attack. Works with other POWs in a vitamin-syrup factory.

1945	On February 13–14, U.S. and British air forces firebomb Dresden, killing 135,000. Vonnegut and other POWs, quartered in the cellar of a slaughterhouse, survive, he later writes that they emerged to find "135,000 Hansels and Gretels had been baked like gingerbread men." Works as a "corpse miner" in the aftermath of the bombing; on May 22, Vonnegut repatriated. Marries childhood friend Jane Marie Cox on September 1 and moves to Chicago.
1945–1947	Studies anthropology at the University of Chicago. Works as police reporter for Chicago City News Bureau.
1947	After master's thesis rejected, moves to Schenectady, New York, to work as publicist for General Electric, where his brother Bernard is a physicist. Begins writing fiction.
1950	First short story, "Report on the Barnhouse Effect," published in *Collier's*, February 11.
1951	Begins writing full-time. Family moves to West Barnstable, Massachusetts, on Cape Cod.
1952	First novel, *Player Piano*, published; sells short stories to magazines, including *Collier's* and the *Saturday Evening Post*.
1953–1958	Publishes short stories, works in public relations, runs a Saab dealership, teaches English at a school for the emotionally disturbed.
1957	Father dies October 1. Sister Alice's husband dies in commuter train accident; Alice dies of cancer less than forty-eight hours later; the Vonneguts adopt their three children.
1959	Second novel, *The Sirens of Titan*, published.
1961	Collection of stories, *Canary in a Cat House*, published.
1962	*Mother Night* published.
1963	*Cat's Cradle* published.
1964	*God Bless You, Mr. Rosewater* published and attracts serious critical attention. Begins publishing essays and reviews in *Venture*, the *New York Times Book Review*, *Esquire*, and *Harper's*.

1965–1967	Begins two-year residency at the University of Iowa Writer's Workshop. Novels reissued as paperback editions become popular with college students, and attract serious critical attention.
1968	Receives Guggenheim Fellowship; revisits Dresden. A collection of short stories, *Welcome to the Monkey House*, published.
1969	*Slaughterhouse-Five; or the Children's Crusade* published and becomes best-seller.
1970	Takes up residence, alone, in New York City; a play, *Happy Birthday, Wanda June*, produced Off-Broadway. Serves as Briggs-Copeland Lecturer at Harvard University. Awarded M.A. from University of Chicago: *Cat's Cradle* accepted in lieu of thesis.
1972	*Between Time and Timbuktu* produced for public television; *Slaughterhouse-Five* released as motion picture. Covers Republican National Convention for *Harper's*, elected vice president of PEN; becomes member of National Institute of Arts and Letters.
1973	*Breakfast of Champions; or Goodbye, Blue Monday!* published; appointed Distinguished Professor on English Prose at the City University of New York.
1974	*Wampeters, Foma, and Granfalloons*, a collection of essays, speeches, and reviews, published.
1975	Son Mark publishes *The Eden Express: A Personal Account of Schizophrenia*.
1976	*Slapstick; or Lonesome No More!* published. It is a critical failure.
1979	*Jailbird* published. First marriage ends in divorce; marries photographer Jill Krementz.
1980	A children's book, *Sun Moon Star*, published in collaboration with illustrator Ivan Chermayeff.
1981	*Palm Sunday: An Autobiographical Collage* published.
1982	*Deadeye Dick* published; *Fates Worse than Death* published in England as pamphlet by the Bertrand Russell Peace Foundation.

1985	*Galápagos* published.

1986   Jane Vonnegut Yarmolinsky, his former wife, dies of cancer in December.

1987   *Bluebeard* published. *Angels Without Wings: A Courageous Family's Triumph over Tragedy*, by Jane Vonnegut Yarmolinsky, published; it is the story of adopting and raising her sister-in-law's children.

1990   *Hocus Pocus* published.

1991   *Even Worse Than Death: An Autobiographical Collage of the 1980's* published. With wife Jill Krementz, files petition for divorce; it is later withdrawn.

1996   Robert Weide's film adaptation of *Mother Night* is released nationally by Fine Line Features. A stage adaptation of *Slaughterhouse-Five* premieres at the Steppenwolf Theatre Company in Chicago.

1997   *Timequake* published. Brother Bernard dies.

1999   Film version of *Breakfast of Champions* is distributed in limited release; *Bagombo Snuff Box* published.

2000   *God Bless You, Dr.* published.

2005   *A Man Without a Country,* edited by Dan Simon, published.

2007   Kurt Vonnegut dies April 11.

2008   *Armageddon in Retrospect* published.

Contributors

HAROLD BLOOM is Sterling Professor of the Humanities at Yale University. He is the author of 30 books, including *Shelley's Mythmaking* (1959), *The Visionary Company* (1961), *Blake's Apocalypse* (1963), *Yeats* (1970), *A Map of Misreading* (1975), *Kabbalah and Criticism* (1975), *Agon: Toward a Theory of Revisionism* (1982), *The American Religion* (1992), *The Western Canon* (1994), and *Omens of Millennium: The Gnosis of Angels, Dreams, and Resurrection* (1996). *The Anxiety of Influence* (1973) sets forth Professor Bloom's provocative theory of the literary relationships between the great writers and their predecessors. His most recent books include *Shakespeare: The Invention of the Human* (1998), a 1998 National Book Award finalist; *How to Read and Why* (2000); *Genius: A Mosaic of One Hundred Exemplary Creative Minds* (2002); *Hamlet: Poem Unlimited* (2003); *Where Shall Wisdom Be Found?* (2004); and *Jesus and Yahweh: The Names Divine* (2005). In 1999, Professor Bloom received the prestigious American Academy of Arts and Letters Gold Medal for Criticism. He has also received the International Prize of Catalonia, the Alfonso Reyes Prize of Mexico, and the Hans Christian Andersen Bicentennial Prize of Denmark.

KATHRYN HUME is Edwin Erle Sparks Professor of English at Penn State University. Her books include *Fantasy and Mimesis: Responses to Reality in Western Fiction* (1984), *Pynchon's Mythography: An Approach to* Gravity's Rainbow (1987), *Calvino's Fictions: Cogito and Cosmos* (1992), and *American Dream, American Nightmare: Fiction since 1960* (2000).

OLIVER W. FERGUSON is emeritus associate professor of English at Duke University. He wrote *Jonathan Swift and Ireland* (1962).

DONALD E. MORSE is emeritus professor of English and rhetoric at Oakland University. He wrote *The Novels of Kurt Vonnegut: Imagining Being an American* (2003).

MÓNICA CALVO PASCUAL is a lecturer at the department of English and German of the University of Zaragoza in Spain. She has written articles on postmodern fiction.

TAMÁS BÉNYEI is associate professor in the department of British studies at the Institute of English and American studies at the University of Debrecin in Hungary. He wrote *Acts of Attention: Figure and Narrative in Post-War British Novels* (1999).

PETER FREESE is professor of American studies at the University of Paderborn in Germany. Among his books in English are *The Ethnic Detective: Chester Himes, Harry Kemelman, Tony Hillerman* (1992) and *From Apocalypse to Entropy and Beyond: The Second Law of Thermodynamics in Post-War American Fiction* (1997).

FUMIKA NAGANO is a 1999 graduate of Keio University. Her graduation thesis was "Nuclear Imagination: Freakish Figures in Kurt Vonnegut's Novels."

JOSH SIMPSON maintains a website at <http://www.wjsimpson.net/>.

GILBERT MCINNIS is a playwright and novelist who is pursuing a doctorate in English, with a dissertation on Vonnegut, at Laval University in Quebec.

KEVIN BROWN is assistant professor of English at Lee University in Cleveland, Tennessee. After earning his Ph.D. in 1996 from the University of Mississippi with a dissertation on Kurt Vonnegut and Mark Twain, he wrote articles on Ralph Ellison, John Barth, and religious topics.

Bibliography

Allen, William Rodney. *Conversations with Kurt Vonnegut.* Jackson: University Press of Mississippi, 1988.

——— . *Understanding Kurt Vonnegut.* Columbia: University of South Carolina Press, 1991.

Bellamy, Joe David, ed. *The New Fiction: Interviews with Innovative American Writers.* Urbana: University of Illinois Press, 1974.

Berryman, Charles. "After the Fall: Kurt Vonnegut," *Critique* 26 (1985): pp. 96–102.

Bradbury, Malcolm. *The Modern American Novel.* New York: Oxford University Press, 1983.

Broer, Lawrence R. *Sanity Plea: Schizophrenia in the Novels of Kurt Vonnegut.* Tuscaloosa: University of Alabama Press, 1994.

Bryant, C. D. B. "Kurt Vonnegut, Head Bokononist," *New York Times Book Review* (6 April 1969): pp. 2, 25.

Burhans, Clinton S., Jr. "Hemingway and Vonnegut: Diminishing Vision in a Dying Age," *Modern Fiction Studies* 21 (1975): pp. 173–191.

Crichton, J. Michael, "Sci-Fi and Vonnegut," *New Republic* 160 (26 April 1969): pp. 33–35.

Davis, Todd F. *Kurt Vonnegut's Crusade.* Albany, N. Y.: State University of New York Press, 2006.

Gardner, John. *On Moral Fiction.* New York: Basic Books, 1978.

Hartshorne, Thomas L., "From *Catch-22* to *Slaughterhouse-Five:* The Decline of the Political Novel," *South Atlantic Quarterly* 78 (1979): pp. 17–33.

Hassan, Ihab. *Contemporary American Literature.* New York: Ungar, 1974.

185

———. *Paracriticisms*. Urbana: University of Illinois Press, 1975.

———. *The Postmodern Turn*. Columbus: Ohio State University Press, 1987.

Hearell, Dale. "Vonnegut's Changing Women," *Publications of the Arkansas Philological Association* 22 (Fall 1996): pp. 27–35.

Hendin. Josephine. *Vulnerable People: A View of American Fiction Since 1945*. New York: Oxford University Press, 1978.

Hume. Kathryn. "The Heraclitian Cosmos of Kurt Vonnegut," *Papers on Language and Literature* 18 (1982): pp 208–224.

———. "Kurt Vonnegut and the Myths and Symbols of Meaning," *Texas Studies in Language and Literature* 24 (1982): pp. 429–447.

———. "Vonnegut's Self-Projections: Symbolic Characters and Symbolic Fiction," *Journal of Narrative Technique* 12 (1982): pp. 177–190.

Irving, John. "Kurt Vonnegut and His Critics." *New Republic* 181 (22 September 1979): pp. 41–49.

Karl, Frederick R. *American Fictions 1940–1980*. New York: Harper & Row, 1983.

Klinkowitz. Jerome. *The American 1960's*. Ames: Iowa State University Press, 1980.

———. *The Vonnegut Effect*. Columbia: University of South Carolina Press, 2004.

Klinkowitz, Jerome, and Donald L. Lawler, eds. *Vonnegut in America*. New York: Delacorte Press/Seymour Lawrence, 1977.

Lundquist, James. *Kurt Vonnegut*. New York: Ungar, 1976.

Marvin, Thomas F., and Kathleen Gregory, eds. *Kurt Vonnegut: A Critical Companion*. Westport, Conn.: Greenwood Press, 2002.

Merrill, Robert, and Peter A. Scholl. "Vonnegut's *Slaughterhouse-Five:* The Requirements of Chaos," *Studies in American Fiction* 6 (1979): pp. 65–76.

Morse, Donald E. "Kurt Vonnegut's *Jailbird* and *Deadeye Dick:* Two Studies of Defeat," *Hungarian Studies in English* 22 (1991): pp. 109–119.

———. *Kurt Vonnegut*. San Bernardino, Cal.: Borgo, 1992.

———. "Kurt Vonnegut: The Antonio Gaudi of Fantastic Fiction," *Centennial Review* 42 (Winter 1998): pp. 173–183.

———. *The Novels of Kurt Vonnegut: Imagining Being an American*. Westport, Conn.: Praeger, 2003.

Mustazza, Leonard. "A Darwinian Eden: Science and Myth in Kurt Vonnegut's *Galápagos*," *Journal of the Fantastic in the Arts* 3 (1991): pp. 55–65.

Olderman, Raymond. *Rewind the Waste Land: The American Novel in the Nineteen-Sixties*. New Haven, Conn.: Yale University Press, 1972.

Pieratt, Asa B., Jr., Julie Huffman-Klinkowitz, and Jerome Klinkowitz, eds. *Kurt Vonnegut: A Comprehensive Bibliography*. Hamden, Conn.: Shoe String Press/Archon Books, 1987.

Reed, Peter. *Kurt Vonnegut, Jr.* New York: Warner Paperback Library, 1972.

Reed, Peter, and Marc Leeds. eds. *The Vonnegut Chronicles.* Westport, Conn.: Greenwood Press, 1996.

Scholes, Robert. *The Fabulators.* New York. Oxford University Press, 1967.

————. *Fabulation and Satire.* Urbana: University of Illinois Press, 1979.

Scholl, Peter A. "Vonnegut's Attack upon Christendom," *Newsletter of the Conference in Christianity and Literature* 22 (Fall 1972): pp. 5–11.

Schriber, Mary Sue. "Bringing Chaos to Order: The Novel Tradition and Kurt Vonnegut, Jr.," *Genre* 10 (1977): pp. 283–297.

Thomas, P. L. *Reading, Learning, Teaching Kurt Vonnegut.* Confronting the Text, Confronting the World. New York, N. Y.: Peter Lang, 2006.

Uphaus, Robert W. "Expected Meaning in Vonnegut's Dead-End Fiction," *Novel* 8 (1975): pp. 164–175.

Wilson, Loree. "Fiction's Wild Wizard," *Iowa Alumni Review* 19 (June 1966): pp. 10–12.

Acknowledgments

Hume, Kathryn. "Vonnegut's Melancholy," *Philological Quarterly*, Volume 77, Number 2 (Spring 1998): pp. 221–238. Copyright © 1998 The University of Iowa Press. Reprinted by permission of the publisher.

Ferguson, Oliver W. "History and Story: Leon Trout's Double Narrative in *Galápagos*," *Critique: Studies in Contemporary Fiction*, Volume 40, Number 3 (Spring 1999): pp. 230–238. Reprinted with permission of the Helen Dwight Reid Educational Foundation. Published by Heldref Publications, 1319 Eighteenth St., NW, Washington, D.C. 20036-1802. Copyright © 1999.

Morse, Donald E. "Sensational Implications: Kurt Vonnegut's *Player Piano* (1952)," *the AnaChronist* (2000): pp. 303–314. Copyright © 2000 *the AnaChronist*. Reprinted by permission of *The AnaChronist*, Agnés Péter, editor.

———. "The 'Black Frost' Reception of Kurt Vonnegut's Fantastic Novel, *Breakfast of Champions* (1973)," *Journal of the Fantastic in the Arts*, Volume 11, Number 2 (2001): pp. 143–153. Copyright © 2001 *Journal of the Fantastic in the Arts*. Reprinted by permission of the editor, W. A. Senior, editor, Florida Atlantic University Press and the *Journal of the Fantastic in the Arts*.

Pascual, Mónica Calvo. "Kurt Vonnegut's *The Sirens of Titan:* Human Will in a Newtonian Narrative Gone Chaotic," *Miscelánea: A Journal of English*

189

and American Studies, Volume 24 (2001): pp. 53–63. Copyright © 2001 *Miscelánea: A Journal of English and American Studies.*

Bényei, Támas. "Leakings: Reappropriating Science Fiction—The Case of Kurt Vonnegut," *Journal of the Fantastic in the Arts,* Volume 11, Number 4 (2001): pp. 432–453. This article first appeared in the *Hungarian Journal of English and American Studies,* Volume 6, Number 1 (2001): pp. 132–144, Zoltan Abadi-Nagy, editor. Reprinted by permission of the editor and the *Hungarian Journal of English and American Studies.* Copyright © 2001 *Hungarian Journal of English and American Studies.*

Freese, Peter. "Kurt Vonnegut's *Player Piano;* or, 'Would You Ask EPICAC What People Are For?'," *Arbeiten aus Anglistik und Amerikanistik,* Volume 27, Number 2 (2002): pp. 123–159. Copyright © 2002 Peter Freese. Reprinted by permission of the author.

Nagano, Fumika. "Surviving the Perpetual Winter: The Role of Little Boy in Vonnegut's *Cat's Cradle,*" *Journal of the American Literature Society of Japan,* Volume 2 (2003): pp. 73–90. Copyright © 2003 Fumika Nagano. Reprinted by permission of the author and the American Literature Society of Japan.

Simpson, Josh. "This Promising of Great Secrets: Literature, Ideas, and the (Re)Invention of Reality in Kurt Vonnegut's *God Bless You, Mr. Rosewater, Slaughterhouse-Five,* and *Breakfast of Champions* Or 'Fantasies of an Impossibly Hospitable World': Science Fiction and Madness in Vonnegut's Troutean Trilogy," *Critique: Studies in Contemporary Fiction,* Volume 45, Number 3 (Spring 2004): pp. 261–271. Reprinted with permission of the Helen Dwight Reid Educational Foundation. Published by Heldref Publications, 1319 Eighteenth St., NW, Washington, D.C. 20036-1802. Copyright © 2004.

McInnis, Gilbert. "Evolutionary Mythology in the Writings of Kurt Vonnegut, Jr.," *Critique: Studies in Contemporary Fiction,* Volume 46, Number 4 (Summer 2005): pp. 383–396. Reprinted with permission of the Helen Dwight Reid Educational Foundation. Published by Heldref Publications, 1319 Eighteenth St., NW, Washington, D.C. 20036-1802. Copyright © 2005.

Brown, Kevin. "'A Launching Pad of Belief': Kurt Vonnegut and Postmodern Humor," *Studies in American Humor,* Volume 3, Number 14 (2006): pp. 47–54. Copyright © 2006 Kevin Brown. Reprinted by permission of the author.

Index